T0303764

VIA FERRATAS OF THE FRENCH ALPS

by Richard Miller

CICERONE

2 POLICE SQUARE, MILNTHORPE, CUMBRIA LA7 7PY
www.cicerone.co.uk

© Richard Miller 2014
First edition 2014
ISBN: 978 1 85284 648 0
Printed in China on behalf of Latitude Press Ltd.
A catalogue record for this book is available from the British Library.
All photographs © Richard Miller 2014

Dedication

This book is dedicated to my family, with grateful thanks
for their generous help and encouragement.

Advice to Readers

While every effort is made by our authors to ensure the accuracy of guidebooks as they go to print, changes can occur during the lifetime of an edition. If we know of any, there will be an Updates tab on this book's page on the Cicerone website (www.cicerone.co.uk), so please check before planning your trip. We also advise that you check information about such things as transport, accommodation and shops locally. Even rights of way can be altered over time. We are always grateful for information about any discrepancies between a guidebook and the facts on the ground, sent by email to info@cicerone.co.uk or by post to Cicerone, 2 Police Square, Milnthorpe LA7 7PY, United Kingdom.

Warning

Using via ferratas can be a dangerous activity carrying a risk of personal injury or death. It should be undertaken only by those with a full understanding of the risks and with the appropriate experience to evaluate them. Via ferratists should be correctly equipped for the routes undertaken, understand how to use the equipment, and ensure that the equipment used is in a working state. While every care and effort has been taken in the preparation of this book, readers should be aware that conditions on the routes can be highly variable and can change quickly. Natural and artificial holds and fixed self-belaying equipment may become loose or fall off, and rockfall, snow and ice can affect the character of a route. These can materially alter the risks involved in undertaking a via ferrata. Signposts, cairns and other landmarks mentioned in the text for navigational purposes may also change.

Except for any liability that cannot be excluded by law, neither Cicerone nor the author accepts liability for costs or damage of any nature (including damage to property, personal injury or death) arising directly or indirectly from the information in this book.

Front cover: Approaching the top of Via Ferrata l'Aiguillette du Lauzet (Route 51)

CONTENTS

Mountain safety

Most of the routes in this guidebook take place in a mountainous environment. Every activity in the mountains has its dangers, and all participants should take responsibility for themselves and their companions. It is important that you familiarise yourself with the potential dangers that exist in such a setting, as outlined in the Introduction. In the event of an accident, you should be aware of the standard methods of seeking assistance (below). A mobile phone may be of use, but do not rely solely on this as coverage is sometimes patchy. You may also choose to carry a personal locator beacon, which can be set to alert authorities to your position using GPS in the case of an accident or can be used if you are in difficulty, as an additional safety measure.

International Distress Signal *(emergency only)*
Six blasts on a whistle (and flashes with a torch after dark) spaced evenly for one minute, followed by a minute's pause. Repeat until an answer is received. The response is three signals per minute followed by a minute's pause.

Helicopter Rescue
The following signals are used to communicate with a helicopter:

Help needed:
raise both arms
above head to
form a 'Y'

Help not needed:
raise one arm
above head, extend
other arm downward

Emergency telephone numbers
PGHM (Peloton de Gendarmerie de Haute Montagne):
☎ 04 50 53 16 89; Emergency services: ☎ 112 (mobile phones)

Weather reports
(If telephoning from the UK, the dialling code is: 0033)
Chamonix: ☎ 08 92 68 02 74, www.meteo.fr or ☎ 3250

Note Mountain rescue can be very expensive – be adequately insured.

Map key

⊕ start	⟵ walking path
⊕ finish	⟵ VF grade 1
⊕ alternative finish	⟵ VF grade 2
⟲ return path	⟵ VF grade 3
◤ escape point/path (various colours)	⟵ VF grade 4
❗ crux (very strenuous)	⟵ VF grade 5
⊜ bridge	– – – path or VF hidden from view
⊜ two-wire bridge	㉒ location of VF
⊜ three-wire bridge	Ⓐ Ⓑ Ⓒ location of VF stage
◕ balance beam	⊏A483⊐ major road
⊞ ladder	=D123= minor road
⬤ tunnel (route)	- - - - unsurfaced road
⊗ Tyrolean traverse	⊏----⊐ tunnel (road)
P parking	⟘ cable car
⚲ church	▪▪▪▪ railway line
✝✝✝ cemetery	⬭ lake
▪ building	～ river/stream
⊕ airport	⬭ urban area
	//// steep terrain

7

VIA FERRATAS OF THE FRENCH ALPS

ROUTE LISTING

Route		Stage		Grade	Exposure	Seriousness	Page
Geneva and the Northern Alps							
1	VF Fort l'Ecluse			2	2	A	50
2	VF Jacques Revaclier			2	3	A	52
3	VF des Saix de Miolène	A	Tronçon du Cabri	2	2	A	56
		B	Tronçon du Chamois/Tronçon du Bouquetin	4	3	A	58
4	VF du Rocher de la Chaux	A	La Tête de l'Éléphant	3	5	A	61
		B	L'Oeil de l'Éléphant	5	5	A	63
		C	Mini Via Ferrata	1(3)	2	A	65
5	VF du Saix du Tour			3(4)	3	B	66
6	VF du Mont			3	3	A	70
7	VF de Curalla			2	3	B	74
8	VF de la Tour du Jallouvre			4	5	C	77
9	VF Yves Pollet Villard			3(4)	3	B	81
10	VF de Thônes – La Roche à l'Agathe	A	1ère Partie	4	3	A	86
		B	2ème Partie	5	4	A	87
11	VF d'Ugine			1	2	C	89
12	VF Le Roc du Vent			2	3	C	93
Chambéry							
13	VF de la Guinguette	A	Itinéraire de la Grotte	3	2	A	102
		B	Itinéraire les Buis	4	5	A	103
14	VF Roc du Cornillon	A	Parcours Primevère à Oreille d'Ours	2	3	A	106
		B	Parcours Rocher du Cornillon	1	2	A	108

8

Route		Stage		Grade	Exposure	Seriousness	Page
15	VF École de Rossane			1(2)	1	A	109
16	VF Savoie Grand Revard	A	Parcours le P'tchi	4	3	B	114
		B	Parcours Grotte à Carret	5	5	B	116
17	VF La Grotte du Maquis			1	3	B	118
18	VF de Roche Veyrand	A	1ère Partie	2	3	B	122
		B	2ème Partie	4	5	B	124
Tarentaise							
19	VF du Cochet			2	2	B	129
20	VF du Levassaix			1	1	A	132
21	VF du Lac de la Rosiere			2(1)	2	A	134
22	VF de la Croix des Verdons			3	4	C	136
23	VF des Grosses Pierres			5	3	A	140
24	VF du Plan du Bouc	A	Parcours en Arête	2	2	B	144
		B	Parcours en Falaise	1	2	B	146
25	VF de Pralognan	A	VF de la Cascade de la Fraîche	3(2)	3	A	149
		B	Parcours Ouistiti	1	1	A	151
26	VF des Bettières	A	Eperon des Croës	2	2	B	153
		B	Grand Pilier and La Vire des Barmes	3	3	B	154
		C	Le Surplomb Jaune	4	3	B	156
27	VF Roc de Tovière	A	1ère Partie	2	2	B	159
		B	2ème Partie	3	4	B	160
		C	3ème Partie	5	5	C	161
28	VF Les Plates de la Daille			3	5	B	164

9

Route		Stage		Grade	Exposure	Seriousness	Page
Maurienne							
29	VF d'Andagne	A	Itinéraire Pierre Blanc	1	1	B	171
		B	Itinéraire Guy Favre	2	4	B	172
30	VF du Col de la Madeleine			2	3	A	174
31	VF du Pichet			2(1)	2	A	177
32	VF du Diable	A	VF Les Angelots	1	1	A	181
		B	VF Les Diablotins	2	2	A	183
		C	VF La Descente aux Enfers and La Montée au Purgatoire	4	4	A	184
		D	VF Le Chemin de la Vierge	3	4	A	186
		E	VF La Traversée des Anges	3	4	A	188
		F	VF La Montée au Ciel	3	4	A	189
		G	VF Les Rois Mages	5	5	A	191
33	VF de L'École Buissonnière			1	1	A	193
34	VF du Télégraphe	A	VF Col des Pylônes	1	2	B	196
		B	VF Fort du Télégraphe	2	4	B	198
35	VF de Poingt Ravier			1	1	A	200
36	VF du Rocher Saint Pierre	A	1ère Partie	4(1)	3(1)	A	204
		B	2ème Partie	3	3	A	207
37	VF de Comborsière			1(2)	2	A	208
38	VF de St-Colomban-des-Villards	A	VF École du Rocher de Capaillan	1	1	A	213
		B	VF de la Chal	3	3	A	214
39	VF de l'Adret	A	La Passerelle	3	3	A	217
		B	Le Bastion	4	4	A	219

Route		Stage		Grade	Exposure	Seriousness	Page
Grenoble							
40	VF de la Cascade de l'Oule	A	Parcours par la Vire des Lavandières	3	4	A	225
		B	Parcours par le Grand Dièdre	5	5	A	228
41	VF Les Prises de la Bastille	A	Falaises VICAT	3	2	A	231
		B	Falaises de la Bastille	4(3)	2	A	233
42	VF du Croix de Chamrousse	A	VF Les Trois Fontaines	2	3	B	236
		B	VF Les Lacs Roberts	3	2	B	238
43	VF de l'Alpe du Grand Serre	A	VF de la Cascade	1	1	A	241
		B	VF du Grand Bec 1ère Partie	1	2	B	243
		C	VF du Grand Bec 2ème Partie	4	4	B	245
44	VF de l'Alpe d'Huez	A	Itinéraire des Gorges de Sarenne/ Découverture	2	3	B	248
		B	Itinéraire de Pierre-Ronde/Sportif	3	3	B	250
45	VF Cascade de la Fare	A	Les Passerelles	2(3)	2	B	253
		B	La Cascade	2(3)	3	B	255
46	VF Cascade de la Pisse			3	5	B	256
47	VF Les Perrons			2	2	A	260
48	VF de St-Christophe-en-Oisans	A	1ère Partie	3	3	B	264
		B	2ème Partie	1	1	B	266
49	VF des Mines du Grand Clôt			2	3	C	267
50	VF d'Arsine			2	3	A	270
Briançon							
51	VF l'Aiguillette du Lauzet			2	3	C	276
52	VF du Rocher du Bez			1	1	A	280

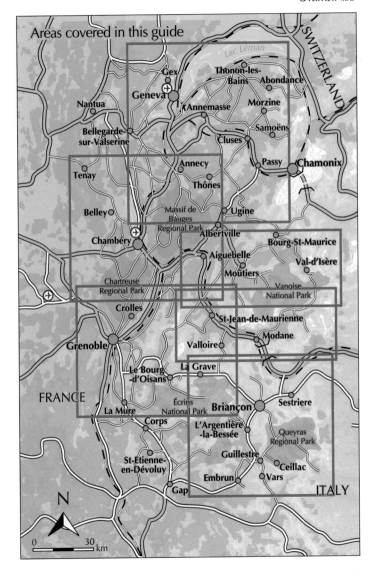

*Enjoying views of Mont Blanc
from near the top of the
Falaise de Curalla (Route 7)*

INTRODUCTION

The Pointe de Chardonnière (2723m) and Sixt-Fer-à-Cheval, seen from the Barme aux Corbés (Route 6)

The sheer beauty and variety of the French Alps are compelling reasons to visit and explore some of the most spectacular scenery in Europe. Much visited for winter sports and mountaineeering (and a favourite destination for skiers), the region also offers great opportunities for summer mountaineering activity, hill walking and now via ferratas. Experienced users of via ferratas, looking for a new region to explore, will find plenty of inspiration in this book. Alternatively, if you are planning a holiday in the area and want to try your hand at something different, the easier routes described here will provide a sound introduction to this increasingly popular activity.

Modern via ferratas originate in the Italian Dolomites and were first created in the late 19th century to assist early tourists with mountaineering ascents by replacing ropes with fixed cables and metal rungs. The system was then adopted in World War I to allow the conduct of warfare from the mountaintops by Italian and Austrian troops. In more recent times they have been rediscovered by Italian mountaineering enthusiasts and, in the late 1980s, the first routes were constructed in France.

The via ferratas of the Italian Dolomites can be quite different from the French routes. The former tend to be fixed mountaineering paths, most similar to summer mountaineering routes, whereas the latter are more likely to be sports routes, closer to scrambling or rock climbing. French via ferratas often seek out the steepest and most vertigo-inducing terrain, requiring a reasonable level of fitness and a decent head for heights.

While some of these routes may challenge even experienced rock climbers, the majority should be within the reach of any strong hillwalker. The quality of the fixed protection found on the routes, in the form of cables, rungs and other more exotic elements, is normally very high. This standard is maintained by regular checks carried out under the direction of the local authority and ensures that, if properly used, you should have a safe and enjoyable excursion. Bon courage!

WHEN TO GO

The via ferratas described in this book are located over a fairly large area, and the range of altitudes at which they are found, from 200m to over 2700m above sea level, is also considerable. A few of the routes may be practicable all year; most, however, will be open from spring until late autumn. In practice, this will vary to a large degree, depending on altitude, latitude and, above all, weather. As the area is predominantly mountainous, the weather can be hard to predict, with heavy snowfall possible, even during high summer. During spring and early

Satisfied via ferratists enjoy views of the Massif des Bornes from the top of the Via Ferrata Yves Pollet Villard (Route 9)

summer there may be packed snow on higher-altitude routes. In autumn the weather may well be settled and reasonably warm, but there is also the chance that higher routes may have some fresh snow on them.

The information box at the top of each route lists its recommended season. A handful of routes are also subject to local by-laws (*Arrêté Municipal*), governing when they may be accessed. Where such restrictions apply, this is also noted at the top of the route. Periodically, routes may also be closed for maintenance.

The French high season runs from early July to late August, with the first two weeks of August being busiest. Routes will be more crowded during this period and accommodation will fill up more quickly. During spring and autumn, accommodation prices are lower, and availability is rarely a problem. September can be a good time to visit, although some tourist services start to close towards the end of the month.

GETTING TO THE ALPS

There are plenty of good road, rail and air links between the UK and the French Alps and travel between the two has never been easier. A passport is required to enter France and should be kept on your person at all times as a form of ID (a legal requirement). UK, Irish and other EU citizens do not require a visa. Citizens of the US, Canada, Australia and New Zealand can visit the country for up to 90 days without a visa. For further information on entry requirements see www.diplomatie.gouv.fr.

The most conveniently located airport with flights to and from the UK is Geneva. Grenoble and Chambéry currently receive flights from the UK only over the winter (but it may be worth checking if there is a summer schedule when planning your trip). Further afield, Lyon, Nice, Marseille, Basel and Turin all have direct air links with a number of UK airports. Eurostar (www.eurostar.com) offers fast trains that run directly between London and Paris. From there, the French high-speed train (TGV) and local rail network (www.voyages-sncf. com) have links with many of the destinations covered in this book.

It is possible to reach Paris from the UK by bus (www.eurolines.co.uk), which is normally cheaper than Eurostar. There are also buses from the UK to Geneva, Basel, Turin and Aosta. There are numerous ferries between the UK and France, with the Dover to Calais route offering the shortest sea journey (see www.directferries.co.uk for a list of connections). Allow seven to nine hours for the journey from the northern French ports to the Alps.

GETTING AROUND

While it is possible to visit many of these routes without the use of a car or public transport, this will not be practical for most people. Travelling

The Arvieux Valley and western Queyras Massif, seen from the Col d'Izoard (above Route 63)

by car or motorbike remains by far the most convenient way to visit the area covered. A number of the routes are in remote locations that are not well served by buses or trains.

By car

France has an extensive network of well-maintained roads that, by British standards, can be eerily quiet. A toll is levied on most motorways (*Autoroutes*) but other roads are mostly free of any charge. Some of the high alpine passes may not be open during the early spring until clear of snow, and may be closed on certain days during the summer for the Tour de France and other events. See Appendix D for websites that give details of such closures.

There is not space here to set out all of the rules of the road, but you should familiarise yourself with them prior to travelling; any infringement of regulations is now taken very seriously by the French police. See www.driving.drive-alive.co.uk for more information. All right-hand drive vehicles must have deflectors affixed to their headlights to avoid dazzling oncoming traffic. Non-French registered vehicles must also display their country of registration (for example GB sticker or plate). Additionally, drivers are required to carry the following: driving licence, proof of vehicle ownership and proof of insurance. Note that French police can stop and search vehicles or ask to see proof of identity. It is a legal requirement that a warning triangle be carried in the car as well as a high-visibility vest for each occupant, which should be kept within reach. From July 2012, it is also mandatory to carry two breathalyser kits in the car.

You should consider carrying snow chains if visiting at any time other than during high summer. They are compulsory in mountainous areas during the winter. If you are hiring a car, you should check that all the aforementioned items are included in the rental, or whether you have to provide them yourself.

For those who use in-car GPS navigational tools, the GPS coordinates of each route are provided at the top of each individual route description. GPS devices can normally be rented as part of car hire, but doing so is typically less cost effective than buying your own or using a mobile app. Finding a petrol station is rarely a problem, although they are increasingly reliant on automated distributors. Such machines normally accept chip-and-pin Visa and Mastercard credit cards. Supermarket stations typically have the lowest prices, with the cost of petrol similar to that in the UK. Diesel is around 10 per cent less expensive.

If you choose to hire a car, you can do so from airports and some larger rail stations, and it is best arranged prior to travelling (see Appendix D). Be sure to check the small print for any hidden charges or excesses and check the vehicle, before driving it, for any marks or damage.

By rail or bus

France has an excellent rail network, which is serviced by fast and modern trains. Prices are reasonable and

The lower Maurienne Valley, as seen from the top of Via Ferrata du Télégraphe (Route 34)

delays fairly rare. While this may be very useful in getting to and from the Alps, once in the mountains coverage is largely limited to the main valleys. The cheaper alternative of long-distance bus travel within France is currently extremely limited, but may improve in the future.

The local bus network within each administrative area (*Département*) varies in quality, but in general covers a fairly wide area with a limited number of journeys per day. If you intend to visit the routes by bus, be prepared for a rather time-consuming and complicated experience. Timetables, which should be studied well in advance, are normally available on the internet (see Appendix D) or through local tourist offices.

On foot or bicycle
Perhaps the most rewarding way to visit the routes detailed here is on foot. While not as easy as taking a car, this will certainly give you the greatest opportunity to enjoy the surrounding countryside. There are lots of long-distance walking paths in the French Alps, a number of which pass close to the via ferratas, and a trip combining both activities is entirely possible. While there is not space here to detail such an itinerary, the GR5 path, for example – as described in Paddy Dillon's *The GR5 Trail* (Cicerone: second edition, 2013) – could be combined with a visit to 19 of the routes described, as well as several more to the north and south of the area covered.

Cycling is hugely popular in France, and the Alps are home to a number of the most arduous stages of the Tour de France. In spite of the many narrow winding roads that cross the Alps, cycling in the region is relatively safe as both French law and custom encourage other road users to give bikes plenty of room. For those who enjoy hill climbing, quite a few of the via ferratas are situated close to the most popular passes for this activity. For cyclists who prefer a more sedate approach, there are numerous well-marked bike routes throughout the French Alps, details of which are available from local tourist offices. See *Cycling in the French Alps* by Paul Henderson (Cicerone: second edition, 2008; reprinted with updates, 2013), for more information.

LANGUAGE

A lack of spoken or written French should be no bar to visiting the French Alps. The area is a popular tourist destination for many English-speaking people and as such plenty of locals will have at least a smattering of English. This is almost always the case in tourist offices and, to a lesser degree, in businesses catering to tourists, for example accommodation providers or outdoor retailers. That said, a little spoken French will go a long way and even a few words or stock phrases will be appreciated by the locals. Appendix C sets out a

The suspension bridge at the start of Via Ferrata Sportive/Noire (Second part) (Route 58, Stage D)

brief summary of French phrases and words that may be of use on the via ferratas and in interpreting French maps and signs.

COSTS

In addition to the expense of travelling to and around the Alps, accommodation and food, the cost of the actual activity should be limited. The specific equipment required to use the via ferratas (see Equipment), can be bought from climbing and hillwalking shops or through the internet (see Appendix D). A kit consisting of helmet, harness, self-belaying lanyard, rest lanyard and gloves should cost between £150 and £250. A Tyrolean traverse pulley costs about £55. Within the French Alps, you should be able to purchase these items in most larger towns and villages (although it may be considerably more expensive than doing so before leaving home).

If you prefer to rent the equipment, you can do so for €10–20 per day. Some places will offer rental for longer periods at a better rate, but will require a substantial deposit.

If you wish to hire a guide to accompany you on a via ferrata this will cost between €25 and €60 per person, depending on the route and the number of people in the group. Only two of the routes featured in this book require the payment of a small access fee (Routes 54 and 57). Additionally, a handful of routes involve the optional use of a cable car or funicular, for which a charge of €5–10 is levied.

ACCOMMODATION

The majority of towns, villages and resorts will have at least one place to stay, and there will usually be a number of different options. Prices and availability vary a great deal, so be prepared to do some research before you visit to obtain the most suitable accommodation. If you prefer not to book in advance, choices may be limited. However, outside the French high season (mid-July to late August) there is normally little difficulty in obtaining lodgings without an advance booking. During these few weeks – when the French take their holidays en masse – even campsites may be full by late afternoon. Additionally, alpine tourist accommodation often closes for several months during the autumn, so from late September onwards you should book in advance.

Hotels vary in quality, from the luxurious (and expensive), which you can find in major destinations, such as Geneva, to the basic. See www.accorhotels.com for an extensive list of motel-style accommodation. For mid-range hotels, often with some character, see www.logishotels.com, and for something more upmarket see www.viamichelin.com. Note that prices in France are normally per room, not per person. Alternatively, if you wish to rent a small house or cottage (*gîte*), see www.gites-de-france.com. Typically, these are let on a weekly basis and this can be a good option if you want to stay in one

Approaching the defensive fosse above the Falaises de la Bastille. Grenoble and the River Isère are seen in the background (Route 41, Stage B)

place. This website also lists bed and breakfast options. In France these are known as *chambres d'hôte*, and tend to be fairly upmarket.

For those on a more modest budget, campsites are an excellent option and are by far the most common form of accommodation in the French Alps. Most are spacious and clean and some offer a wide range of facilities (pool, restaurant, wifi and so on), although these tend to be a little more costly. Almost all campsites also offer caravan pitches and many have cabins to rent. The best value campsites are normally Campings Municipal, which are operated by the local commune. A tent pitch (*emplacement*) for two people with car and electricity typically costs between €12 and €20 per night. There are several websites listing campsites, such as www.campingfrance.com.

Another good budget option is *gîtes d'étape*. These are the French equivalent of private hostels and normally contain a dormitory as well as private rooms. A bed in the dorm should cost €10–20 per night, and dinner, bed and breakfast (demi-pension) €30–45. See www.gites-refuges. com for a full list. This site also lists mountain refuges, but these will be of limited use as most of the via ferratas are situated at lower altitude in the main valleys. Local tourist offices will also have full details of accommodation in each area. See the individual routes and Appendix D for relevant website addresses.

MAPS

It is likely that the majority of readers will visit these routes by car; to that end a good, up-to-date, road atlas is highly recommended. Most of the routes cover a small area and make use of their own purpose-built approach and descent paths. For this reason, a topographical map will be of limited use.

However, for a handful of longer mountain routes such as the Via Ferrata d'Ugine (Route 11) or Via Ferrata l'Aiguillette du Lauzet (Route 51), one may come in handy. In any event, if you plan to extend your outing beyond the via ferrata or just wish to have a better appreciation of the surrounding landscape, a topographical map will be useful. The Institut Géographique National (IGN) produces the standard range of French topographic maps, which are of a similar quality to British Ordnance Survey maps. The most suitable series is the IGN Carte de Randonnée TOP25 series, which has a blue cover. These are widely available from newsagents and tourist offices throughout France and can also be ordered online. The IGN website (www.geoportail.fr), which features scalable topographical and satellite maps, is also extremely useful.

ROUTE GRADING

All the routes in the book have been given three grades. The first is for technical difficulty, the second for

(clockwise from top left): typical via ferrata stemple/rung; fingerhold; footplate; small stemple

exposure, and the third for the seriousness of the surrounding environment.

Technical grade
This indicates the overall technical difficulty of the route or stage and is the most important grading. It is based on how strenuous the route is, the degree of technical movement required, how sustained and/or committing and the difficulty of any bridges or other components requiring balance. The technical grade takes only limited account of the length of the route but gives particular weight to the difficulty of any crux points. Appendix A lists the routes in order of technical grade (1–5) and by approximate difficulty, relative to each other, within each grade.

1   Very few or no strenuous components, involving basic scrambling at most. Suitable for competent and fit hillwalkers.

2   Occasional strenuous moments. Very small overhangs may be present but these are spaced well apart. May also be technical sections requiring some scrambling skills. Suitable for those with such skills or in good physical condition.

3   Fairly strenuous at times, but such moments are well spaced out. Small to medium overhangs may be present. Occasionally, you may be required to clip

your via ferrata lanyard under pressure. Possible technical sections requiring good scrambling skills. Suitable for those with such skills or in good physical condition.

4 May contain isolated large overhangs, long fairly strenuous and/or sustained sections. You may be regularly required to clip your via ferrata lanyard under pressure. May involve technically complex sections requiring basic rock-climbing skills. Bridges may require a reasonable sense of balance. Suitable for those with some rock-climbing ability or in very good physical condition.

5 May contain a number of passages that are strenuous, sustained and committing. Technically complex sections, requiring low-grade rock-climbing skills, may be present. You may often have to clip your via ferrata lanyard under pressure. Bridges may require a good sense of balance. Suitable for proven rock climbers or those in excellent physical condition.

Exposure
Exposure is a measure (graded 1–5) of how much empty space there appears to be beneath you and, therefore, how good a head for heights you are likely to require. Routes graded 1 will probably place you near drops of

10 to 20m, with any more exposed positions not being too 'immediate'. Routes graded 5 will probably involve positions with several tens or hundreds of metres of air directly underfoot. That said, the individual grades do not reflect any specific set of criteria but are solely relative to each other. The grade, ultimately, reflects only the opinion of the author, but should assist readers in assessing whether a route is suitable. Many people find that the more exposure they experience, the less effect it has. So, if you struggle at first with this aspect of via ferratas, persevere and you are likely to find that your head for heights improves.

Seriousness
This grade (A–C) indicates the overall seriousness of the environment in which the route is situated. The grade is based on the following criteria: the proximity of the route to towns/villages; altitude; the likely effects of rapidly worsening weather; the danger posed by rockfall, and the general nature of the terrain.

A The route is in or near a town, village or resort. It is at a relatively low altitude and rockfall is not a particular issue. Escape in the event of a sudden deterioration in weather would not normally be problematic.

B The route may be somewhat distant from any population centre

The exposed ladder (grade 5) at the top of the Grande Dièdre, on Via Ferrata de la Cascade de l'Oule (Route 40, Stage B)

Climbing the third set of bluffs encountered on the Via Ferrata de St-Christophe-en-Oisans, with the River Vénéon directly underfoot (Route 48, Stage A)

and/or at moderately high altitude. Escape from the route in the event of a sudden deterioration in the weather may not be entirely straightforward. Rockfall may be an issue.

C The route is relatively far from any population centre and/or at a relatively high altitude. A sudden deterioration in the weather could have serious consequences. Rockfall may be an issue and the nature of the terrain may demand particular care.

In general, the routes described are situated in comparatively benign settings and the majority are graded A, with only a few graded C. However, it is important to remember that deteriorating weather can cause any route to become a much more serious undertaking. See Dangers for more information on this subject. It is also the case that the nature of terrain can change over time. In particular, rock quality can deteriorate. This has resulted in the temporary or permanent closure of several French via ferratas.

The grades assume that a route is undertaken when it is clear of snow and ice, and during periods of reasonable weather. In more challenging conditions, routes may be much harder. Additionally, the technical difficulty of a route can change over time due to polishing of the rock, or minor amendments to the fixed equipment made during inspections.

THE FRENCH GRADING SYSTEM

Many French via ferratas have a semi-official grade, provided by the company that built the route. Typically, these grades run from *Facile* (easy) to *Extrêmement Difficile* (extremely difficult). Although the French mountaineering grading system (IFAS) uses the same nomenclature, these two grading systems are entirely unrelated. The individual grades have no defined meaning and the system is not applied consistently to all routes. Therefore, it is not used in this guide.

EQUIPMENT

To climb a via ferrata, you will require the following equipment. If in any doubt as to what to get and how to use it, consult with the staff at a climbing shop.

Climbing harness

Either a sit harness or a full-body harness can be used, depending on personal preference. It should be comfortable, close-fitting and light, and you must understand how to fasten it correctly. It is strongly recommended that a full-body harness be used for children, or by adults who carry a lot of weight around the waist. In the event of a fall, this form of harness will reduce the possibility of the via ferratist turning upside down. If this happens with an inadequately tightened sit harness, there is a risk that the climber may fall out of it.

Via ferrata kit (clockwise from top left): VF lanyard with rest lanyard (quickdraw) attached, harness, helmet, gloves, security rope and belay device

Climbing helmet

This should be worn at all times while on the via ferrata or below steep rock. Adjust the helmet for comfort before starting the route.

Via ferrata shock-absorbing lanyard

This consists of a shock-absorbing mechanism and two lengths of kernmantle rope or climbing webbing, on the ends of which are special karabiners designed for via ferratas. The shock-absorbing element may consist of a metal friction device through which the rope runs, or a sealed length of webbing bonded together by stitching, which absorbs energy by progressively tearing apart when put under extreme pressure. A number of these kits are now available from various climbing equipment manufacturers. The style of via ferrata

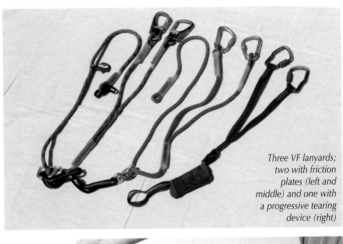

Three VF lanyards; two with friction plates (left and middle) and one with a progressive tearing device (right)

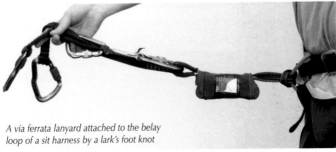

A via ferrata lanyard attached to the belay loop of a sit harness by a lark's foot knot

lanyard detailed above is known as 'Y-shape'. You may encounter the older 'V-shape' via ferrata lanyard, where only one half of the lanyard was clipped onto the cable at once. These are now considered obsolete and should be avoided. It is possible to construct a via ferrata lanyard by yourself, but instructions on how to do so are beyond the scope of this book, and it is not recommended.

The via ferrata lanyard should be attached to the belay loop of your harness via a lark's foot knot. Never use a karabiner to attach the via ferrata lanyard to the harness. In the event that such a karabiner is shock-loaded by a dynamic fall, there is a chance that it may break. Any via ferrata lanyard that has been placed under significant stress, such as from holding a fall, is excessively worn, or that has passed its use-by date, should be replaced. Read the instructions that come with the lanyard and follow them. See Moving safely for information on how to use the lanyard correctly.

Rest lanyard
In addition to the via ferrata lanyard you should carry another lanyard to hang off when taking a rest in exposed positions. The via ferrata lanyard is typically too long for this purpose and it is better not to put the shock-absorbing element under unnecessary strain. Some proprietary via ferrata lanyards come with an additional loop fitted below the shock absorber, to which a screwgate karabiner can be attached to construct a rest lanyard. With such a design, it is imperative that, when not being used to rest on, the karabiner be left hanging rather than attached to your harness, as this may bypass the shock absorber.

To construct your own rest lanyard, use either a quickdraw with a screwgate karabiner on each end or a climbing sling with one screwgate karabiner. The sling should be attached to the belay loop of your harness via a lark's foot knot and be just long enough to allow you to rest at a comfortable distance from the

SAFETY CHECK

Before purchasing or using any of the equipment listed above check that it is certified to EN Standard or UIAA Standard, how long the item has been in stock (components have a shelf-life), and that it has not been subject to a product recall. There were recalls of well-recognised brands of via ferrata lanyards in both 2011 and 2012, some of which may still be on sale from retailers unaware of those recalls. To check which items have been affected, see www.theuiaa.org/certified_equipment. Always buy your via ferrata gear from a high-quality retailer and always check it before, during and after use. If in any doubt whatsoever, replace it.

Taking a rest on the balance beam near the top of Via Ferrata du Grand Bec 1ère Partie, while still securely attached to the cable by a via ferrata lanyard (Route 43, Stage B)

rockface. The rest lanyard is intended to assist with resting only, and under no circumstances should be used in place of a shock-absorbing via ferrata lanyard. It will not protect you from the effects of a dynamic fall.

Tyrolean traverse pulley

Routes 15 and 37 both contain an optional Tyrolean traverse, designed to be used with a specific model of pulley. Unfortunately, the models differ, with Route 15 requiring a Petzl Tandem Cable pulley (yellow), and Route 37 a Petzl Tandem Speed pulley (grey). Details of these devices can be found at www.petzl.com. You will also need thick full-finger gloves. See Tyrolean traverses (page 38) for more information on how to use the pulley.

Gloves

Whether or not you choose to wear gloves is a matter of personal preference. They will offer protection against general wear as well as cuts caused by frayed cables (which are rare), but may give less grip than bare hands. There are a number of brands of fingerless gloves designed specifically for via ferratas.

Footwear

There is no specific type of via ferrata shoe and you may see people wearing a wide variety of footwear on the routes, from light sandals to heavy mountaineering boots. Whatever you wear, it should be comfortable, and give good grip on rock, ideally with a Vibram sole. Although trainers will

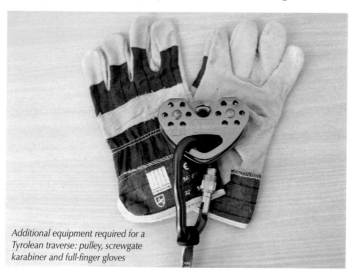

Additional equipment required for a Tyrolean traverse: pulley, screwgate karabiner and full-finger gloves

often suffice, stiff walking or summer mountaineering boots will probably offer more grip and protection. Larger boots are recommended for the handful of longer mountain routes, such as Via Ferrata Le Roc du Vent (Route 12), but may feel a bit bulky on the more delicate passages found on some via ferratas. Rock-climbing shoes are not required for any of the routes, but may be worth considering on some of the most difficult, particularly for shorter climbers who will be required to use rock holds more often. Rock-climbing approach shoes offer a good compromise, but are expensive. Regular use of via ferratas tends to wear through the soles used on climbing and mountaineering footwear rather quickly.

Clothing

This should be appropriate to the mountainous situation and current weather forecast. Even when mild, it is sensible to carry a warm and waterproof coat, in case of a sudden change in the weather. Via ferratas can take a heavy toll on garments, so whatever you wear should be durable. Before setting off ensure that there is nothing loose in your pockets, any zips are done up, and laces are tightly fastened. Spectacle wearers should consider securing their glasses with a small lanyard.

The following additional items are recommended: mobile phone, whistle, water bottle, emergency blanket, pen and paper, compass, sunscreen, small medical kit and a camera (preferably with an anti-shake feature and on a lanyard to secure it). Consider taking a length of lightweight climbing rope, a belay device and some quick-draws if your party contains children or climbers that require extra security (see Roped progression; page 35).

Hiring via ferrata equipment

Via ferrata kits can be hired throughout the region, and in most cases there will be somewhere close to each route that hires out the necessary gear. Local tourist offices often rent out the equipment or will be able to advise on where it can be obtained. Usually, you will be required to leave a deposit of around €20, or your passport. As with your own equipment, thoroughly check all hired gear for any signs of damage prior to use. See page 30 for information on recalled via ferrata lanyards. These should be hired only if you are satisfied that they have been returned to the manufacturer and verified as safe.

Protection for climbers on a via ferrata takes the form of a cable that is anchored to the rock at regular points. Via ferratists should ensure that they are attached continuously to the cable by both of the karabiners at the end of their via ferrata lanyard, except at the point where they move from one section of cable to the next. At each of these anchor points, take one of

The limestone slabs encountered on the first stage of
Via Ferrata de Roche Veyrand are protected by numerous
stemples for both hands and feet (Route 18, Stage A)

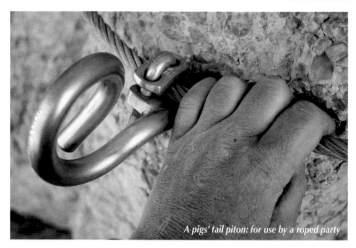

A pigs' tail piton: for use by a roped party

the karabiners off the cable, while the other is still attached, and place it around the next section of cable, ensuring that both karabiners are fully closed.

The length of cable between anchors, known as the run-out, varies from one metre to as much as 10m. Normally, the more challenging the movement required on any one passage, the shorter the run-out will be. Assuming you are correctly attached to the cable, this system assures that, in the event of a fall, you will never drop more than a few metres. However, a fall still has the potential to result in injury, and is to be avoided if possible. On longer run-outs, or particularly strenuous overhangs, you can further reduce the potential fall distance by clipping one of the karabiners of your via ferrata lanyard

onto a rung or other element of the fixed protection situated between the cable anchor points. This can be moved up from one rung to the next as you progress but, if you do this, the other karabiner should always remain attached to the cable.

Roped progression

Parties with children, or those requiring extra assurance, should use a rope in addition to the via ferrata lanyard used by each member of the party. The rope should be attached to the belay loop of each person's harness via a re-threaded figure of eight knot (for the ends) or a figure of eight knot on a bight (for the middle). Keep the rope reasonably taut, with a gap of 5 to 8m between each climber. Many via ferratas are equipped with pigs' tails pitons, through which the rope should

35

A roped-up party crossing the Pont du Calvaire (Route 10, Stage A)

be threaded by the lead climber. If these are not present, use quickdraws placed onto the fixed protection by the lead climber instead. If properly organised, there should always be an anchor point between each member of the party. The last climber should unthread the rope from the pigs' tails (or collect the quickdraws). Additional security on strenuous sections can be given by the use of a belay plate. If you wish to secure your party with a rope but are not confident of your ability to use this equipment correctly, consider hiring a guide.

Further advice

- Try to avoid the two strands of your via ferrata lanyard becoming excessively twisted or tangled.

If this happens, stop, unclip one strand at a time and untwist it.
- Put your weight on your legs in preference to your arms. On strenuous sections, keep your arms straight, as bent arms will tire more quickly. If your arms or legs are feeling strained, try to change posture regularly.
- You may find some sections of via ferratas more challenging, depending on your height. Put simply, the shorter you are, the more difficulty you will have with sections of vertical climbing; the taller you are, the more difficulty you will have with traversing. Bear this in mind when choosing routes.
- Rock-holds are not always immediately obvious, especially on

harder routes, and occasionally you may have to search for them.

- On a few of the hardest routes you may occasionally have to 'smear' your boots on the rock. To smear is to use the friction of the sole of your footwear against a vertical (or near vertical) surface, in the absence of rungs or horizontal footholds. Shorter climbers are more likely to have to use this technique.

- Always try to maintain three points of contact on the rock, fixed protection or the cable.

- There is no such thing as poor via ferrata style. Climb using the rock, the cable and fixed protection in whatever manner feels safest and most enjoyable.

- Some bridges can be quite wobbly but all are well secured and protected. Some, particularly the two-wire and three-wire variants, can feel extremely exposed.

- Try to avoid having more than one climber clipped onto any single section of cable at the same time. Normally you should leave enough room between climbers so that, should the higher climber fall, there is no risk that they will hit the lower one.

- The majority of routes have an indicated direction of travel (*sens de l'itinéraire*). Do not go against the flow.

- It is not uncommon to see people passing each other in relatively precarious positions. If a faster party wishes to pass you, you should assent to this only if you are entirely comfortable with the proposition. Should you

Crossing the suspension bridge on Parcours le P'tchi, with Chambéry and the Chartreuse Massif in the background (Route 16, Stage A)

find your progress blocked by a slower party, wait patiently until you consider that it will be possible to pass them safely. In such circumstances, a polite request to pass is rarely refused.

• Many approach and return paths pass over steep and slippery ground and require care. Despite this, they are not normally protected by cable except where exposure is also a factor.

Tyrolean traverses

Only two of the via ferratas in this book contain a Tyrolean traverse, both of which are optional. These are not traditional rock-climbing Tyrolean traverses, which require a belayer, but single cables that are traversed by force of gravity. Of all the different elements found on via ferratas, Tyrolean traverses present the greatest potential risk of accident if misused. Many supervised Tyrolean traverses exist, including a few that are adjacent to routes in this book. The uninitiated should consider trying one of these before using a traverse incorporated into a via ferrata.

To use a Tyrolean traverse, place a climbing sling onto the belay loop of your harness by a lark's foot knot. Attach the other end of the sling to a screwgate karabiner. Place your pulley onto the Tyrolean traverse cable and attach it to the karabiner (with the screw tightened). Your rest lanyard (see Equipment) may be suitable for this purpose, but your via ferrata

self-belaying lanyard is not. This latter item should remain attached to the via ferrata cable until ready to start on the Tyrolean, and then be clipped onto the gear loop of your harness.

Ensure that your arms are at a comfortable distance from the cable, so that you can reach it, at a point behind the pulley, with both hands. Tie up long hair, to avoid the possibility of it snagging in the pulley. The speed at which you travel will depend upon the force with which you start, the angle of the traverse, your weight, the type of pulley used and wind resistance. You can reduce the possibility of your body spinning around by placing both (gloved) hands on top of the pulley. If you stop short of the end of the traverse, you will need to pull yourself along; be very careful not to snag fingers or gloves in the pulley.

Only one person at a time should use a Tyrolean traverse and any specific instructions at the start of the traverse should be followed.

CLIMBING WITH CHILDREN

French via ferratas are an ideal way to introduce children to the pleasure and satisfaction that can be gained from outdoor activities. Although many relatively difficult via ferratas are climbed by appropriately supervised children, the lower grade routes are typically more suitable. Ideally, in addition to standard via ferrata equipment, children should wear a full-body harness and be attached to an adult by rope (see Roped progression; page 35). In the event of a fall, small children may be too light to benefit from a shock-absorbing lanyard and it is therefore essential that they be secured by rope. The following routes, which are easy and have closely spaced fixed protection, are designed specifically with children in mind. They are also well suited for adult beginners.

4 VF du Rocher de la Chaux,
    Stage A Mini Via Ferrata
15 VF École de Rossane
17 VF la Grotte du Maquis
21 VF du Lac de la Rosiere
24 VF du Plan du Bouc,
    Stage B Parcours en Falaise
25 VF de Pralognan,
    Stage B Parcours Ouistiti

27 VF Roc de Tovière,
    Stage A 1ère Partie
29 VF d'Andagne,
    Stage A Itinéraire Pierre Blanc
32 VF du Diable,
    Stage A Les Angelots
33 VF de L'École Buissonnière
35 VF de Poingt Ravier
38 VF de St-Colomban-des-Villards,
    Stage A VF École du Rocher de Capaillan
43 VF de l'Alpe du Grand Serre,
    Stage A VF de la Cascade
52 VF du Rocher du Bez
55 VF de la Schappe
57 VF de l'Horloge
60 VF du Torrent de la Combe
61 VF Gorges d'Ailefroide,
    Stage A Via Facile

A family party crossing the Passerelle de l'Ou Izès (Route 6)

DANGERS

Weather

In common with all mountain ranges, the French Alps are subject to rapid and unpredictable changes in the weather. Prior to setting out on a via ferrata, you should obtain an up-to-date weather forecast. Meteo France, the French state weather service, is the best source of information, with forecasts tailored specifically to the Alps. This can be obtained from www.meteofrance.com, or via television and radio broadcasts. Tourist offices will normally post a recent forecast, which is sometimes available in English. Otherwise, the staff should be able to translate the French-language forecast for you.

Light rainfall should not normally prevent the use of a via ferrata, although it may reduce the grip offered by rock-holds. Routes should be avoided altogether during or after periods of snowfall or when icy. At higher altitude, routes may ice over at any time of year during cold snaps. After snowfall, or during spring or early summer on higher-altitude routes, avalanche may be a risk. Routes should also be avoided when storms are forecast, due to the risk of lightning strike.

Should you find yourself caught out on a via ferrata by bad weather then, if possible, leave by the nearest escape path. If unable to do so, take shelter until the worst has passed. If lightning is present try to isolate yourself from the surrounding rock. If your pack is large enough, sit on it and distance yourself from any metal items, such as walking poles or ice

The Belledonne Massif from the Col de la Croix de Fer (near Route 37)

axes. The via ferrata cable and other metallic elements conduct electricity, so if it is possible to move away from them without compromising safety, do it. Avoid high points such as summits or ridges. Stay in the open and avoid sheltering in caves and other shallow indentations in the rock or under boulders and trees. If these features are struck by lightning, the electricity will take the most economical route to ground, which may be via you. Open depressions in the ground can be a relatively safe place to take shelter.

Hypothermia is also a risk during sudden storms, when the temperature may drop considerably. Put on any spare clothing and try to keep dry. Conversely, during hot periods, you should be aware of the risk of sunburn and heat exhaustion. Carry sunscreen and plenty of water.

Loose rock and fixed protection failure

The fixed equipment used to protect French via ferratas, as well as the rock surrounding the route, is normally checked regularly. However, you should exercise common sense and, if in any doubt about the quality of a hold, give it a solid whack with your boot or fist. If it moves or sounds hollow, do not rely on it to take your weight. Report any equipment in a dangerous state, or conspicuously loose rock, to the local tourist office.

If there are climbers above you, be aware of the possibility that they may dislodge stones as they progress. Be similarly wary of knocking stones onto anyone below. If you do so, warn them of the risk (see Appendix C).

Dogs

In recent years a number of wolves were reintroduced to the French Alps, having been eradicated from the area in the 1930s. As a result of their increasing predation of sheep, shepherds have been encouraged to guard their flocks with Pyrenean mountain dogs, known locally as *pastous*. These live with the sheep while on high pastures. Although it is exceptionally unlikely that you will see wolves, you may well meet a pastou. Although they look like a large pale golden retriever, they share none of that breed's placidity and by instinct will act aggressively to anyone they perceive to be a danger to their flock. To avoid the possibility of attack, try to give any flock of sheep or goats encountered on the hill as wide a berth as possible. However, it is often not easy to differentiate the dog from its flock until it has started to approach. Should you encounter one or more pastous, they will most likely check you out, perhaps with a show of aggression, and then dismiss you as a threat. Do nothing to dissuade them of this opinion, and maintain a calm demeanour while attempting to move away from the flock. Keep any poles or cameras, which they may find threatening, discreetly stored.

A mountain rescue team practising on the Parcours Grotte à Carret (Route 16, Stage B)

ACCIDENTS AND MOUNTAIN RESCUE

Every year many thousands of people use via ferratas without suffering any sort of problem. Nevertheless, accidents, some of them fatal, do occur on these routes. There is no authoritative source of information on the causes of accidents, but it is highly probable that the majority result from the incorrect use of personal self-belaying equipment or failing to clip onto the cable.

If you have an accident and require rescue, you must raise the alarm (see Mountain safety for information; page 6). French mountain rescue teams are trained in via ferrata rescue techniques, but their service is not free of charge. Therefore, it is essential that you are appropriately insured.

INSURANCE

In addition to the standard terms of travel insurance, you should ensure that your policy covers the use of via ferratas. This activity should be named specifically within the policy document. You should also check that the routes you intend to visit are not higher than the maximum altitude permitted by the policy. The British Mountaineering Council and Austrian Alpine Club both offer cover that is well adapted to mountaineering activity.

Additionally, European Union citizens should obtain a current European Health Insurance Card (previously know as an E111 form) prior to travelling. This entitles you to a discount on emergency healthcare (search 'EHIC' at www.nhs.co.uk), but should not be thought of as an alternative to travel insurance.

USING THIS GUIDE

The routes are divided into six chapters, each representing a distinct geographic area. However, this division is highly arbitrary and you should combine routes from different areas based on whatever criteria suits you best. A close inspection of the route descriptions and accompanying sketch maps and topo diagrams will reveal that a fair number of routes contain stages of different grades, and it is worth taking time to find the option that best suits your requirements. If uncertain of your abilities, do not start with a high-grade via ferrata but pick one of the easiest routes; if comfortable with it, consider trying something harder. Note that any references to the true left or true right of a river or stream should be taken to mean your left or right when facing the direction in which the water flows. Also note that all distances for sections of via ferrata mentioned within route descriptions are approximate.

The sketch map at the top of each route is highly schematic and not to scale. These maps are designed to assist with navigation to the routes by car and then to the start of the route on foot. The large majority of approach and return paths are well marked with signs, waymarks and cairns, so navigation is rarely complicated. For most routes, an annotated photo is also provided. This shows the line taken by the via ferrata together with other details. Readers should use these illustrations, in conjunction with the route description, to assess whether the via ferrata is suitable for them and, in some cases, for navigational advice once on the route.

Mont Blanc seen from the highest point on Via Ferrata Le Roc du Vent (Route 12)

Lac de Roselend seen from the top of the Roc du Vent (Route 12)

Route descriptions

The following information is given at the start of each route or stage description.

Location

The nearest village, town or resort to the route and the administrative area (Département) in which it is situated, as well as its GPS coordinates.

Length

Unless otherwise noted, this is the estimated length of the via ferrata only and does not include the approach and return paths.

Ascent/Descent

The total height gain and loss that the route or stage involves, taking into account both the via ferrata and its approach and return paths. The figure is not exact and minor undulations have not been accounted for. For some multi-stage routes, the ascent/descent figure stated in the route overview box is not the sum of the figures given in the individual stage overviews (Route 14, for example). This is due to differing approach and return paths.

Route grading

The technical grade, exposure and seriousness of the route or stage.

Total time

An approximate indication of the time needed to complete the route or stage, including a breakdown of the times required for the approach

path and return path as well as for the via ferrata itself. Stated times assume that the reader has a reasonable level of fitness and do not allow for anything other than short breaks. Congestion can have a major effect on times, as 'overtaking' can be impractical. Should you find your progress blocked by a slow party, the time required to complete the route may be considerably increased. For some multi-stage routes, the total time given in the route overview differs from the combined times of the stage overviews, due to differing approach and return paths (Route 13, for example).

Highest altitude

The maximum altitude gained while on the route.

Map

The relevant map number from the IGN TOP25 series.

Technical notes

Direction: the main direction faced by the route or stage, which will have a bearing on the effects of the weather. For example, on sunny days south-facing routes may be uncomfortably hot, while on cold mornings north-facing routes may be unpleasantly damp.

Escape points: many routes feature one or more places where it is possible to escape from the via ferrata onto easier ground. For routes that are split into multiple stages, the number given in the route overview box is the total number of escape points for the whole route. The number given in each individual stage overview box is the number of escape points within that stage only. As some escape points are located between the end of one stage and beginning of another, the total number of escape points listed in route overviews is not necessarily always the sum of those listed in stage overviews. In addition, as well as escape points leading off via ferratas and onto easier ground, some multi-stage routes feature escapes that lead from a more difficult stage onto an easier stage (Route 4, for example).

When to visit

An approximate indication of the typical season during which a route is open. In practice, this will vary depending on the prevailing weather. Some routes may be closed by the local commune over the winter. If visiting in late autumn or early spring check with the local tourist office as to whether or not the route is open.

Useful websites

In most instances these are for the local tourist office. As well as detailing what the local area has to offer, these are potential sources of up-to-date information on routes regarding alterations or closures and may list places to hire gear or guides. Note that a number of these websites are for ski resorts, which typically have separate front pages for winter (*hiver*) and summer (*été*), with information relevant to the via ferrata listed on the summer page.

KEY POINTS TO REMEMBER

- Knowledge of basic French will be useful but is not essential.
- Before deciding to climb a route, read the entire route description.
- If unsure of your abilities, start with an easy route and progress from there (see Appendix A).
- Make sure that you understand how to set up and use your personal safety equipment correctly.
- Always check the state of your safety equipment before each use, particularly if you have hired your gear.
- Do not hesitate to hire a guide if you require extra assurance.
- Do ensure that you are adequately insured.
- It is a good idea to check in advance with the local tourist office whether a route is open.
- Have a back-up plan in the event of a sudden change in the weather.

GENEVA AND
THE NORTHERN ALPS

Mont Blanc and Passy, as seen from the second balance beam on Via Ferrata de Curalla (Route 7)

INTRODUCTION

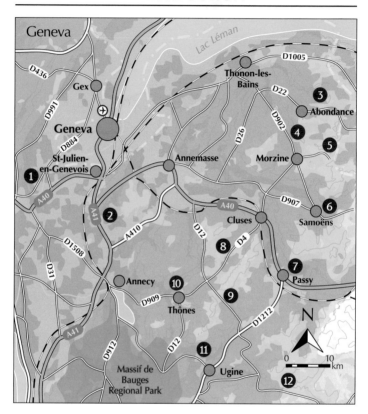

Geneva is actually in Switzerland, but serves as a convenient starting point for the routes in the area, being a major regional transport hub. There are air links with a number of UK cities and it takes three to four hours to reach Geneva by train from Paris.

Once there, the A41 motorway leads south to Chambéry and Grenoble, and the A40 east to Chamonix and the Mont Blanc tunnel. Located on the Genevois Plain, Geneva is effectively an enclave within France, being separated from the rest of Switzerland

The Giffre Massif, seen from the top of Via Ferrata de la Tour du Jallouvre (Route 8)

by Lac Léman (Lake Geneva). The city is home to a number of national and international organisations and financial institutions, lending the city a cosmopolitan air.

In the event of poor weather, there are plenty of the usual tourist attractions associated with a city; be warned, however, that if you intend spending any time here it can be very expensive. Anyone on a limited budget should consider staying over the border at Saint Julien-en-Genevois or Annemasse. Further afield there are plenty of towns, villages and resorts that would make a good base, with the attractive lakeside town of Annecy particularly recommended.

The area covered in this chapter encompasses the Chablais, Haute-Giffre, Bornes, Aravis and Beaufortain ranges within the Alps as well as the southern end of the Jura Massif, which is a separate range from the Alps. These ranges are more accessible than some of those of higher altitude to the east and south, and have a relatively long summer season. The 12 via ferratas described are spread out over a fairly wide area, so allow plenty of travel time if you intend to visit several of them. The routes are fairly representative of French via ferratas, being quite varied in both style and difficulty.

For tourist information see the websites listed in Appendix D.

ROUTE 1

Via Ferrata Fort l'Ecluse

Location	Léaz, Ain (GPS: Lat. 46° 7′ 11.92″ N Long. 5° 53′ 24.78″ E)
Length	400m
Ascent/Descent	170m
Route grading	technical grade: 2; exposure: 2; seriousness: A
Total time	1hr 30mins (approach: 10mins; route: 1hr; return: 20mins)
Highest altitude	590m
Map	3330OT
Technical notes	direction: SW; escape points: 0
When to visit	March to November

Strategically located overlooking the River Rhone at a point where it forces a path through the tail-end of the Jura Massif, the Fort de L'Ecluse guards a major approach route to Geneva. The eponymous via ferrata, which scales bluffs running between the lower and upper bastions of the fort, involves a pleasant and straightforward ascent offering fine views of the river and the Genevois

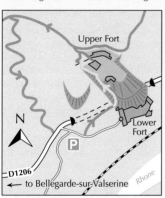

Plain. South facing and situated at low altitude, the route can be visited for much of the year and is suitable for beginners. A visit to the fort, which has been the site of military conflicts from Roman times until the 1940s, is recommended. The fortress is open to visitors from mid-June to mid-September, 1000 to 1830 (entry €5). In 2013 an additional via ferrata/ropes course was added to the internal walls of the Upper Fort (€25 fee); see www.varappe-evolution.com.

Access
From Bellegarde-sur-Valserine drive 10km to the east on the **D1206**. Just prior to entering a tunnel, which

passes under the fort, turn right and park. If coming from Geneva, take the D884 and D984 to reach the D1206 just prior to its passage through the tunnel. Turn left at the exit of the tunnel and park.

Crossing the two-wire bridge beneath the Upper Fort

Approach

From the car park, head towards the **Lower Fort** and turn left up a signposted path, which leads directly to the start of the route.

Route

The initially direct climb soon turns into a long rising traverse to the left. Any strenuous moments are brief and well spaced out and there are plenty of opportunities to rest. Once the walls of the **Upper Fort** are reached, cross a balance beam and two-wire bridge, both of which are short and unexposed. After the via ferrata ends, continue ascending, ignoring any unmarked descent paths, until the entrance to the Upper Fort is reached.

Return
Follow green arrows heading northwest on a metalled track. After 10mins turn left as signposted and descend to the car park.

ROUTE 2
Via Ferrata Jacques Revaclier

Location	Pomier (near Présilly), Haute-Savoie (GPS: Lat. 46° 4′ 46.02″ N Long. 6° 6′ 25.63″ E)
Length	500m
Ascent/Descent	200m
Route grading	technical grade: 2; exposure: 3; seriousness: A
Total time	1hr 45mins (approach: 25mins; route: 1hr; return: 20mins)
Highest altitude	1020m
Map	3430OT
Technical notes	direction: W; escape points: 0
When to visit	April to October
Useful websites	www.genevois-nature.fr; www.maisondusaleve.com

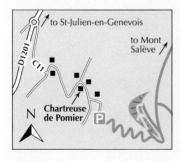

While undoubtedly brief, this via ferrata is still a tempting proposition due to its position on the western flanks of Mont Salève. This long escarpment runs south from Geneva and is much used by the inhabitants of that city for hiking, climbing and paragliding. The local authority asks that you exercise particular discretion if visiting this route during spring, due to the possibility of peregrine falcons nesting in the vicinity.

Note that there are two other cabled routes on Mont Salève, the Vires Büttikofer and Etournelles, both located above Collonges-sous-Salève. These involve sections of unprotected and exposed scrambling and should not be undertaken other than with a local guide.

Access
From St-Julien-en-Genevois drive south on the **D1201**. At a roundabout take the **C11** and drive to **Chartreuse de Pomier**. From there, follow signs for 'Parking Promeneurs' until you come to a parking area with a large boulder at its centre.

Approach
Look out for a small yellow sign for Les Convers. Follow the indicated track, which winds steeply uphill through dense forest, until you reach an information panel for the via ferrata.

The Genevois Plain from the exposed final part of the route

There are 79 bolted rock-climbing routes in the vicinity of the via ferrata, graded 3–7.

Route

Walk without any noticeable difficulty until emerging from the woods onto a pleasantly bulging rock-face. Continue, with intermittent protection, past some impressively overhanging bolted rock-climbing routes. ◄ Just beyond the point where you pass a memorial to the mountaineer after whom the route is named (who died in an accident elsewhere), the nature of the route changes. Both exposure and difficulty increase as you edge out onto sheer rock and ascend for 20m to the finish. This final section is short but moderately strenuous and offers good views of the countryside surrounding Geneva.

Return

A narrow path follows red waymarks uphill for a little way until joining a larger path. Turn left to extend your visit to Mont Salève, or right to descend and rejoin the approach path.

ROUTE 3
Via Ferrata des Saix de Miolène

Location	La Chapelle-d'Abondance, Haute-Savoie
	(GPS: Lat. 46° 17′ 41.71″ N Long. 6° 45′ 52.44″ E)
Length	900m
Ascent/Descent	225m
Route grading	technical grade: 2–4; exposure: 2–3; seriousness: A
	(all stages)
Total time	3hrs 30mins
Highest altitude	1250m
Map	3528ET
Technical notes	direction: SE; total escape points: 3
When to visit	April to October

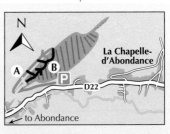

The picture-postcard Abondance Valley constitutes the perfect ideal of an alpine setting: small, chalet-filled villages surrounded by pastures and overlooked by high mountains. The Saix de Miolene, a line of high bluffs dominating the north side of the valley above La Chapelle-d'Abondance, is perhaps the best vantage point from which to enjoy this magnificent location. The via ferrata is of good quality throughout and is divided by escape paths into several sections of increasing difficulty. The upper parts of the route should not be underestimated. Although they contain fewer conspicuously strenuous passages than some other routes of similar grade, the full route is quite long and fairly tiring. Due to the presence of nesting peregrine falcons, the route is closed beyond the second escape path from 15 March to 10 July. There is another via ferrata, of approximately the same difficulty, just over the Swiss border at Champéry.

Access
La Chapelle-d'Abondance is on the **D22**, between Thonon-les-Bains and Monthey (in Switzerland). The car

park, which is at the western end of the village beneath an old quarry, is indicated by a sign with a large white outline of a climber.

STAGE A
Tronçon du Cabri

Length	350m
Ascent/Descent	75m
Route grading	technical grade: 2; exposure: 2; seriousness: A
Time	2hrs (approach: 15mins; route: 1hr 15mins; return: 30mins)
Technical notes	escape points (within stage): 0

Approach
Crossing the Pont du Goleron

A more-or-less level path (Sentier du Menhir) leads through woodland in a westerly direction to the foot of the bluffs on your right.

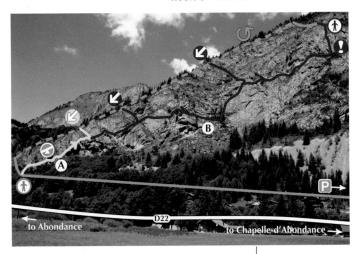

Route

Initially, the route gains 20m in height as it climbs around the toe of the bluffs. Once the southeast face is reached, continue with a gently rising traverse until an outside corner is reached. Exposure along this section is somewhat mitigated by the treetops just below you. Turn the corner and traverse for a few metres to a short balance beam, the Pont du Goleron, using large pockets in the rock for the hands. This is one of the few places along the entire route to use rock handholds, with most progress being aided by abundant stemples.

Beyond the beam, a mildly strenuous climb of a couple of metres, followed by more traversing, leads to a shallow bay where a rest can be taken. The climbing traverse continues more steeply with a few brief and mildly strenuous moves to reach a second shallow bay. From here, cross a 10m-wide blank wall on stemples with plenty of exposure and some effort required. After a little more traversing, Stage A ends at a third shallow bay. There is an escape path on the left.

STAGE B
Tronçon du Chamois/Tronçon du Bouquetin

Length	550m
Ascent/Descent	150m (225m, if combined with Stage A)
Route grading	technical grade: 4; exposure: 3; seriousness A
Time	3hrs 15mins (approach: 15mins; route: 2hrs 25mins (both stages combined); return: 35mins)
Technical notes	escape points (within stage): 2

Route

To continue, edge out onto an exposed position on a blank wall. This is similar in nature to the one crossed near the end of the first stage. More blank walls follow, interspersed with short sections of easier traversing. A broad bay is reached, with a second escape path climbing to the left. Cross the bay on an easy path, and arrive at the Traverse de Coucou. This crosses an impressively smooth rockface for 25m utilising a small horizontal weakness in the rock.

The strenuous Traverse de Coucou

Some of the foot placements are hidden and fairly small, and the traverse is likely to leave you with aching arms.

Climb up around a narrow buttress to reach a ledge, which is followed without any difficulties until arriving at a large tree. This spot (Le Jardin de Miolene) is one of the few places on the route with shade. From here, the route gains 65 vertical metres up a series of steep climbs and traverses (La Para Nera). This ascent is tiring but contains no noticeably strenuous moves. At the top a narrow ledge passes an escape path on the left and leads to the Traversée des Poupées. This takes a gradually rising line across a series of vegetated ledges and bare slabs until arriving at a steep climb of 15m. The final 5m of the climb ascend an open corner and are fairly tough.

Above this, another narrow ledge, where a rest can be had, leads to the Mur du Saix Rouge. This is climbed for 70 vertical metres and contains a few small passages that are slightly overhanging. Depending on your height, some moves may be fairly awkward due to the placement of the rungs and you may need to make use of a number of small hand and rock foot placements. At the top of the climb, the cable continues along much easier ground for a further few minutes before terminating.

Return
Descend carefully until the start of the route is reached and return along the approach path.

DENT D'OCHE OPTION

Although it cannot really be considered to be a via ferrata, the path traversing the nearby Dent d'Oche (2221m) is well worth an ascent for anyone in the area. The route contains several exposed sections of scrambling, which are protected by cable. It is situated a little to the north of the Abondance Valley and is best accessed from the small village of Bernex, which can be reached from Évian-les-Bains. There is a staffed refuge on the summit of the peak, from which there are exceptional views, taking in the entire sweep of Lake Geneva. The ascent climbs for 1010m from Parking La Fétiuère (above Bernex); allow 5–7hrs for the round-trip.

ROUTE 4

Via Ferrata du Rocher de la Chaux

Location	St-Jean-d'Aulps, Haute-Savoie
	(GPS: Lat. 46° 14′ 36.65″ N Long. 6° 38′ 51.63″ E)
Length	700m
Ascent/Descent	795m
Route grading	technical grade: 3–5; exposure: 5; seriousness: A (all stages)
Total time	5hrs 25mins (if all stages climbed consecutively)
Highest altitude	1173m
Map	3528ET
Technical notes	total escape points: 0
When to visit	May to October

This new route, opened in the summer of 2011, scales a feature known locally as the Tete de l'Éléphant. Driving north from Morzine, the reason for

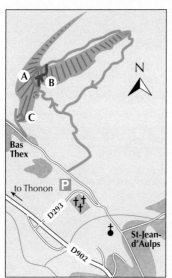

the name soon becomes apparent, as an approximation of an elephant's head can clearly be seen on the Rocher de la Chaux, to the northwest of St-Jean-d'Aulps.

There are two routes on the rock, with the easier one ascending the 'trunk' of the elephant and the harder route its 'face', as well as an easier third option nearby. Both routes are athletic, sustained and exceptionally airy, with the exposure being particularly 'immediate' for most of their length. There are few good places to take a break on either route, so a rest lanyard is essential. The second route is considerably more arduous and sustained than the first, although the most difficult passages are fairly well spaced apart. As such, the route would be a good option to try before tackling one of the most difficult via ferratas in the book, such as the Grotte à Carret (Route 16, Stage B) or Grand Dièdre (Route 40, Stage B). An easier third option, the Mini Via Ferrata, could be completed as a warm-up for the other routes, or by children and beginners who want to dip their toes in the water. The routes on the Rocher de la Chaux are closed each year from 15 April to 15 May to protect the kidding of chamois.

Access
Driving south on the **D902** from Thonon-les-Bains, turn left onto the **D293** just before **St-Jean-d'Aulps**. Follow this for 200m and park next to a cemetery and information panel for the via ferrata.

STAGE A
La Tête de l'Éléphant

Length	300m
Ascent/Descent	375m
Route grading	technical grade: 3; exposure: 5; seriousness A
Time	2hrs 30mins
	(approach: 25mins; route: 1hr 30mins; return: 35mins)
Technical notes	direction SE; escape points (within stage): 0

Approach
Briefly walk uphill to a minor road and turn left. Immediately beyond the first intact building on your right a small sign indicates the point where you leave the road. Take a path, with orange waymarks, that climbs steeply uphill through forested slopes.

Route
A straightforward climbing traverse leads to the Pilier de Chantemerle, a vertical climb of 50m. This is quite steep, but initially not too strenuous. In common with the rest

The reward for your efforts: a view of Mont Blanc

of the route, as well as the adjacent route, progress is almost exclusively on stemples, with only very occasional contact made with the rock. Towards the top of this first climb, several mildly demanding moves lead to a short, vertiginous traverse around a corner, beyond

which is a balance beam. The 4m-long beam (Le Pont de Saint Guérin) feels extremely airy and is equipped with a cable only just tight enough to avoid having to rely on balance alone.

Pass the escape path from the harder route and continue with a climb of 30m. This involves a few slightly strenuous moves and leads to a steep traverse up to the second escape path from the harder route. Continue to traverse steeply, with a gradual decline in the angle of ascent leading to the junction with the other route. From here, walk easily up the grassy hillside to the end of the cable. ▸

The platform above the end of the route affords fine views of Mont Blanc (4810m), in the distance, as well as of St-Jean-d'Aulps, now far below you.

Return

Keep your gear on as the return path involves some easy cabled sections. Follow a path up the ridgeline, and then descend forested slopes to meet your approach path.

STAGE B
L'Oeil de l'Éléphant

Length	300m
Ascent/Descent	375m (750m, if combined with Stage A)
Route grading	technical grade: 5; exposure: 5; seriousness: A
Time	2hrs 30mins
	(approach: 25mins; route: 1hr 30mins; return: 35mins)
Technical notes	direction: SE; escape points (to Stage A): 2

Route

Start as for Stage A: within 10m diverge from the easier route and climb straight up the face for 35m and cross the Traversée du Doute. This steeply rising traverse of 15m constitutes the first real challenge, being both noticeably strenuous and the first point at which the exposed nature of the route can be properly appreciated. Arrive at the Mur des Lamentations, a vertical climb of 20m with some reasonable overhangs on it.

A little more steep traversing brings you to the first escape point.

If you really struggled with the first section, consider taking the easier route as the next part is just as arduous but even more exposed. This consists of a long rising traverse, occasionally interrupted by some overhangs. The largest of these, near the top of the section, is the eponymous Oeil de l'Éléphant (crux). This involves a highly muscular and airy move part-way along a generally strenuous passage of 15m. The second escape point is found a little way above this.

The third and final section may come as a disappointment or a relief depending on how you have found the route so far. Begin with a climb followed by a traverse, both of a few metres each and all somewhat overhanging. Difficulty then reduces significantly along with a marginal drop in exposure as a long rising traverse is followed. The cable tops out onto a grassy hillside before rejoining the easier route.

STAGE C
Mini Via Ferrata

Length	100m
Ascent/Descent	45m (795m, if combined with preceding stages)
Route grading	technical grade: 1 (variant: 3); exposure: 2; seriousness: A
Time	45mins (approach: 10mins; route: 25mins; return: 10mins)
Technical notes	direction: W; escape points (within stage): 0

Approach
From the parking place briefly walk uphill to a minor road and turn left. Follow the road, passing the junction with the path for the other stages, and continue to a rock-climbing area above the hamlet of **Bas Thex**. A little way beyond an information panel, take the first path to the right and immediately you will see two via ferrata lines alongside many bolted sports climbing routes.

Route
Ascend the left-hand cable. Scale a just off-vertical slab for 25m to a narrow ledge. Either continue climbing for 10m or walk along the ledge to the right to take a harder variant. This harder option begins by ascending through a moderate overhang for a few metres before continuing up to join the other route. Another alternative is to continue along the ledge to the right to join the descent route. From the top of the climb, the cable heads right and descends broken ground without particular difficulty.

ROUTE 5

Via Ferrata du Saix du Tour

Location	Avoriaz, Haute-Savoie
	(GPS: Lat. 46° 11' 25.86" N Long. 6° 46' 39.88" E)
Length	600m
Ascent/Descent	225m
Route grading	technical grade: 3 (variant: 4); exposure: 3; seriousness: B
Total time	3hrs 15mins
	(approach: 20mins; route: 2hrs 25mins; return: 30mins)
Highest altitude	2023m
Map	3528ET
Technical notes	direction: SW; escape points: 3
When to visit	May to October

The ski resort of Avoriaz cannot be described as the most attractive of places. During the summer, this jumble of architecturally dubious apartment blocks typically resembles a building site, but this is more than compensated for by the beauty of its mountain setting as well as the presence of a high-quality via ferrata crossing heavily striated bluffs above the resort. With several escape points and two variants, the via ferrata offers a wide variety of challenge; however, the general standard is reasonably demanding, especially for the first half of the route. There is quite a lot of rock contact in places and a pair of boots with good grip, and a rest lanyard, are recommended. The route is situated at a relatively high altitude and due consideration should be given to the effects of poor weather. Watch out for some loose rock on and above the route.

*Avoriaz, from the
Passage du Berger*

Access
From Morzine, follow the **D338** to the ski resort of
Avoriaz. The resort is theoretically car-free for most of
the year, so you may have to park on its outskirts. Walk
(or drive if permitted) through the centre of the resort via
Rue des Traîneaux. At the bottom of the road look out for
a large via ferrata information panel next to a small car
park and a **Sherpa supermarket**.

Approach
From the Sherpa supermarket, walk downhill along a
gravel track for a minute and then turn left at a sign for
the via ferrata. Follow a clear path up grassy slopes to the
base of the bluffs.

Route
Start with a climbing traverse (l'Emotion). This gives a
good idea of the nature of the rest of the route. A short
down-climb on hidden stemples is followed by an awkward move around a corner. Arrive at the first escape
point.

The next part (Le Passage du Génépi) follows a gradually rising line until a somewhat strenuous climb of 10m
brings you to a narrow, airy ledge. Follow this until a second, similarly strenuous climb of 10m. A little beyond
here, you are presented with two options:

1   Keep left to take a straightforward route that ascends gradually around a shallow bay in the cliff-face.

2   Alternatively, go right to cross the slightly wobbly 20m-long bridge (Pont de la Vot'nette) and climb up for 15m. This climb is quite strenuous, with one move halfway up, at the most exposed point, being particularly tricky. Depending on your height you will probably have to make one or two smears with your boots.

Above this, the two routes rejoin and difficulty reduces as the second escape point is passed, heading off to the left along the Sentier des Moutons. To the right is a good rest spot next to a shallow cave (La Grotte des Ardoisiers). Beyond this, a lengthy cabled walk along the Passage du Berger and Balcon du Lac follows. This is briefly interrupted by an easy climbing traverse (La Traversée du Bénitier) before more walking leads to a short climb up the hillside. Above this is a second split in the cable and another choice of options:

1 Go straight up for the harder option, which involves
climbing through a short but fairly heavy overhang
(La Surplomb du Saix).

2 Go right for a much easier climb.

Both routes quickly re-converge after 15m of ascent.
Either head steeply uphill to take the third escape, or
descend a little to your right to continue.

This final part follows a long, more-or-less level
traverse (Le Passage du Rasoir), crosses a three-wire
bridge (Le Pont de Vorlaz), then climbs around and up a
tower (La Pointe du Tour). Progress is not very strenuous
but there are a few delicate moves and the climb around
the tower feels noticeably exposed. The three-wire bridge
is 10m long and reasonably stable. Above the tower the
cable continues back along the narrow ridge of the Saix
du Tour without difficulty. Assuming a clear sky, compensation for your efforts comes in the form of extensive
views of the surrounding mountains and valleys. The row
of peaks just visible over the Swiss border is the Dents du
Midi (highest point 3178m).

*Crossing Le Pont de
Vorlaz to arrive at
La Pointe du Tour*

Return

Continue along the ridge, passing many wild flowers in early summer, and descend to a ski piste. Follow this in the same direction until the first turn to the left, which descends down a gravel road to the centre of Avoriaz. If you are parked on the outskirts of the resort, do not turn left but instead continue straight ahead.

ROUTE 6
Via Ferrata du Mont

Location	Sixt-Fer-à-Cheval, Haute-Savoie (GPS: Lat. 46° 3′ 21.48″ N Long. 6° 45′ 28.39″ E)
Length	800m
Ascent/Descent	240m
Route grading	technical grade: 3; exposure: 3; seriousness: A
Total time	2hrs 45mins (approach: 25mins; route: 2hrs; return: 20mins)
Highest altitude	1010m
Map	3530ET
Technical notes	direction: S; escape points: 3
When to visit	March to November

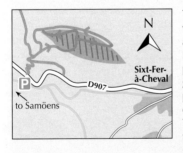

This well-designed and scenic via ferrata is extremely popular, and can often be quite crowded. Don't let that put you off as it has plenty to offer, being a good mid-grade route with several escape points and the unusual option of a long descending traverse. The immediate area is well worth further exploration, especially the nearby Cirque du Fer-à-Cheval, a vast natural amphitheatre. Situated at a comparatively low altitude and south facing, the route can be a reasonable option when poor weather prevents access to some of the more elevated routes in the area.

Looking down at the Gorges des Tines from the Passerelle de l'Ou Izès

Access
From Cluses, follow the D902 to Taninges and, from there, the **D907** through Samoëns towards **Sixt-Fer-à-Cheval**. Some 5km beyond Samoëns, at the Gorges des Tines, park on the right of the road, next to the Snack des Tines café.

Approach
Cross the road to a signpost and take the indicated path, which winds steeply uphill through dense tree cover. Turn

left at the first junction encountered, and follow more signs and red triangles to the start of the route.

Route
Initially the route is very easy, involving a long cabled walk up a broad ledge, the Vire à l'Ours, which is briefly interrupted by a short climb. At the end of the ledge, the cable climbs up to a shallow cave, the Barme aux Corbés, and the route becomes a little more serious. Move out onto the rockface and climb up the Dalle des Paresseux for 40m. The ascent is well protected and not particularly arduous but feels reasonably airy.

Above the climb, go left to take the first escape point (*Sortie directe*) or right to continue with a short airy traverse. This leads to a vegetated area, which is a good place to take a break before passing around a corner (La Becque) and crossing a 13m-long plank bridge (Passerelle de l'Ou Izès). On the other side of the bridge, which is not very stable and quite exposed, a traverse of 20m length leads to a short ladder. The first 10m of the traverse is a little overhanging and reasonably strenuous.

Above the ladder a further airy traverse leads to a second escape point. Descend a little from here to the Traversée de l'Ally and follow a long, generally rising, traverse on a mixture of narrow ledges and steep slabs, passing another escape point along the way. The slabs contain a few slightly strenuous moves but are well protected with plenty of rungs. A short climb then passes through a small overhang to reach the top of the bluffs. Descend along the Chemin du Retour until signs indicate a left turn for the Vire du Raffour. Keep right to continue descending by the Chemin du Retour or go left and descend to the top of the Dalle des Paresseux and turn right. The Vire du Raffour utilises a system of gradually descending vegetated ledges. While progress is mostly quite easy, there are several passages of mildly strenuous downclimbing.

A small traffic jam near the first escape point

Return
Keep your gear on, as the descent path contains one short, easy, cabled section. Having passed this, quickly rejoin the approach path.

ROUTE 7

Via Ferrata de Curalla

Location	Plateau-d'Assy, Haute-Savoie
	(GPS: Lat. 45° 56' 19.09" N Long. 6° 41' 43.88" E)
Length	400m
Ascent/Descent	350m
Route grading	technical grade: 2; exposure: 3; seriousness: B
Total time	2hrs 45mins
	(approach: 30mins; route: 1hr 30mins; return: 45mins)
Highest altitude	1420m
Map	3530ET
Technical notes	direction: S; escape points: 0
When to visit	May to October

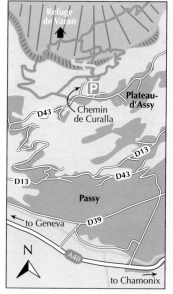

While this via ferrata makes for a pleasant outing in its own right, its greatest virtue is the outstanding views it affords of Mont Blanc (4810m). The route is exposed to the full breadth of the southern aspect of this iconic mountain and its associated peaks, and given clear weather you should be treated to an exceptional panorama. In the event that Mont Blanc is wreathed in cloud, consolation comes in the form of extensive views of the Arve Valley and the busy town of Passy. The ascent involves only a few brief strenuous moments but lacks any escape, is fairly exposed throughout, and contains several bridges that require a steady head for heights. As such, the route is suitable only for confident beginners. A visit to the nearby Refuge de Varan and further exploration of the Massif de Fiz would make for a worthwhile extension.

Access
Drive to **Passy**, some 15km west of Chamonix and the Mont Blanc tunnel. From Passy, follow signs for **Plateau-d'Assy** on a road (**D43**) that ascends the hillside to the north Just after the plateau is reached and the road levels off, look out for a signpost for the via ferrata indicating a left turn up the **Chemin de Curalla**. After 300m, park on the left.

Approach
Follow a steep path, turning first right then left at sign-posted junctions.

Route
Climb up the cliff-face for 35m, making use of abundant fixed protection, until the route levels off. Then follow a gently rising traverse across a series of narrow ledges for 50m. This quickly becomes quite exposed, but is

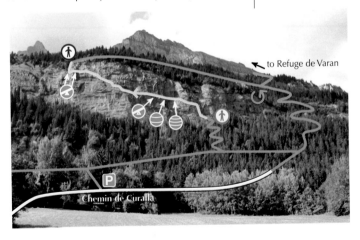

The Pont du Varan and Pont d'Assy

Crossing the Pont de Varan with the Aiguille Verte (4122m) in the background

otherwise fairly easy. The ledges disappear and a gap of 18m is crossed by a three-wire bridge, the Pont de Varan. Immediately beyond this a second gap of 7m is crossed by a two-wire bridge, the Pont d'Assy. Both bridges are a little slack and the brief move between the two, which passes around a corner, is one of the most strenuous parts of the route.

Beyond the bridges, the route passes over a balance beam and continues with a long rising traverse, interspersed with brief vertical sections of climbing. This is well protected where necessary and not particularly strenuous. There are several places where it is possible to rest. Having gained quite a bit of height, cross a second balance beam and pass around a corner. Overcome a third balance beam and climb up for 15m to the top of the cliff. This final climb is the most exposed and strenuous part of the route, so if you are feeling tired take a break and admire the views before going around the corner.

Return
Head east until a broad track is reached. Descend to return to the parking, or alternatively ascend for 30mins to visit the **Refuge de Varan**.

ROUTE 8
Via Ferrata de la Tour du Jallouvre

Location	Le Grand-Bornand, Haute-Savoie (GPS: Lat. 45° 59′ 20.53″ N Long. 6° 28′ 3.49″ E)
Length	1100m
Ascent/Descent	620m
Route grading	technical grade: 4; exposure: 5; seriousness: C
Total time	4hrs 30mins (approach: 30mins; route: 3hrs; return: 1hr)
Highest altitude	2040m
Map	3430ET
Technical notes	direction: SW; escape points: 1
When to visit	Closed 15 November–15 May

This is the perfect via ferrata for mountain lovers. The route scales the steep southeastern flanks of the Pic de Jallouvre (2408m), one of the pale limestone peaks of the Aravis Massif, and offers extensive views of the surrounding

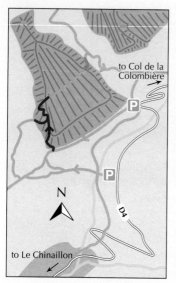

mountain ranges. The via ferrata is of high quality and makes good use of the heavily eroded karstic terrain. It is fairly long, occasionally strenuous, and in its latter stages, supremely exposed. Although there is an escape path part-way along, the outing should be undertaken only by those in a decent state of fitness and when the weather forecast is good. In addition to the fine views, your efforts should be rewarded by a close encounter with yellow-billed choughs (a relative of the crow), chamois or Alpine ibex. This latter species of hardy mountain goat is known in France as a *bouquetin*.

Access

From Annecy, follow the D909 to St-Jean-de-Sixt and then the D4 to Le Grand-Bornand. Continue on the **D4** in the direction of the Col de la Colombière for around 10km (passing through **Le Chinaillon**). Shortly before the col, there is a parking area with a via ferrata information panel to the left of the road. The route can be started from here, or alternatively – for a more level approach path – drive on for 1km to a hairpin bend. Park on the left, next to some piles of rubble.

Approach

The path from the lower parking is well signposted and descends and then ascends the shallow valley between the car park and the southwest end of the cliff-face opposite. From the higher parking area, follow an unmarked path running parallel to the cliff-face (which contains several bolted sports climbing routes) until the first cable is encountered.

Route

Start by following a leftwards rising traverse that gradually bends around the cliff-face. Other than a few short steps progress is straightforward until the cable leads across some large slabs beneath an overhang (Arche du Bouquetin). The climb through the overhang is brief but quite arduous due to the placement of the rungs, which are fairly small. Some smeary holds on the slightly polished rock may be helpful to shorter climbers.

Above the overhang, a long scramble gains 200m in height up a 70° slope until a semi-detached pillar (Tour du Jallouvre) comes into view. Gradually descend for 30m to meet the escape path (Sortie à Fred). The escape route follows a wide ledge that leads down to a path descending back towards the lower parking area.

If continuing, climb up to the 15m-long suspension bridge (Passerelle du Gypaète) and, once crossed, ascend the smooth face of the pillar for 30m, on stemples. This climb, although lacking any overhangs, is moderately strenuous and contains a few slightly awkward moves. From the top of the climb, a gently rising traverse around the edge of the pillar is followed. The traverse, which is in a marvellously exposed position, crosses down-sloping slabs and passes over a shallow depression by means of a 5m-long balance beam. Gain more height over broken terrain until the edge of an arête (Arête de la Faim) is gained.

Both exposure and difficulty diminish somewhat from here as the arête is followed back to the main body of the mountain. A short descending scramble off the arête leads to some wonderfully flowing limestone slabs, which are ascended with minimal difficulty to the finish. From here,

Approaching the top of the Tour du Jallouvre

there are extensive views to the east, with the top of Mont Blanc (4810m) prominent behind Pointe Percée (2753m), which is the highest peak of the Aravis Massif. There are also good views of the Giffre Massif to the northeast.

Return

Keep your gear on for the descent. The return path, which is a little hands-on in places, follows cairns across the side of the mountain and then descends at a moderate angle down a weakness in some bluffs. The descent, which is cabled, drops for 40m. There is normally a herd of ibex grazing in the vicinity of these bluffs. Once the cable ends, follow a particularly slippery path down scree slopes to return to the upper car park. Another path heads down the valley from here to the lower car park.

ROUTE 9
Via Ferrata Yves Pollet Villard

Location	La Clusaz, Haute-Savoie
	(GPS: Lat. 45° 52′ 44.31″ N Long. 6° 27′ 5.33″ E)
Length	700m
Ascent/Descent	410m
Route grading	technical grade: 3 (variant: 4); exposure: 3; seriousness: B
Total time	3hrs 45mins
	(approach: 20mins; route: 2hrs 40mins; return: 45mins)
Highest altitude	1800m
Map	3531OT
Technical notes	direction: S; escape points: 0
When to visit	Closed 15 November–15 May

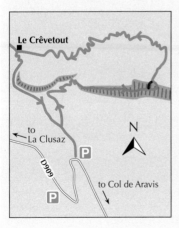

This via ferrata is located above the Col de Aravis, between the archetypal Savoyard villages of La Clusaz and La Geittaz. Together with an adjacent area of bolted rock-climbing routes (the Rocher des Aravis), the route was erected in memory of a famous local mountaineer. If there is such a thing as a typical via ferrata, this route might be it, being of middling grade and averagely exposed. That should in no way put you off an ascent, as the route is cleverly designed to make excellent use of ledges running across a long escarpment, the Rocher de Borderan.

Gaining height near the start of the route

Access
From Annecy, take the **D909**. Pass through La Clusaz and continue in the direction of the Col de Aravis. Approximately 5.5km from the centre of **La Clusaz** and 2km before the col, park in a small lay-by to the left of the road. Additional parking is available 400m down the hill.

Approach

A well-signposted path leaves the road, just below the parking area. The path, which passes a large information panel for the via ferrata, leads steeply uphill to the base of the bluffs. There are numerous bolted rock-climbing routes on the cliffs to the left of the path.

Route

Having gained a little height up some easy ledges, the route follows a long and gradually rising line across the bluffs. Initially, this uses a number of fairly wide ledges, is quite easy and not very exposed. This does not last for long, as the ledges soon narrow and the ground drops away. Gain some height up the bluffs, now progressing mostly on stemples, with a large drop directly beneath you. The route levels off and follows a long ledge (Le Mur du Bon Geste), which leads out above a massive overhang, passes around a corner, and disappears. The ledge reappears, in a much-reduced form, on the other side of a large gap, which is crossed via a 15m-long bridge, the Arvi Pa'ssrelle. This is particularly airy but quite stable.

The ledge continues along the face at the same angle, now with more exposure and a few slightly strenuous moves, until a brief climb leads up some low-angle slabs (La Dalle aux Lapiaz). There is a good place to rest at the top of the slabs, which are followed by more traversing.

Looking down on the Col de Aravis and Arvi Pa'ssrelle

This is easier and less exposed than the previous sections and leads to a junction. Continue to the right to take the Sortie des Aravis, which leads to the end of the route via an easy scramble up a short chimney. For a harder exit, go left for the Sortie a la R'tourne. This climbs vertically on stemples for 25m, and then passes through one short but pronounced overhang, which is directly above the junction.

Return

Admire the view, then descend to the left, following cairns and signs for 'Retour de la Via Ferrata', to **Le Crêvetout**. From there, turn left, taking the Route du Col de Aravis, to return to the car park.

ROUTE 10
Via Ferrata de Thônes – La Roche à l'Agathe

Location	Thônes, Haute-Savoie (GPS: Lat. 46° 53' 2.65" N Long. 6° 19' 17.86" E)
Length	600m
Ascent/Descent	285m
Route grading	technical grading 4–5; exposure 3–4; seriousness: A (all stages)
Total time	2hrs 30mins
Highest altitude	895m
Map	3431OT
Technical notes	direction: SW; total escape points: 2
When to visit	May to October

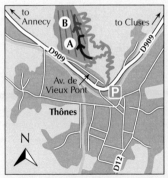

Once considered to be one of the hardest via ferratas in France, this high-quality route has now been surpassed in difficulty by a handful of newer itineraries. Nevertheless, it remains a very enjoyable outing and is one of the easier top-grade via ferratas and a good option for those who wish to try their hand at one of the harder routes for the first time. However, the Surplomb de l'Ermite, a short optional climb near the top, involves the most strenuous and sustained single section of climbing to be found on any route in this book.

Access
Upon entering **Thônes**, take the second exit from the first roundabout (if driving from Annecy on the **D909**) and follow signs to the via ferrata car park (next to the bus station).

STAGE A
1ère Partie

Length	325m
Ascent/Descent	190m
Route grading	technical grade: 4; exposure: 3; seriousness: A
Time	1hr 30mins (approach: 5mins; route: 1hr; return: 25mins)
Technical notes	escape points (within stage): 0

Approach

The Pont du Calvaire is less strenuous if crossed facing outwards

Follow signs for the via ferrata back along the D909 for 70m and then for 100m along the **Avenue de Vieux Pont** to a via ferrata information board. Take a path that zig-zags up the hillside, ignoring any side-paths, until a sign indicates a turn to the left.

Route

After a brief climb, cross an 11m-long two-wire bridge (Pont du Calvaire). This is reasonably stable and is easier to cross facing outwards. Exposure is already abundant and will only increase as you follow a fairly direct line up the cliff. There are plenty of short demanding passages, which are generally in the most exposed positions. Between these are sections of easier climbing, utilising steep ledges, which offer a number of small places to rest. Stage A ends a little over halfway up the route. An escape path heads off to the right.

STAGE B

2ème Partie

Length	275m
Ascent/Descent	95m (285m, if combined with Stage A)
Route grading	technical grade: 5; exposure: 4; seriousness: A
Time	2hrs 30mins (approach: 5mins; route: 1hr 50mins (both stages combined); return: 35mins)
Technical notes	escape points (within stage): 1

Route

Above the first escape point, the route continues in a similar fashion as before; sections of difficult climbing with short overhanging positions interspersed with easier ledges and traverses. This is only a little more demanding than the first stage. Having arrived at a broad ledge, you are presented with three different choices. Either walk along the ledge to the right to escape, scale

The Surplombe de l'Ermite is one of the
hardest sections of via ferrata in France

the outward-facing ladder for 13m or, to the left, climb the 12m-high Surplomb de l'Ermite.

The latter option is overhanging for most of its length and consequently puts a lot of strain on the arms. The rungs are closely spaced and cable run-outs are very short, which is just as well, given the number of people who fail to hang on and end up dangling in mid-air. A rest lanyard is essential, and should you 'come off', do not hesitate to take a long rest or climb back down rather than continue. The ladder, although exceedingly airy, is recommended for anyone who is not entirely confident of his or her upper body strength. Above the climb or ladder, steep flowing limestone slabs, which are mostly free of stemples, make for a pleasant finale as you ascend the final 30m to the finish.

Return

Having enjoyed the bird's-eye view of Thônes, descend steeply to the right. Keep your gear on, as the return path is partially cabled. At a junction in the path, either go right to rejoin the approach path or keep left to return more directly to the car park. This follows the Chemin de la Chapelle du Calvaire, which passes a series of Stations of the Cross.

ROUTE 11
Via Ferrata d'Ugine

Location	Ugine, Savoie
	(GPS: Lat. 45° 47' 38.15" N Long. 6° 25' 37.64" E)
Length	10km (approx. 1400m cabled)
Ascent/Descent	1020m
Route grading	technical grade: 1; exposure: 2; seriousness: C
Total time	6hrs (approach: 1hr; route: 2hrs 30mins; return: 2hrs 30mins)
Highest altitude	2409m
Map	3531OT
Technical notes	direction: all; escape points: 1 (but see Route below)
When to visit	Closed 16 October–14 May

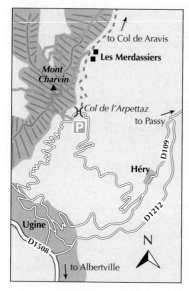

As a fixed mountaineering path, rather than a 'sports' via ferrata, this route is a relative rarity in France. Despite the lack of thrills compared to some other via ferratas, it is still a worthwhile outing for any mountain lover. The summit of Mont Charvin (2409m) offers outstanding panoramas of the surrounding ranges including good views of the Mont Blanc Massif to the east. Although the route is mostly well protected, it is as much a long, easy, summer-mountaineering trip as a via ferrata. Note that this is the longest route covered in the book and involves more height gain than any other route. As such, it requires a reasonable level of fitness and, due to the nature of the terrain and limited escape options, should not be undertaken in poor weather.

Access

From **Ugine**, follow signs up a narrow minor road in the direction of the Col de l'Arpettaz. Alternatively, if approaching from the north along the **D1212**, turn right onto the **D109** and drive to **Héry**, just beyond which a minor road ascends to the **Col de l'Arpettaz**. Park at Les Bassins, which is 1km to the south of the col. For those with robust vehicles, it is also possible to make a highly scenic approach from the Col de Aravis (see Route 9) along a rough vehicle track.

Approach

An increasingly steep path zigzags up the slope towards an obvious weakness in the line of bluffs.

Route

The steep walk turns into an easy scramble as some small rock steps are overcome. Just above this, a large information panel indicates the start of the cable. Follow this up

You may not have the summit of Mont Charvin to yourself

a broad low-angle gully (the **Golet de la Trouye**), keeping an eye out for indistinct red waymarks. This initial passage is typical of the entire route, which consists of steep and slippery unprotected walking, interspersed with sections of easy scrambling protected by cable. Once the top of the cliffs is reached follow red and white waymarks (ignore any old red waymarks) up the southwest arête of Mont Charvin to the summit.

From the summit, it is possible to escape down a path to the northwest, which leads to the Col des Porthets. This is recommended only in extremis, however, as there is no easy way to return to the car park via this route that does not involve an excessively long journey. Having taken in the wide-ranging views from the top of Mont Charvin, descend via the east arête until a little before the lowest point of the ridge is reached, where the **Pas de l'Ours** commences. This point is rather unobtrusive, so look out for an information panel immediately to the right of the path. Descend a short way and traverse along a narrow shelf, between two bands of rock, for 250m.

Return

The path descends steeply until blocked by a long line of bluffs. The seemingly interminable Sentier des Martines is then followed to a point where it is possible to descend to some chalets (**Les Merdassiers**). From there, turn right and follow a gravel road back towards the Col de l'Arpettaz and the car park.

ROUTE 12

Via Ferrata Le Roc du Vent

Location	Plan de la Lai, Haute-Savoie
	(GPS: Lat. 45° 41′ 34.90″ N Long. 6° 40′ 12.05″ E)
Length	850m
Ascent/Descent	550m
Route grading	technical grade: 2; exposure: 3; seriousness: C
Total time	4hrs 15mins
	(approach: 50mins; route: 2hrs 45mins; return: 40mins)
Highest altitude	2360m
Map	3532OT
Technical notes	direction: all; escape points: 2
When to visit	June to September

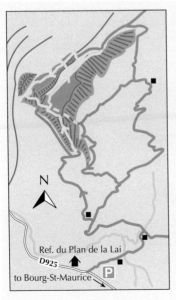

This is arguably the most scenic of any of the routes in this book, and is certainly one of the most popular. The summit of the Roc du Vent is an exceptional viewpoint, offering a wide-ranging panorama of much of the Beaufortain and Vanoise ranges as well as of Mont Blanc, while Lac de Roselend lies below. For this reason, and bearing in mind the relatively high altitude of the route, it is strongly recommended that the via ferrata be climbed when the weather is clear. Although the route is neither technically demanding nor especially strenuous, it is fairly long, involves quite a lot of rock contact and contains a few very brief sections of unprotected easy scrambling. A torch is required to complete the final, optional, section of the route.

Access
From Albertville follow signs for 'Beaufortain' and take the **D925** to Beaufort and continue on the same road to **Refuge du Plan de la Lai**. Park just beyond the refuge. The departure point is indicated by a large information panel for the via ferrata.

Approach
Follow signs for the via ferrata along a clear path, initially shared with the GR5 walking route. Just before a chalet, turn left off the main path and ascend steeply in the direction of the large bluffs. If in any doubt as to where to go, head for the large white sign at the base of the bluffs. If this is not visible from below due to low cloud, consider leaving the route for a clearer day.

Route
The first passage of the via ferrata consists of a long climb up a succession of low-angle slabs, with the main cliff-face immediately below and to your left. These can be slippery and are often a little damp. Protection is adequate rather than abundant and you may find yourself

The first part of the route ascends a series of low-angle slabs

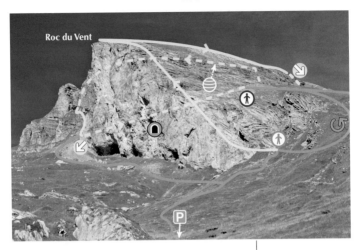

hauling up the cable in preference to using the rock. After the angle briefly eases, it again steepens for the final 30m of ascent until a narrow grassy ridge is attained. The cable ends and a clear path is followed along the edge of the ridge, with views across a massive cleft in the mountain-top to the second part of the route.

The cable starts again at the end of the ridge and descends along similar ground to that which you have recently ascended. While the descent is not strenuous, it can be slightly awkward and care should be taken, par-ticularly for the first few metres. Having deposited you at the end of the gigantic slot in the mountaintop, the cable again ends. It is possible to escape to the right at this point.

To continue, cross the slot and climb (the cable having recommenced) up the side of one of the towers that runs along the slot's other side. Walk along the top of the tower and cross to the second tower by a three-wire bridge. This is 19m long and can feel quite unstable, especially in gusty conditions. Given that Roc du Vent means 'Windy Rock', such conditions are not unusual.

95

Looking across the massive cleft in the top of the mountain, with the Mont Blanc range behind

Cross the top of the second tower, in the direction of two large cairns. This is not cabled and some care is required at two points that involve short, unexposed descents. Beyond the cairns the cable recommences and a short, quite awkward, descent of a few metres follows before the cable ends again. The cabling hereafter is not continuous but is present on the most trying parts of the descent.

Once at the base of the ridge that you initially climbed, either escape to the right by descending to the start of the route, or enter a low tunnel. The tunnel, rather improbably, was built as part of a failed scheme to construct a road running the length of the high French Alps. After 100m, emerge onto a platform, with the initial ascent route now at your back.

Return

Take the broad track to the northeast to join the GR5 path, or for a more direct descent, head down the unmarked path immediately to your right. This path is steep and can be slippery, so requires care.

CHAMBÉRY

*Lac du Bourget and Aix-les-Bains from Parcours
Primevère à Oreille d'Ours (Route 14, Stage A)*

INTRODUCTION

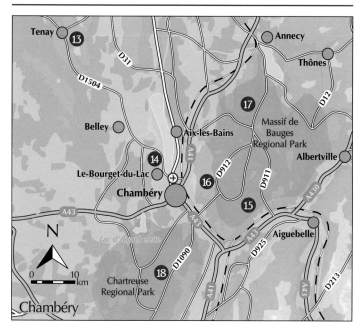

The small city of Chambéry, scenically located in a wide valley between two mountain ranges, is the capital of the Savoie department. The city centre is interesting historically, having been the capital of the Duchy of Savoy, which covered much of the western Alps until its annexation by France in 1860. All bar one of the routes in this chapter are situated fairly close to Chambéry, so it makes sense to set up a base in or near the city. There is a good range of accommodation within the city, but if you wish to camp you will need to head a little way out of it, to Le-Bourget-du-Lac, Aix-les-Bains or Lac d'Aiguebelette.

The city can be reached by direct high-speed train from Paris and there are good road links with Paris, Lyon and Geneva. Additionally, there is a small airport, but it does not currently receive flights from the UK during the summer. Most of the routes in this chapter are located in the Chartreuse and Bauges massifs, which are considered part of the lower Pre-Alps. The chapter also includes one route (Route 13) that is located at the southern end of the Jura mountains. Due to the relatively modest altitude of these ranges, the routes have a fairly long season, and can be visited from early spring to late autumn. They are mostly sports routes, which involve little rock contact, and several of them are suitable for novices.

For tourist information see the websites listed in Appendix D.

Admiring the view from Itinéraire les Buis (Route 13, Stage B)

ROUTE 13
Via Ferrata de la Guinguette

Location	Hostiaz, Ain
	(GPS: Lat. 45° 54′ 58.00″ N Long. 5° 31′ 9.79″ E)
Length	1050m
Ascent/Descent	60m
Route grading	technical grade: 1–4; exposure: 2–5; seriousness: A
	(all stages)
Total time	3hrs 30mins
Highest altitude	760m
Map	3231OT
Technical notes	direction: W; total escape points: 2
When to visit	March to November

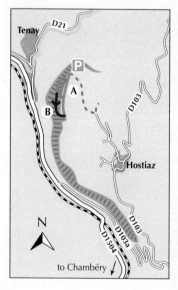

This excellent route is everything a French via ferrata should be; strenuous, airy and set against a wonderfully scenic backdrop. The landscape of the surrounding district consists of rolling forested plateau intersected by deep, steep-sided gorges. It is on the side of one such gorge, carved out by a tributary of the River Albarine, that the route has been built, high above the cramped town of Tenay. The via ferrata has been considerably extended in recent years and the full route is not to be underestimated. While only periodically difficult, it is at times very exposed and those without a strong head for heights may feel they have bitten off more than they can chew.

There is another route nearby, the Via Ferrata de la Charbotte. This scales bluffs adjacent to the Chute de l'Albarine, an impressive waterfall to the northeast of Tenay. The route, which is reportedly quite easy, is private and can be undertaken only in the company of a guide. For further information, see www.natureaventure.blog4ever.com.

Access

Drive to **Tenay** on the **D1504**, between Chambéry and Abérieu-en-Bugey. Some 2.4km to the south of Tenay, take a turning to the east and follow a narrow road (**D103a/ D103**) for 7km to **Hostiaz**. From the centre of the village

Commencing the strenuous and heavily exposed traverse on Itinéraire les Buis (Stage B)

(via ferrata information board) follow signs for a little over 2km to a parking area. The final part of this road is unpaved, but should be passable by two-wheel-drive cars.

STAGE A
Itinéraire de la Grotte

Length	350m
Ascent/Descent	20m
Route grading	technical grade: 3; exposure: 2; seriousness: A
Time	1hr 45mins
	(approach: 10mins; route: 1hr 20mins; return: 15mins)
Technical notes	escape points (within stage): 2

Approach
From the car park make your way to the nearby viewpoint and orientation table. After taking in the views of the picturesque Albarine Valley and Tenay, head left and pass a via ferrata information panel. Follow a clear path

for a few minutes until the start of the route is indicated by a sign on your right.

Route

Descend without much difficulty until you are presented with a choice of routes. La Grotte starts on the left (to skip this stage and tackle only Les Buis continue to descend: see Stage B). A brief, slightly strenuous, descent leads to a short two-wire bridge. Continue descending, via a ladder (Échelle de Tychodrome), until the route levels off.

The cable then traverses the cliff-face, utilising a number of short balance beams. This does not feel too exposed, and due to the lack of height gain or loss, progress is not too arduous. Escape is possible two thirds of the way along or, more strenuously, towards the end (via a wooden ladder, Échelle a Perroquet). Otherwise descend slightly to join with Les Buis and continue with this or, if you have had enough, return to the north via the first, easy, part of Les Buis.

STAGE B

Itinéraire les Buis

Length	700m
Ascent/Descent	40m (60m, if combined with Stage A)
Route grading	technical grade: 4; exposure: 5; seriousness: A
Time	2hrs 30mins or 3hrs 30mins (approach: 10mins; route: 2hrs (3hrs if combined with Stage A); return 20mins)
Technical notes	escape points (within stage): 0

Route

Having descended from the junction with the start of Stage A, an easy traverse is followed along a fairly broad ledge. Due to the surrounding boxwood (from which the route takes its name), exposure is minimal. At the point where La Grotte descends from above, the ledge narrows considerably and the foliage gives way to magnificent

The crux of the route: the Surplomb Jaune

views (and considerable exposure). The route then follows a slightly descending traverse along the cliff-face until a metre-wide ledge is reached.

Have a rest at this point before taking on the hardest part of the route, the Surplomb Jaune. This consists of an ascending, slightly overhanging, traverse of 15m. This is strenuous in places and somewhat awkward and is followed by a dramatically exposed traverse utilising a long horizontal weakness in the face. From the ledge to the end of the traverse there is little opportunity to rest your arms.

The dahu, a very rare species of mountain goat, can occasionally be seen in the vicinity of the bridge.

Eventually, the cable returns to easier ground and a rather wobbly 15m-long suspension bridge is crossed. ◄ The route then gains 30m, briefly passing through one final moderate overhang, before returning to the top of the bluffs.

Return

Follow the obvious path to the north to return to the start of the route and the car park.

ROUTE 14
Via Ferrata Roc du Cornillon

Location	Bourdeau, Savoie
	(GPS: Lat. 45° 41' 33.05" N Long. 5° 50' 52.05" E)
Length	370m
Ascent/Descent	220m
Route grading	technical grade; 1–2; exposure: 2–3; seriousness: A
	(all stages)
Total time	2hrs 15mins
Highest altitude	845m
Map	3332OT
Technical notes	total escape points: 2
When to visit	March to November

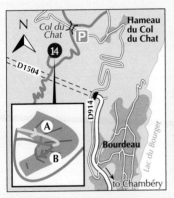

The Roc du Cornillon is justly popular with walkers, being blessed with fine views of Chambéry and of Lac du Bourget – the largest glacial body of water wholly within France. A viewing platform has been built on top of the large buttress, which juts out from the Mont du Chat, and from here much of the lake can be seen. For those who prefer a more energetic experience, two small via ferratas have been constructed, both of which run horizontally around the flanks of the buttress. The first is noticeably exposed but not particularly physical. The second is short and very easy. Both are well suited for beginners but, for the views as well as the quality of the routes, may be enjoyed by climbers of all abilities.

Access

From Chambéry, follow the **D1504** in the direction of Belley. A little way past the entrance to the village of **Bourdeau**, turn left up the **D914**. At a junction immediately beyond **Hameau du Col du Chat** keep left and continue to the **Col du Chat**. Park on the left, next to a set of information panels.

STAGE A
Parcours Primevère à Oreille d'Ours

Length	250m
Ascent/Descent	220m
Route grading	technical grade: 2; exposure: 3; seriousness: A
Time	1hr 45mins
	(approach: 35mins; route: 45mins; return: 25mins)
Technical notes	N and E; escape points (within stage): 1

Approach
A clearly marked path winds steeply uphill to the **Roc du Cornillon**, glimpses of which may be seen overhead, through dense tree cover, as you ascend. The first route starts from the back of the rock, the second from near the viewing platform on its summit.

Route
Leave a wooden platform through a gate and begin to edge out onto the north face of the Roc du Cornillon. Little use is made of the smooth limestone, with progress being mostly via metal rungs and wooden planks. The route quickly leaves the cover of the trees, revealing fine views of Lac du Bourget and much exposure, the latter being quite 'immediate'. Halfway along the face, pass an escape path on your right and then cross two balance beams. The first beam is 5m and the second 2m long, and both are in quite airy positions.

Continue around the face, losing a little height, until reaching the top of a ladder. Descend the ladder, facing outwards and then climb through a short tunnel. Exposure eases as the route passes around the vegetated east face of the Roc du Cornillon to arrive at the base of a

Although exposed, progress along the edge of the Roc de Cornillon is quite easy due to the abundance of stemples

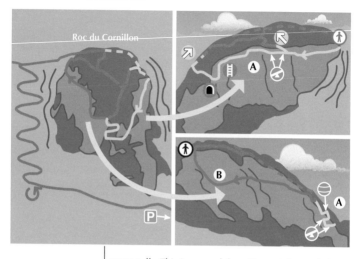

steep gully. This is crossed three times; twice on balance beams and once on a two-wire bridge. Above the gully, turn right to finish via an escape path, or left to continue with the next stage.

STAGE B
Parcours Rocher du Cornillon

Length	120m
Ascent/Descent	220m (220m, if combined with Stage A)
Route grading	technical grade: 1; exposure: 2; seriousness: A
Time	1hr 30mins or 2hrs 15mins (approach: 35mins; route: 30mins (1hr 15mins if combined with Stage A); return: 25mins)
Technical notes	direction: S; escape points (within stage): 0

Route
This short and very simple route gradually gains height up the south face of the Roc du Cornillon. Stemples are plentiful and closely spaced, allowing you to concentrate

on the fine views across the lake to the Aix-les-Bains, a large town known for its thermal springs.

Lac du Bourget and the Bauges Massif from the Parcours Rocher de Cornillon

Return
Walk off the back of the Roc du Cornillon and descend via your approach path.

ROUTE 15

Via Ferrata École de Rossane

Location	Aillon-le-Jeune Station, Savoie (GPS: Lat. 45° 36′ 43.02″ N Long. 6° 5′ 45.95″ E)
Length	300m
Ascent/Descent	110m
Route grading	technical grade: 1 (variant: 2); exposure: 1; seriousness: A
Total time	1hr 45mins (approach: 10mins; route: 1hr 20mins; return: 15mins)
Highest altitude	1050m
Map	3432OT
Technical notes	direction: SW; escape points: 2
When to visit	March to November

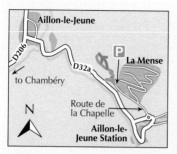

As suggested by the name, this is a 'school route' aimed specifically at beginners and children. Most of the elements found on via ferratas are present, and fixed protection is abundant and closely spaced. While the immediate setting – on a hillside surrounded by trees – is not the most scenic, the via ferrata is nevertheless pleasant and makes a good introductory route (especially so for those with an uncertain head for heights as there is little exposure). There are a number of signs posted along the route giving a simple explanation of the principles of via ferrata use.

Note that if you intend to use the optional Tyrolean traverse at the end of the route, you will need to bring a yellow Petzl Tandem Cable pulley.

Access

From Chambéry follow the D912 to St-Jean-d'Arvey, then the **D206** to **Aillon-le-Jeune**. From there take the **D32a** to **Aillon-le-Jeune Station**. Upon entering the station turn left and shortly thereafter, at a roundabout, left again (signed for **La Mense**). Drive to the end of **Route de La Chapelle** and park.

Approach

Follow a well-signposted path that zigzags steeply uphill to a small cave (the Grotte du Nant de Rossane).

Route

Climb up from the cave mouth and follow an easy traverse to the base of a 6m-high ladder. At the top of this, a little more climbing brings you to an 8m-long three-wire bridge, which is stable and not at all exposed. A mildly strenuous traverse of 20m then leads to a break in the cable, where it is possible to escape from the route.

A minute's walk brings you to the second part of the route. This involves an easy, unexposed traverse

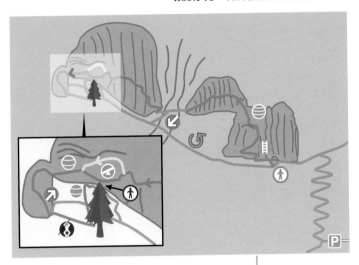

along scrambly ground for 50m to a split in the cable. Continue by crossing a balance beam and then gaining some height, or take the variant and go right to tackle a brief but pronounced overhang of 2m and then traverse for 15m (grade 2).

The two routes quickly rejoin just before a 12m-long two-wire bridge crosses a large scoop in the cliff-face. The bridge, which is a little awkward to use, is the most airy part of the route. Down-climb for 10m and either finish or use the small Tyrolean traverse. This is 20m long and deposits you on the trunk of a tree, from where a short two-wire bridge leads to the end of the route.

Return

A clear path returns to the start of the route, from where you should retrace your approach.

ROUTE 16
Via Ferrata Savoie Grand Revard

Location	St-Jean-d'Arvey, Savoie
	(GPS: Lat. 45° 36' 41.50" N Long. 5° 59' 35.94" E)
Length	860m
Ascent/Descent	480m
Route grading	technical grade: 4–5; exposure: 3–5; seriousness: B (all stages)
Total time	7hrs 20mins (if both stages climbed consecutively)
Highest altitude	1223m
Map	3332OT
Technical notes	direction: S; total escape points: 0
When to visit	March to November

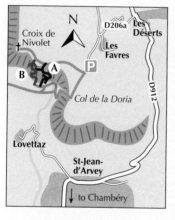

The Parcours Grotte à Carret is the hardest route in this book and one of the most difficult via ferratas ever constructed. With only one – rather belated – escape point (and that leading only onto the easier Stage A as opposed to leaving the via ferrata), it should not be undertaken by anybody who is not entirely confident of their abilities. A combination of heavy overhangs, sparse (and often small) handholds and a particularly nerve-racking bridge make for a truly challenging experience. If all this sounds like too much, consider instead the adjacent Parcours le P'tchi, which, while still relatively demanding, is much easier. This also gives you the option (via the Trottoir) of completing only the final part of the harder route.

Whichever line you take, there are exceptional views of Chambéry and its surrounds throughout the ascent. The Bauges Massif, upon the edge of which the route is perched, merits further exploration. The nearby Croix de

Nivolet, in particular, is worth a visit for even better views of Chambéry. Signposted paths lead to this obvious eminence, situated to the west of the via ferrata, from the vicinity of the bottom and top of the route.

Access

From Chambéry, drive east on the D912 to **St-Jean-d'Arvey** and continue until **Les Déserts**. Turn left onto the **D206a**, pass through **Les Favres** and follow signs for Parking Doriaz. Alternatively, for a longer day, start from **Lovettaz**, accessed via a minor road from St-Jean-d'Arvey. This adds 250m of height gain and 1hr to the outing.

Traversing between the Grotte de l'Oeil and suspension bridge, on Parcours le P'tchi (Stage A)

STAGE A
Parcours le P'tchi

Length	450m
Ascent/Descent	240m
Route grading	technical grade: 4; exposure: 3; seriousness: B
Time	3hrs 45mins
	(approach: 45mins; route: 2hrs 30mins; return: 30mins)
Technical notes	escape points (within stage): 0

Approach

Pass to the right of some farm buildings and follow a clear, well-signposted track through woodland and fields until you reach the Col de la Doria. Descend steeply, passing an area of bolted rock-climbing routes, and cross the Ruisseau de la Doria on a small bridge. ◄ Follow a signed path that ascends scree slopes towards the obvious cave mouth (**Grotte à Carret**).

The rock-climbing area contains 23 bolted routes, graded 5–7.

One of the short, strenuous passages on the initial part of Parcours le P'tchi

Alternatively, from just before the bridge, take a path on the right, which ascends steeply to the Trou de la Doria. This leads to a short, easy, section of via ferrata, which passes behind a highly picturesque waterfall that bursts out of a hole in the rock-face. You should put your via ferrata gear on before climbing this. Beyond the waterfall, follow a path that contours below the cliff-face until joining the more direct approach to the Grotte à Carret described above. ▶

The cave is named after Jules Carret, who excavated prehistoric remains there in the 1880s. He had the adjacent house built so that he could live nearer the diggings.

Route
From the cave, descend a little to the right to locate the start of the route. A large blank wall is climbed and then traversed to the right on stemples until more broken ground is reached. A number of short strenuous passages have to be overcome, but there are also plenty of places to rest and progress eases as the route begins to traverse back to the left.

Take a breather in the **Grotte de l'Oeil**, a small cave that should offer some shade, and continue the increasingly arduous traverse until a 32m-long suspension bridge is reached. Although relatively benign, the bridge is nevertheless avoidable by a cabled route on the right. At the end of the bridge, either turn left and descend

115

Two balance beams on the final part of Parcours le P'tchi

strenuously to take the **Trottoir**, as mentioned above, or continue ascending. If you choose the first option, take extreme care not to dislodge any loose stones as you are directly above the Grotte à Carret. Alternatively, the final part of le P'tchi crosses two balance beams and scales a steep wall for 25m to the top of the bluffs.

Return
Having taken in the fine views from the Belvedere du Rocher de Charvetan, situated at the top of the route, follow a broad track back through woods to the parking. The track is signposted, but if in doubt look out for yellow waymarks.

STAGE B
Parcours Grotte à Carret

Length	410m
Ascent/Descent	240m (480m, if combined with Stage A)
Route grading	technical grade: 5; exposure: 5; seriousness: B
Time	3hrs 45mins
	(approach: 45mins; route: 2hrs 25mins; return: 35mins)
Technical notes	escape points (to Stage A): 1

Route
The route starts towards the back of the Grotte à Carret. Climb up and around the cave wall and, upon emerging from the entrance, ascend steeply to a small ledge under a broad scoop in the rock-face. The ledge, although extremely exposed, is a good place to have a rest before tackling the crux of the route, which is immediately above this point.

Follow a steeply rising traverse up the heavily overhanging wall of the scoop. The small metal handholds found here and on several other parts of the route can be quite awkward to use. Prior to moving, you may need to plan ahead the order in which you use the handholds and, depending on your height, some smearing on the rock may be necessary. Above the scoop, traverse across a blank, airy wall and cross an inside corner on a small two-wire bridge. Continue via a balance beam and an enormous flake, which is passed with the aid of two more balance beams.

Above the flake, another heavily overhanging wall is ascended strenuously to reach the three-wire bridge that has been overhead for most of the route. This is 35m long, a little wobbly and massively exposed; enjoy!

If, having crossed the bridge, you've had enough, turn right along the **Trottoir** to escape and finish via the Parcours le P'tchi. ▶ Otherwise, turn left, cross a rather cramped balance beam beneath a roof within a large hollow, and follow an arduous traverse for several metres to a tiny platform. The final vertical 25m of climbing is broken into two sections, with a small ledge between them. Progress is quite strenuous and once again involves small metal handholds and possible smearing foot placements that require some thought.

This is also a good option if you want to have a rest, as partway along the Trottoir there is a small cave that offers some shade.

Return
Follow a narrow path to the east to join the return path from the top of Parcours le P'tchi (see above).

ROUTE 17
Via Ferrata La Grotte du Maquis

Location	Semnoz/Gruffy, Haute-Savoie
	(GPS: Lat. 45° 47' 32.75" N Long. 6° 6' 6.11" E)
Length	150m
Ascent/Descent	340m
Route grading	technical grade: 1; exposure: 3; seriousness: B
Total time	2hrs (approach: 40mins; route: 30mins; return: 50mins)
Highest altitude	640m
Map	3431OT
Technical notes	direction: W; escape points: 0
When to visit	March to November

The principal attraction of this short via ferrata is the extensive view of the pre-alpine countryside to the west of the Montagne du Semnoz. The route also offers the chance to visit an historic hideout used by World War II resistance fighters. While it is not the easiest route to locate, a brief visit is worthwhile for these reasons and also for the abundance of wild flowers that grow in the area, at their best from late spring to early summer.

There is another route in the vicinity, the Via Ferrata de la Roche du Roux, which is private and can be undertaken only with a guide. The route, which is located above the Col de la Forclaz and the village of Montmin, affords fine views of Lac d'Annecy, the second largest lake in France. It is reportedly of moderate difficulty and involves a Tyrolean traverse, a two-wire bridge and some abseiling. See www.montagnesensation.com for more information.

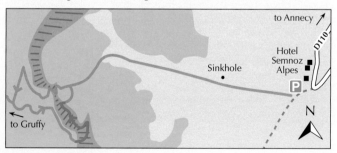

Access

The easiest approach by car is from Annecy. From the south of the city, follow signs for Le Semnoz and take the D41. The road climbs up the northern end of the Montagne du Semnoz for 18km to the Crêt du Chatillon and then becomes the **D110**. Drive for a further kilometre to just beyond the **Hotel Semnoz Alpes** and park to the right of a hairpin bend.

Approach

From the parking area head across a grassy slope in a westerly direction. This may involve crossing temporary cattle fences. Within one minute, you should see some conifers below you, to your right. Trend a little to your left, with a slight valley opening up between you and the conifers. Pass a fenced-off sinkhole and pick up a faint unmarked path. Follow this down the centre of a broad ridgeline, passing a few wooden posts marked with green and yellow arrows. Then pass a sign for 'Viuz Gruffy' and continue on this path, passing more signs and, once in the forest, yellow and blue waymarks.

The path descends to the northwest then turns sharply back to the southwest. At the next hairpin bend, take a path to your left. The point where you leave the main path is not obvious, but is next to a yellow and blue waymark on a tree. If you reach a length of chain

The Albanais Plain from the Crêt du Chatillon

119

protecting a steep descent, you have gone too far and
should backtrack a little. The subsidiary path, which is
initially unmarked, is narrow and slippery. After the first
few minutes of progress, you should see a number of
cairns indicating the correct route. Continue beneath
large bluffs until the path ends and the start of the cable is
visible above you to the left.

Route
Climb up and continue to the left above a break in the
cable. The cable recommences at a short easy climb up
to a ledge, which is wide enough to walk along without
difficulty. Pass a wood store and turn a corner. From here
on, the route feels quite airy, as the ledge passes across
the bluffs below which you have just traversed. Wide-
ranging views can be enjoyed from the ledge, with Lac
du Bourget visible to the southwest and the expansive
Albanais Plain running to the northwest.

The cable rises a little and disappears into a small
notch in the rock. This is actually the entrance to the
Grotte du Maquis, a cave used by French Resistance
fighters during World War II. It is easy to appreciate why
the cave was used; despite affording unrestricted views
of the surrounding area, it is all but invisible from below.
Once you have examined the few souvenirs of the cave's
former occupants, descend and continue along the bluffs.
The ledge narrows considerably for 3m and a mildly
strenuous traversing move is aided by some rungs. This is
also the most exposed part of the route. Beyond here the
ledge continues for a little way before a climb up into the
forest arrives at the end of the cable.

Return
At this point, look up and notice a break in the low
bluffs above you. Follow an unmarked path that zigzags
uphill for 35m, aiming for the break. Scramble easily for
a couple of metres through the break and emerge onto
flower meadows. Turn left and walk for 50m to rejoin the
approach path.

ROUTE 18
Via Ferrata de Roche Veyrand

Location	St-Pierre-d'Entremont, Savoie
	(GPS: Lat. 45º 25′ 5.32″ N Long. 5º 51′ 18.25″ E)
Length	900m
Ascent/Descent	660m
Route grading	technical grade: 2–4; exposure: 3–5; seriousness: B (all stages)
Total time	4hrs 15mins
Highest altitude	1300m
Map	3333OT
Technical notes	total escape points: 2
When to visit	March to November
Useful websites	www.chartreuse-tourisme.com; www.parc-chartreuse.net

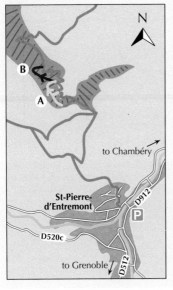

This relatively new via ferrata is situated at the heart of the Chartreuse Massif, halfway between Chambéry and Grenoble. The area is famous for the eponymous liqueur made originally by monks at the nearby Grande Chartreuse Monastery, but is also known for the scenic beauty of its landscape, which mostly consists of long limestone ridges running from north to south. It is a popular walking destination in spring and early winter, when the higher peaks to the east are snowbound.

The first stage is quite playful, with only one briefly strenuous moment. The second stage is a little more demanding and you should be sure of your abilities before

121

commencing. While it is easy enough to begin with, difficulty gradually builds up (together with the amount of exposure) until the crux: a sharp and extremely airy overhang near the top of the route. Both stages are well designed, with plenty of protection, but also make good use of the pale limestone that predominates throughout the route.

Access
St-Pierre-d'Entremont can be reached by either the **D912** from Chambéry (follow signs for 'Massif de la Chartreuse') or the **D512** from Grenoble (follow signs for 'P.N.R. de la Chartreuse'). Park on the north side of the village, between a church and the post office.

STAGE A
1ère Partie

Length	450m
Ascent/Descent	490m
Route grading	technical grade: 2; exposure: 3; seriousness: B
Time	2hrs 30mins (approach: 45mins; route: 1hr; return: 45mins)
Technical notes	direction: SW; escape points (within stage): 1

Approach
Cross the road bridge over the River Cozon and turn left. Almost immediately turn right as indicated and follow a series of well-signposted paths that become increasingly steep. After a stiff, but well-shaded, climb of 300m, keep left at a signposted junction. Descend a little then climb up through shrubs to the base of the cliff.

Route
After an initial climbing traverse to the left, cross a short easy balance beam. The angle of ascent then reduces as a series of low-angle slabs are overcome with the aid of closely spaced rungs. At the top of these, a little

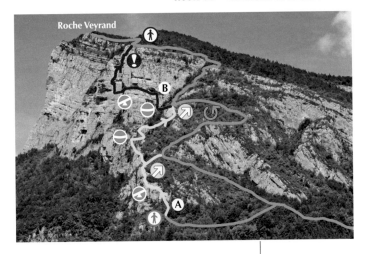

way past an escape point, a steep, moderately strenuous wall is climbed for 10m. Beyond this the climbing continues, interspersed with short walking sections, with a 17m-long suspension bridge crossed a little way before Stage A's end. This is slightly wobbly but unexposed.

Closely spaced rungs ease progress on the first stage

STAGE B
2ème Partie

Length	450m
Ascent/Descent	170m (660m, if combined with Stage A)
Route grading	technical grade: 4; exposure: 5; seriousness: B
Time	4hrs 15mins (approach: 45mins; route: 2hrs 30mins (both stages combined); return: 1hr)
Technical notes	direction: S; escape points (within stage): 0

The suspension bridge at the start of Stage B

Route

Start by crossing a second suspension bridge, which is 30m long and similar in nature to the first. Beyond the bridge, climb up for 25m to gain a ledge that quickly leads to a shallow cave. Depending on the angle of the sun, this might be a better place to rest than the top of the first stage, which lacks shade. Exposure increases drastically at this point, as you continue traversing around the cliff-face on a downward-sloping ledge. Pass around a corner and cross a balance beam to a gravelly bay. This makes a good place to take a breather before tackling the rest of the route, which is fairly sustained.

Continue to the left along the ledge and then follow a series of climbs and traverses up the just off-vertical cliff-face. Towards the top of the cliff, having moved back to the right, scale a short chimney and then tackle the crux of the route. This involves edging out under, and then overcoming, a short but pronounced overhang. The traverse is rather cramped and the overhang

Crossing the exposed balance beam. St-Pierre-d'Entremonte can be seen in the background

Approaching the crux of the route

feels particularly 'out there' but both are well protected. Beyond this the angle eases considerably for the final 20m of easy climbing.

To extend your outing by continuing to the summit on the signposted path, add 130m of ascent and 30mins. This additional effort is especially worthwhile on clear days when the expansive views of the rolling countryside to the west will be at their best.

Return

A rough path descends steeply through low scrub to the approach path. This has several sections of cable on it, so you should keep your gear on.

TARENTAISE

Climbers descending Le Curé on Via Ferrata
de la Croix des Verdons (Route 22)

INTRODUCTION

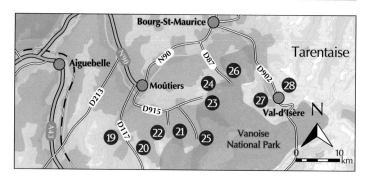

The Tarentaise Valley encompasses the upper reaches of the River Isère, from Moûtiers in the west to Val-d'Isère at its eastern extremity. All the routes in this chapter are situated just to the south of the valley, within the northern half of the Vanoise Massif, on the edge of the Vanoise National Park. This national park covers more than 50,000ha and boasts many extensively glaciated peaks. At a height of 3855m, Grande Casse is the tallest of these mountains and the highest point in France outside of the Mont Blanc and Écrins massifs.

The area is home to several world-famous ski resorts, some of which have constructed via ferratas to attract summer visitors. These include the highest route in the book (Route 22) as well as one of the most challenging (Route 27). There is a motorway from Chambéry as far as Moûtiers (the A43, A430 and N90), and from there a main road (still the N90) runs the length of

the Tarentaise Valley. There is also a rail line as far as Bourg-St-Maurice, halfway up the valley. From here, there is a road link with Courmeyeur and Turin in Italy, via the Col du Petit St-Bernard.

The Tarentaise Valley offers plenty of places in which to base yourself, with the normal range of accommodation available. Most hotels, gîtes d'étape and campsites have a fairly short season, so if planning to visit during the spring or autumn, consider booking ahead. However, most of the routes in this chapter are situated at a relatively high altitude and, depending on the weather, may be open only during the summer. With one notable exception (Route 27), all these via ferratas are sports routes and do not involve large amounts of rock contact. A number of the lower-grade routes are specifically designed for beginners.

For tourist information see the websites listed in Appendix D.

ROUTE 19
Via Ferrata du Cochet

Location	St-Martin-de-Belleville, Savoie
	(GPS: Lat. 45° 22' 14.01" N Long. 6° 29' 26.43" E)
Length	700m
Ascent/Descent	430m
Route grading	technical grade: 2; exposure: 2; seriousness: B
Total time	2hrs 30mins
	(approach: 25mins; route: 1hr 30mins; return: 35mins)
Highest altitude	2023m
Map	3433ET
Technical notes	direction: E; escape points: 1
When to visit	April to October
Useful websites	www.st-martin-belleville.com; www.guides-menuires.com

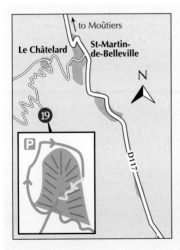

The Belleville Valley occupies the western end of the Vanois Massif and is home to several picturesque mountain villages (and a not so picturesque ski resort). Le Cochet, a prominent lump overlooking one of these villages, St-Martin-de-Belleville, is now the site of a pleasant and simple via ferrata. The route scales the steep, heavily eroded, eastern flank of the peak by a straightforward line unadorned with bridges, beams or other elements. Although the ascent is quite easy, there is a lot of loose rock in the vicinity of the route. Be careful not to dislodge stones on to anyone below.

Le Cochet

Access

The Belleville Valley from the penultimate vertical section

Take the N90 to Moûtiers, which is situated halfway between Albertville and Bourg-St-Maurice. From Moûtiers, head south on the **D117**, to **St-Martin-de-Belleville**. From

there, follow signs for **Le Châtelard**. Above Le Châtelard, turn left (via ferrata sign) and continue up a steep, narrow road that quickly becomes unsurfaced. Follow this road for around 2.5km then turn left. A further 150m brings you to a small car park below two chalets.

Approach
Walk uphill, passing the chalets, to reach a junction. Take the left-hand path, and walk around the northern flank of a steep-sided hill (**Le Cochet**). Once on the eastern side of the hill, the path gains height up a scree slope until arriving at the base of some heavily eroded bluffs.

Route
Start by climbing up a broken buttress for 25m. Much use is made of large rock-holds for both hands and feet, with an occasional stemple for additional assistance. There is a break in the cable as a narrow path is briefly followed to the left. More climbing on reddish broken rock and gravelly paths gradually leads back to the right. The bluffs then steepen considerably and a long climb of 40m leads directly up the face. This feels quite airy towards the top but is well protected throughout by numerous rungs. This leads to a broad ledge with an escape path on the right. Finish by descending to the left and climbing a final section of steep, broken, rock for 25m.

Return
Ascend a little to the summit of Le Cochet (2023m), which is surmounted by a cross and some orientation tables. Briefly walk to the south, where a sign indicates the start of the return path. This path is quite steep and slippery in places, and is protected by a short section of cable. To extend your outing a little, do not take this path, but instead keep left and head to the Col de la Fenêtre. From here, turn right to return to the car park.

ROUTE 20
Via Ferrata du Levassaix

Location	Levassaix, Savoie
	(GPS: Lat. 45° 20' 21.49" N Long. 6° 31' 53.51" E)
Length	350m
Ascent/Descent	195m
Route grading	technical grade: 1; exposure: 1; seriousness: A
Total time	1hr 45mins (approach: 15mins; route: 1hr; return: 30mins)
Highest altitude	1880m
Map	3534OT
Technical notes	direction: SW; escape points: 1
When to visit	April to October
Useful websites	www.lesmenuires.com; www.guides-menuires.com

This modest route, which is designed for children and beginners, involves few difficulties and will not occupy too much of your time. While lacking the ostentation of some other routes in the area, it makes the most of the small rock outcrop on which it is built and is ideally situated to enjoy good views of the western Vanoise Massif. Being fairly short, it is perhaps best completed as a warm-up prior to visiting the nearby Via Ferrata du Cochet (Route 19).

Access
Take the N90 to Moûtiers, which is situated halfway between Albertville and Bourg-St-Maurice. From Moûtiers, head south on the **D117**, passing through **St-Martin-de-Belleville**, until the turning for **Levassaix** is reached. Park by the side of the main road, immediately beyond the turning, next to a yellow via ferrata information panel.

Approach
Walk up the road for 100m and then take the path indicated by a sign for the via ferrata. Follow more signs uphill to the base of some low bluffs.

Route

Climb up onto a detached boulder for a few metres then cross a 6m-long three-wire bridge. The bridge is fairly stable and not at all exposed. The route then gains a little height up a stout arête before trending to the right up several short rock steps. Walk along a broad ledge until the cable briefly climbs up a bizarrely sculpted wall beneath a large overhang. Descend a little and continue to the right along a ledge, without gaining much height. The cable then passes around a shallow bay, crossing a short balance beam at the mid-point.

Scale the other side of the bay for 10m to a small platform, from where there are views to the south of the rather out-of-place **Les Menuires** ski resort. Continue up the platform to finish or turn left and recross the bay on a plank bridge, which is quite stable. On the other side, step off the bridge and immediately turn around and recross the bay, this time on stemples and a two-wire bridge. This is not strenuous, as the 8m-long bridge is stable, but is the most exposed part of the route. After a couple more short rock steps, the route ends at the top of the bluffs.

The two-wire bridge at the end of the route

Return

A path to your right quickly descends to rejoin the approach path.

ROUTE 21

Via Ferrata du Lac de la Rosiere

Location	Courchevel 1650 Moriond, Savoie
	(GPS: Lat. 45° 24' 27.54" N Long. 6° 40' 4.13" E)
Length	600m
Ascent/Descent	40m
Route grading	technical grade: 2 (variant: 1); exposure: 2; seriousness: A
Total time	2hrs (approach: 15mins; route: 1hr 30mins; return: 15mins)
Highest altitude	1550m
Map	3534OT
Technical notes	direction: all; escape points: 3
When to visit	May to October
Useful websites	www.courchevel.com; www.courchnet.com

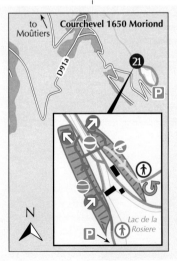

Set above the tranquil turquoise waters of Lac de la Rosiere, this playful via ferrata guarantees a fairly relaxed experience. The line followed is mostly level and not too exposed. The route contains several easy bridges, allows for escape at different points and has lots of fixed protection, which is closely spaced. As such it is an acceptable via ferrata for beginners and children, or during cloudy weather. If you intend to do this route as a warm-up before climbing the nearby Croix des Verdons (Route 22), start fairly early in the morning.

Access
Take the N90 to Moûtiers, which is situated half-way between Albertville and Bourg-St-Maurice. From Moûtiers, follow the D915 and then the **D91a** to **Courchevel 1650**. At a roundabout, turn left up the Rue du Belvédère and, just after the road levels out, turn left again and descend to a car park.

Approach
From the parking area head downhill to a café. Turn left off the main path and walk along the left bank of the lake to arrive at a sign indicating the start of the via ferrata.

Route
Traverse out onto the cliff-face and pass above the lake and a *prise d'eau* (water intake). The water is only 20m below, so this should not feel too exposed. Descend a little to arrive at the first escape point. Either finish by down-climbing for 10m via a ladder or continue by crossing a short, stable, two-wire bridge. A rising traverse then leads past the second escape path (a long easy descent down forested slopes).

Crossing the two-wire bridge just after the first escape point

Briefly descend to a bridge, which crosses the main valley for 35m and is quite stable. On the other side of the bridge, the cable passes the third escape path, which involves a pleasant descending traverse, and continues to the right. Finish by passing across a series of ledges on pale bluffs above the true right of the valley. A short, easy balance beam is crossed part-way along and progress is generally trouble free, with only the final climb of 10m involving one very slight overhang. This passage is very well protected but involves more exposure than the first part of the route.

Return
Turn right to descend to the lake. Continue to the right to return to the approach path near the café.

ROUTE 22
Via Ferrata de la Croix des Verdons

Location	Courchevel 1850, Savoie
	(GPS: Lat. 45° 24' 54.95" N Long. 6° 38' 1.31" E)
Length	800m
Ascent/Descent	250m/530m
Route grading	technical grade: 3; exposure: 4; seriousness: C
Total time	3hrs 45mins
	(approach: 20mins; route: 2hrs 25mins; return: 1hr)
Highest altitude	2739m
Map	3534OT
Technical notes	direction: E; escape points: 1
When to visit	June to September (but note cable car opening dates below)
Useful websites	www.courchevel.com; www.courchnet.com

This is one of only a few proper mountain via ferratas in France, and it is also the highest route in the country. The via ferrata climbs over and around the spiky Arêtes des Verdon, which overlook the famous ski resort of Courchevel.

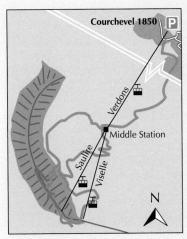

While the surrounding ski slopes may not be to everyone's taste, the accompanying lifts allow easy access to the route, saving much time. Unfortunately, these cable cars (which cost €11 for a return ticket) are open only from early July to late August.

Similar in nature to many via ferratas of the Dolomites, the route is mostly a long mountain scramble with lots of rock contact. That said, there are several passages that are reasonably strenuous and very airy, and care should be taken due to the large volume of loose rock near the route. While it does not match the altitude of some of the via ferratas in Switzerland or Italy, the route is situated in a high mountain environment and should be undertaken only with a clear weather forecast.

Access

Take the N90 to Moûtiers, which is situated half-way between Albertville and Bourg-St-Maurice. From Moûtiers, follow the D915 and then the D91a to **Courchevel 1850**. Park in the underground car park (which should be free of charge during the summer) at the centre of the resort.

Approach

While it is possible to approach the route on foot, this is not recommended as two cable cars lead directly to the start. Purchase tickets for the cable cars from the nearby tourist office. Take the **Verdons** cable car to the Middle Station and then the **Saulire** cable car. If the latter is closed use the **Vizelle** cable car, which leads to the Sommet de la Vizelle. From there, head west along the ridge for 10mins

to the Sommet de la Saulire. Should you choose to walk, add around 3hrs and a painful 950m of height gain.

Route

◀ Leave the Saulire cable car Upper Station and walk to the north, near the crest of the ridge, following a vague path and heading for a white sign. The cable begins near the sign and initially follows an easy route, picking its way up, down and around the heavily broken ridgeline before passing through a narrow gap in the ridge (La Porte). A little beyond this the route begins to gain height up the side of a massive rock pinnacle (**Le Curé**), so named because it is said to resemble a priest praying before the Croix des Verdons, when viewed from Courchevel.

It is worth taking a break on the cramped summit of Le Curé before starting the descent down its north face. Although very well protected with closely spaced rungs and short run-outs, the 35m down-climb passes through a few minor overhangs, and is quite strenuous.

At the bottom of the climb, continue with an easy walk along the ridge, passing an escape path on your right. The route then moves around to the east face of

Just prior to publication of this book, a new route, the Via Ferrata du Panoramic, was constructed near the Saulire cable car Upper Station. Located beneath the Restaurant Le Panoramic, it is reportedly 250m long, contains one two-wire bridge and is of moderate difficulty and quite exposed. Allow an extra 30mins to 1hr.

the ridge beneath the south summit of the Croix des Verdons. This face is scaled directly to the south summit for a length of 100m. Although not entirely vertical, the ascent, which is well protected, passes through a number of small overhangs, and is fairly tiring. An easy scrambling descent loses 50m to arrive at a small col. From here, more straightforward scrambling leads up a broken arête to the main summit of the **Croix des Verdons**. Take in the extensive views of Courchevel and the glaciated peaks of the northern Vanoise Massif and then carefully descend to the east. The descent is made via a scree-filled couloir, which may hold snow early in the summer.

Return

Descend via a steep scree slope. Once below the scree slopes continue on a mixture of paths and ski pistes in the direction of the cable car Middle Station, which should be visible below you. The Verdons cable car is free of charge in descent.

Alternatively, to return from the Middle Station to Courchevel on foot, allow an extra hour. ▶

A further alternative return option was added just prior to publication of this book. Full details are unknown at the time of writing, but a path has reportedly been constructed that allows a direct return to the start of the route via the top of the escape path, and avoids most difficulties. By following this and then retracing the approach route, you can descend to Courchevel from the cable car top station.

A climber admiring the view of La Dent Parrachée (3695m) from near the top of the south summit of the Croix des Verdons

ROUTE 23

Via Ferrata des Grosses Pierres

Location	Champagny-en-Vanoise, Savoie
	(GPS: Lat. 45° 27′ 24.22″ N Long. 6° 42′ 4.40″ E)
Length	200m
Ascent/Descent	30m
Route grading	technical grade: 5; exposure: 3; seriousness: A
Total time	1hr 30mins (approach: 10mins; route: 1hr; return: 20mins)
Highest altitude	1370m
Map	3532OT
Technical notes	direction: SW; escape points: 0
When to visit	Closed 1 November–30 April

Despite its short length and relative lack of exposure, this via ferrata really is suitable only for climbers with plenty of brawn. Progress is not at all technical (there is comparatively little contact with the rock), but the route is quite arduous throughout. While there are no massive overhangs along the way, there are plenty that are moderate. The overall effect is to make the route feel extremely strenuous and quite sustained. The lack of any decent places to rest, especially on the first half of the route, means that a rest lanyard is obligatory. On the plus side, the first 25m is the hardest part, with difficulty gradually

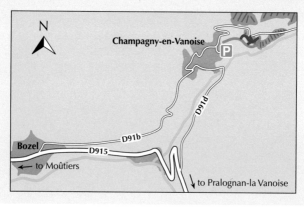

declining thereafter. The via ferrata is a worthwhile test of strength for those of sufficiently robust physique; others should leave well alone and head straight for the nearby Via Ferrata du Plan du Bouc (Route 24). Note that this route will be in shade for most of the morning, when it may be damp.

Access
Take the N90 to Moûtiers, which is situated half-way between Albertville and Bourg-St-Maurice. From Moûtiers, follow the **D915** to **Bozel** and from there, the **D91b** to **Champagny-en-Vanoise**. Drive through the village until a Sherpa supermarket is passed on the left. Immediately beyond the supermarket, turn right and follow signs for the via ferrata until a car park is reached.

Approach
Follow a track heading directly towards the obvious bluffs beneath the main road. Turn left at a junction just below the bluffs.

Although exposed, the balance beam is a good place to take a break

Route

Climb straight up for 15m. This is immediately quite strenuous. If you have any trouble with this first vertical climb, do not continue but return back down the cable. At the top of the climb, traverse for 10m, still strenuously but with the first opportunity for a brief rest halfway along. Climb up for a few metres to a second traverse of 10m, a little easier than the previous one. A climb of 5m, with a pronounced overhang, arrives at a third traverse similar to the last one, followed by another overhanging climb of 7m. This arrives at a short balance beam, after which difficulty decreases a little.

The beam presents no problems and is actually a good place to have a rest. A climb of 5m leads up to a strenuous traverse across to an 8m-long two-wire bridge. There is an awkward move to step onto the bridge, which is crossed facing outwards but is not particularly exposed. Climb up for a few metres, overcoming one final short overhang, to the highest point of the route. Having taken in the views of Champagny and, across the valley, the Croix de Verdon (Route 22), descend along a fairly straightforward path to the end of the cable.

Return
Turn right and descend to the beginning of the route, passing several bolted sports-climbing lines. Alternatively, turn left, ascend a little and follow the road for 1km to visit Via Ferrata du Plan du Bouc.

ROUTE 24
Via Ferrata du Plan du Bouc

Location	Champagny-en-Vanoise, Savoie (GPS: Lat. 45° 27' 33.03" N Long. 6° 43' 16.80" E)
Length	1800m
Ascent/Descent	1020m
Route grading	technical grade: 1–2; exposure: 2; seriousness: B (all stages)
Total time	3hrs 15mins or 4hrs 15mins
Highest altitude	1950m
Maps	3532OT, 3532ET
Technical notes	direction: S; total escape points: 0
When to visit	Closed 1 November–30 April

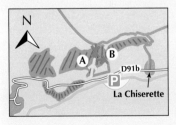

An easier and more scenic neighbour to the preceding via ferrata, this route is ideal for those who want a relatively relaxed experience, and is popular with families with young children. The outing offers a number of different alternatives. Most people ascend by the Parcours en Arête and then ascend and descend the Parcours Commun, which is situated on the steep hillside above the two main stages. They then descend by the Parcours en

Falaise. The following description assumes that the routes are completed in that order.

If you choose to ascend by the Parcours en Falaise, follow its route description in reverse to reach the junction with the Parcours en Arête. You can then return by the same route, or continue up the Parcours Commun, from where there are much better views of the surrounding peaks of the Vanoise National Park. This is also a great option in spring and early summer, when the alpine flower meadows situated above the route are at their best.

Access

Take the N90 to Moûtiers, which is situated half-way between Albertville and Bourg-St-Maurice. From Moûtiers, follow the D915 to Bozel and from there, the **D91b** to Champagny-en-Vanoise. Continue on the D91b for 3km beyond Champagny, passing a small reservoir on your right. Park immediately after the reservoir.

STAGE A
Parcours en Arête

Length	900m
Ascent/Descent	510m
Route grading	technical grade: 2; exposure: 2; seriousness: B
Time	3hrs 15mins or 4hrs 15mins (approach: 15mins; route: 2hrs 50mins (both stages combined, or Stage A and the Parcours Commun); return: 10mins or 1hr 10mins)
Technical notes	escape points (within stage): 0

Approach
Cross the road and follow the obvious path that heads to the left.

Route
Progress is initially very easy as height is gained up a broad ridge. Cabling is intermittent until the ground steepens

and the via ferrata proper commences. Thereafter, a consistently climbing line is followed until the sharp edge of an arête is attained. The highlight of the stage, the arête, is steep but contains no particular difficulties and affords

Climbers ascending the eponymous Parcours en Arête

145

excellent views both up and down the valley. After the
arête ends, ascend steeply through trees until the junction
with the Parcours en Falaise is reached.

Above this point, the Parcours Commun, which is
cabled only intermittently, ascends steeply up the flower-
covered hillside until a junction is reached. After heavy
rain this path can be quite slippery and care is required
in descent.

STAGE B
Parcours en Falaise

Length	900m
Ascent/Descent	510m (1020m, if combined with Stage A)
Route grading	technical grade: 1; exposure: 2; seriousness: B
Time	3hrs 15mins or 4hrs 15mins (approach: 15mins; route: 2hrs 50mins (Stage B and the Parcours Commun); return: 10mins or 1hr 10mins)
Technical notes	escape points (within stage): 0

Descending along the Parcours en Falaise

Route

Descend for 30m via a broad couloir. A long, mostly level, traverse then leads along La Grande Vire, which, as its name suggests, is generally quite wide and does not feel too exposed. Take particular care not to dislodge any stones while following the traverse, as there is a rock-climbing area immediately below. At the end of the traverse, finish with a steep descent of 25m. This is the most demanding part of this stage and, although not strenuous, it is a little awkward in places.

Return

Descend to the car park, ignoring the right fork in the path, which leads to the rock-climbing area. ▶ If you decide to finish at the top of the Parcours Commun, turn right and follow a clear path that descends to the hamlet of **La Chiserette** and, from there, follow the road back to the parking. Allow 1hr 10mins for this option.

The area contains 21 bolted rock-climbing routes, graded 4–6.

ROUTE 25
Via Ferrata de Pralognan

Location	Pralognan-la-Vanoise, Savoie (GPS: Lat. 45° 22′ 42.61″ N Long. 6° 43′ 40.39″ E)
Length	320m
Ascent/Descent	175m
Route grading	technical grade: 1–3; exposure: 1–3; seriousness: A (all stages)
Total time	2hrs 30mins
Highest altitude	1580m
Map	3534OT
Technical notes	direction: SW; total escape points: 4
When to visit	May to October

Situated at the heart of the Vanoise National Park, and adjacent to the lively resort of Pralognan, Via Ferrata de la Cascade de la Fraîche can

make a serious claim to be the most picturesque of all French via ferratas. Set against a backdrop of soaring peaks, the route climbs up by the side of a huge waterfall carved out of attractively sculpted orange granite by the Torrent de Glière. Unsurprisingly, the route, which contains a number of variants, is exceptionally popular and can be rather crowded at times.

The other route here, the Parcours Ouistiti, was designed as a short introductory via ferrata primarily for children, but it can also be completed by beginners or as a warm-up for the main route. It was originally intended to be climbed using roped progression but most of the route has now been fitted with cable and the short sections lacking cable can be protected by clipping into the rungs. As with all routes, younger children should climb only if roped to an appropriately experienced adult.

Access

Take the N90 to Moûtiers, which is situated half-way between Albertville and Bourg-St-Maurice. From Moûtiers, follow the **D915** to **Pralognan-la-Vanoise**. From the entrance to the village follow blue signs for 'Autre Quartiers' and then for 'La Barioz'. At **La Barioz**, turn right at a sign for Le Bieux and then, 80m further on, right again. Follow the **Chemin des Bieux** for 370m to a small parking area. The village can be very busy during the summer, so you may have to park further back.

STAGE A
VF de la Cascade de la Fraîche

Length	250m
Ascent/Descent	140m
Route grading	technical grade: 3 (variant: 2); exposure: 3; seriousness: A
Time	2hrs (approach: 15mins; route: 1hr 20mins; return: 25mins)
Technical notes	escape points (within stage): 2

Approach
From a large information panel, follow signs along a clear path to the base of the waterfall.

The exciting, and damp, variant near the beginning of the route

Route
A straightforward traverse quickly gives way to a choice of routes, with the right-hand option being the harder, and (depending on how heavily the waterfall is flowing) wetter. Once the routes rejoin, the cable continues upwards to arrive at a large platform.

From here there are three options:

1   The easiest is simply to keep ascending in the same direction (the Sortie anti-stress).

2   For a little more effort traverse along the true right side of the stream (La Conque).

3   The third and most exciting option is to cross directly above the waterfall for 15m on a relatively stable two-wire bridge and follow a rising traverse across the angular rock-face (La Traversée des Dieux).

Return
Turn right and descend the true left of the stream to meet the approach

Posing for a photograph on the two-wire bridge

path. For a slightly more scenic descent, turn left and follow the GR55 back to Pralognan, to return in around 35mins. Alternatively, it is possible to make a more rapid return by way of a 400m-long Tyrolean traverse that starts near the top of the route. This can only be organised through prior arrangement with a guide, and costs €12.

STAGE B

Parcours Ouistiti

Length	70m
Ascent/Descent	35m (175m, if combined with Stage A)
Route grading	technical grade: 1; exposure: 1; seriousness: A
Time	45mins (approach: 5mins; route: 35mins; return: 5mins) or, if combined with Stage A, 2hrs 30mins (approach: 15mins; route: 2hrs 10mins; return: 5mins)
Technical notes	escape points (within stage): 2

Approach
Continue up the Chemin des Bieux, passing a rock-climbing area on the right. The route is immediately on the right, just before the hamlet of Les Beaux.

Route
Scale the true left side of a narrow gully, utilising an unusual ladder construction part-way up. Cross the gully on a suspension bridge and, having passed an escape point, descend the other side to a second escape point and two-wire bridge. The bridge, which is 15m long and stable, returns to the other side of the gully and the end of the route.

ROUTE 26

Via Ferrata des Bettières

Location	Peisey-Nancroix, Savoie (GPS: Lat. 45° 31' 7.87" N Long. 6° 48' 8.84" E)
Length	600m
Ascent/Descent	360m
Route grading	technical grade: 2–4; exposure: 2–3; seriousness: B (all stages)
Total time	2hrs 45mins
Highest altitude	1910m
Map	3532ET
Technical notes	direction: SW; total escape points: 2
When to visit	May to October

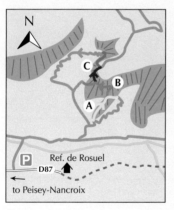

Located right on the doorstep of the Vanoise National Park, it should come as no surprise that this via ferrata affords great views. Although situated on the flanks of two of the park's largest peaks, the heavily glaciated Dôme de la Sache (3588m) and Mont Pourri (3779m), the route is easy to access and fairly straightforward to climb. The via ferrata has three stages of progressive difficulty, with an escape point between each one. As such this is a good route for beginners who want to try something a little harder.

Access

Take the N90 to Landry, part-way between Moûtiers and Bourg-St-Maurice. From Landry, take the **D87** to Peisey-Nancroix. Pass through these two villages and continue in the direction of **Refuge de Rosuel**. Once at the refuge, park on the left of the road, near a large via ferrata information panel.

STAGE A
Eperon des Croës

Length	200m
Ascent/Descent	130m
Route grading	technical grade: 2; exposure: 2; seriousness: B
Time	1hr 15mins
	(approach: 15mins; route: 40mins; return: 20mins)
Technical notes	escape points (within stage): 0

Approach
Head north from the information panel, cross a bridge, and turn right. After 250m, turn left and ascend to the base of the bluffs.

153

Route

Scale a broken spur of rock at a fairly gentle angle. There are a reasonable number of stemples on steeper sections, but most progress is made with the aid of good rock-holds, which are plentiful. Having gained 50m in height, the spur narrows to an arête and the end of Stage A, where you are confronted with a 50m-high pillar. The route's first escape point, which descends easily to the right, is just before the pillar. This first stage is quite a lot easier than the rest of the route, so use the escape if it has been problematic.

STAGE B
Grand Pilier and La Vire des Barmes

Length	200m
Ascent/Descent	130m (260m, if combined with Stage A)
Route grading	technical grade: 3; exposure: 3; seriousness: B
Time	2hrs (approach: 15mins; route: 1hr 20mins (Stages A and B combined); return: 25mins)
Technical notes	escape points (within stage): 0

Route

Climb straight up the front of the pillar (the Grand Pilier). This is not fully vertical and involves only a few slightly strenuous moves. The climb is well protected by numerous stemples but also makes occasional use of knobbly quartzite for handholds. At the top of the pillar, cross a bay by way of a 7m-long three-wire bridge. This is quite slack, but not too exposed. On the other side of the bay descend on rungs for 12m. The last few metres of the descent are overhanging and somewhat strenuous.

Walk along a broad ledge (La Vire des Barmes) to the right for several minutes to arrive at the end of Stage B at an escape point, the Sortie du Clapet. The cabled escape route descends steeply along a slippery path to join the return path.

Ascending the Grand Pilier

STAGE C
Le Surplomb Jaune

Length	200m
Ascent/Descent	100m (360m, if combined with preceding stages)
Route grading	technical grade: 4; exposure: 3; seriousness: B
Time	2hrs 45mins (approach: 15mins; route: 1hr 50mins (all stages combined); return: 40mins)
Technical notes	escape points (within stage): 0

Route
Continue along the broad ledge until arriving at the base of a yellowish wall, which you climb up for 15m on stemples. The upper part of the wall is overhanging and quite strenuous for a few metres. Thereafter difficulty diminishes and a straightforward scramble, up what turns out to be a gigantic flake, follows. Step across a chasm to rejoin the face and continue to gain height until reaching the top of the bluffs and a split in the cable. To extend your outing to include an exploration of the west flank of Mont Pourri, continue up the hill to the right. To finish, go left and descend the side of a broad ravine via a fault. A short ladder leads to the end of the cable.

Return
The descent path, which is obvious and well marked, rejoins the approach route just below the start of the via ferrata.

ROUTE 27
Via Ferrata Roc de Tovière

Location	Val-d'Isère, Savoie
	(GPS: Lat. 45° 27′ 45.31″ N Long. 6° 57′ 49.93″ E)
Length	1400m
Ascent/descent	560m
Route grading	technical grade: 2–5; exposure: 2–5; seriousness: B
	(Stages A and B), C (Stage C)
Total time	5hrs
Highest altitude	2347m
Map	3633ET
Technical notes	total escape points: 2
When to visit	May to October

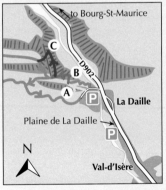

Of the many scenic highlights along the southern approach to the celebrated ski resort of Val-d'Isère, perhaps the most impressive are the huge walls of the Gorges de la Daille. The vast eastern face of the Roc de Tovière, on one side of the gorge, is home to one of the hardest and longest via ferratas in France. Thankfully, the route is split into three stages of increasing difficulty, allowing climbers with less-than-perfect physiques to have a taste of what the full outing offers.

The first stage is suitable for beginners and the second, while quite exposed, is only briefly strenuous. The third stage, despite containing only one especially strenuous passage, is generally quite physical and is also very, very exposed throughout. Additionally, by the standards of French via ferratas, this stage involves much rock contact, and those without some rock-climbing experience may find this rather demanding. This is one of the most rewarding routes described in this book and, if you think that you are up to the challenge, cannot be recommended highly enough.

Just prior to the publication of this book, an alteration was made to the route line of Stage C due to rockfall. Full details of the new line are unknown at the time of writing, but it is understood that the difficulty of the stage is likely to remain unchanged. Further information will be made available under the Updates tab on this book's page on the Cicerone website (www.cicerone.co.uk).

Ascending the Dalle de Lézard. The Aiguille de la Grande Sassière (3747m) is in the background (Stage C)

Access

Driving south from Bourg-St-Maurice on the **D902**, turn right at the first roundabout encountered upon entering **La Daille**, at the north end of **Val-d'Isère**. Cross a bridge and park. There are restrictions on when this car park may be used, but alternative parking is available a little further down the main road, at Parking **Plaine de La Daille**.

STAGE A
1ère Partie

Length	150m
Ascent/Descent	100m
Route grading	technical grade: 2; exposure: 2; seriousness: B
Time	1hr (approach: <1min; route: 35mins; return: 25mins)
Technical notes	direction: S; escape points (within stage): 0

Approach
The start of the route is just beyond the low white bunker-like building.

Route
After a brief climb, a gradually rising traverse is followed along the edge of a low bluff. A longer climb up a broken buttress then leads to a short balance beam. This requires a little care to cross, but is not particularly exposed. A further short climb leads to the end of Stage A before the

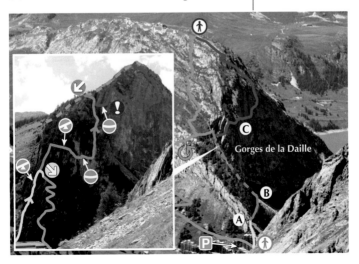

Gorges de la Daille

first escape point of the route. There is quite a bit of contact with the rock throughout this stage, but only a few isolated moves are considerably strenuous.

STAGE B
2ème Partie

Length	600m
Ascent/Descent	160m (260m, if combined with Stage A)
Route grading	technical grade: 3; exposure: 4; seriousness: B
Time	3hrs (approach: <1min; route: 2hrs 20mins (Stages A and B combined); return: 40mins)
Technical notes	direction: E and NE; escape points (within stage): 0

Route

Continue gaining height and then follow a level path across tree-covered slopes, passing over an airy balance beam part-way along. A little height is lost as the path ends adjacent to pale bluffs that drop away precipitously towards the river. These are crossed, with some mildly strenuous moves and plenty of exposure, for 20m. After a short climb up the bluffs and some easy traversing, a 7m-long bridge is crossed. A slightly strenuous climb of 10m up an arête leads to a good spot to take a break.

Ascend a steep scrambly path up a rocky, tree-covered slope and then follow a system of fairly broad ledges up the side of the bluffs. The ledges present few problems and do not feel very exposed, due to the surrounding trees. The ledges continue for several hundred metres, interrupted only once by a short, energetic climb up and around a slight eminence from the bluffs. Towards the top of the ledges and the end of Stage B, the rather daunting bridge and initial climb at the start of the third stage come into view, allowing ample time to consider whether or not to continue. If you have had enough, continue climbing past the end of the bridge, and descend along the obvious path to return to the car park.

The airy 42m suspension bridge at the beginning of the third stage

STAGE C
3ème Partie

Length	650m
Ascent/Descent	300m (560m, if combined with preceding stages)
Route grading	technical grade: 5; exposure: 5; seriousness: C
Time	5hrs (approach: <1min; route: 4hrs (all stages combined); return: 1hr)
Technical notes	direction: E; escape points (within stage): 0

Overcoming the crux of the route, an exposed and demanding 7m rising traverse

Route

Having crossed the airy 42m-long bridge (which is quite stable), scale a largely featureless wall (Dalle de Lézard). This is interrupted one third of the way up by a pronounced overhang. The overhang is a little harder than it initially appears and involves a steeply rising traverse of 7m. Although not massively strenuous, you will probably have to make use of several small or smeary foot placements, some of which are becoming polished. Above the overhang, which is the crux of the route, the remainder of the climb is well off-vertical, so should present no particular problems.

From the small platform at the top of the wall, follow a gradually descending traverse down a narrow ledge. Although massively exposed, your attention will be primarily focused on placing your feet on the down-sloping rock. Progress eases as the ledge flattens and, having turned a corner, levels off. Continue on the ledge (Traversée de non-retour) along the edge of the bluffs without particular difficulty. After passing around a second corner the ledge narrows somewhat, allowing far greater appreciation of the 250m drop immediately below your right foot. In a few places it disappears for a short distance, necessitating the use of small or smeary rock foot placements.

Eventually the traverse ends at the Pilier Mystérieux, which involves a vertical climb of 25m. At first this is fairly strenuous but then eases off after 5m. Throughout the climb, the rungs are widely spaced and even the tallest climbers will have to use small but good rock-holds for hands and feet in a number of places. Commence a second traverse (Traversée de l'Edelweiss), which is a little shorter than the last but slightly more difficult. This contains many moderately strenuous passages across slabs, using only small rock footholds. The route then climbs up the Montée de la Délivrance for 60m. This is noticeably easier than the previous vertical section and ends at the top of the cliff, with fine views both up and down the valley. The Barrage de Tines, visible to the north, is the tallest such construction in France. From here, the cable winds up the hillside for a long way without any difficulty, until ending next to a large cairn.

Return
Having taken in the views of the surrounding peaks (the glaciated eminence to the southwest is La Grande Motte, 3653m), descend by one of two routes. For a longer and more scenic return, keep right and take a cairned path over the Arête de Tovière, which leads to the GR5 trail. Follow this downhill and then take a signposted path, to your left, which returns directly to La Daille. For a more rapid descent from the large cairn, go left and follow a narrow path that winds through snow barriers to meet the path from the top of the second stage. This route is initially protected by several short lengths of cable, so keep your gear on. It also involves much unprotected, slippery, and exposed walking, which requires particular care.

ROUTE 28

Via Ferrata Les Plates de la Daille

Location	Val-d'Isère, Savoie
	(GPS: Lat. 45° 27′ 45.31″ N Long. 6° 57′ 49.93″ E)
Length	650m
Ascent/Descent	385m
Route grading	technical grade: 3; exposure: 5; seriousness: B
Total time	3hrs 15mins
	(approach: 20mins; route: 2hrs 10mins; return: 45mins)
Highest altitude	2180m
Map	3633ET
Technical notes	direction: SW; escape points: 0
When to visit	May to October

This via ferrata climbs the bluffs on the eastern side of the Gorges de la Daille, directly opposite the Roc de Tovière (Route 27). While considerably less daunting than its near neighbour, the route still involves a fairly challenging ascent. Although well spaced, there are a number of strenuous or awkward passages, in particular a brief descending traverse out onto the main cliff-face. This, together with the exposed nature of the ascent and the lack of any escape, results in a serious undertaking.

Climbing both routes at Val-d'Isère in one day is possible but not recommended, due to the length. If you intend to do this, however, note that the Plates de la Daille will be in shade in the early morning and the Roc de Tovière in shade in the late afternoon. Thus, starting with Route 27 would be the better option.

Access

Driving south from Bourg-St-Maurice on the **D902**, pass the first roundabout encountered upon entering La Daille (at the north end of Val-d'Isère). At the second roundabout, turn right and park at Parking **Plaine de La Daille**.

Approach

Head down Rue de la Daille, which is across the roundabout from the car park. Make your way into the group of houses just to the side of the main road and turn right by some recycling bins and a yellow signpost. Shortly thereafter, turn left at a second yellow signpost and follow a gradually ascending path to the foot of the cliffs.

A good head for heights is required to ascend Les Plates de la Daille

Route

The first part of the route offers a relatively gentle introduction as a rising traverse crosses a series of slabs, grassy shelves and small rock steps. Once near the main cliff-face, the angle steepens as the first wall is tackled. This is 20m high and involves some fairly strenuous moves. Continue to gain height up fairly broken rock until confronted by a short but quite overhanging wall. Once this is overcome the angle again eases and the full extent of the drop just to your left becomes increasingly apparent as more height is gained up mostly easy ground. Eventually, a small platform housing the remains of an antenna is reached. This is a good place to take a break and admire the views of La Daille and Val-d'Isère.

Leave the relative comfort of the top of the bluffs and follow a descending traverse for 20m out onto the main cliff-face (La Traversée de l'Aigle). This feels particularly airy and is slightly awkward in one place, but is very well protected. The cable then leads up a steep, grassy, ledge. The ledge is mostly quite broad, but still feels very exposed. At the end of the ledge, the route steepens

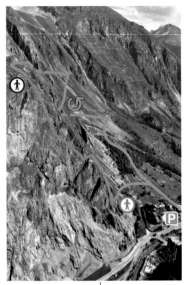

considerably as a long climb leads to the top of the cliff-face and the end of the cable. The climb involves overcoming a few small overhangs and is well protected by abundant stemples. That said, the length and ever-present exposure make for a fairly sustained and arduous finale. There are fine views, from this final section, of Lac du Chevril to the northwest, as well as of the austere east face of the Roc de Tovière.

Return

Take the path to the right, which crosses a broad plateau above the bluffs then zigzags downhill to rejoin the approach path just above La Daille.

The famous resort of Val-d'Isère, seen from the top of the route

MAURIENNE

*Approaching the first balance beam
on Les Diablotins (Route 32, Stage B)*

INTRODUCTION

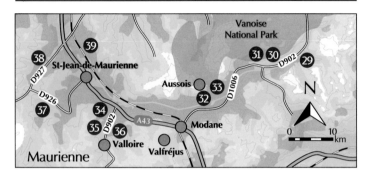

The majority of routes in this chapter are located along the course of the valley of the River Arc. This valley is traditionally divided into two sectors, the Basse-Maurienne and the Haute-Maurienne. The former is relatively built-up and industrial and the latter, which borders the southern boundary of the Vanoise National Park, is sparsely populated and highly scenic. In addition to the Vanoise Massif, the surrounding mountains consist of the Mont-Cenis, Cerces and Arves ranges, which include many of the higher glaciated peaks of the Alps.

The fastest access to the area is from Chambéry via the A43 motorway, which runs as far as Modane and then crosses into Italy. Modane can also be reached by train. There are also road links with the Tarentaise Valley via the Col de la Madeleine and the Col de l'Iseran, which is the highest pass crossed by a paved road in Europe. To the south, Briançon can be reached via Valloire and the Col du Galibier.

Plenty of accommodation of all types is available, both near the routes and in the larger towns and villages. The principal town of the valley, St-Jean-de-Maurienne, offers the widest range of choices and is a good place to base yourself in the Basse-Maurienne. Further up the valley, the summer resort of Aussois is also worth considering as a base, if you intend to spend some time in the area. All of the routes in this chapter are sports routes that do not involve large amounts of rock contact. Most of them are fairly easy with only a handful of more difficult routes. Several of the easier routes would serve as ideal introductions to the activity.

Just prior to publication of this book, a new route called Via Ferrata du Grand Vallon opened at the Valfréjus resort, which is located southwest of Modane. The route involves two moderately difficult sections and one section of high difficulty, contains several bridges and takes two to three hours to complete. For further details see www.valfrejus. com. For tourist information see the websites listed in Appendix D.

Ascending the Échelle de Tichodrome (Route 36, Stage A)

ROUTE 29
Via Ferrata d'Andagne

Location	Bessans/Bonneval-sur-Arc, Savoie
	(GPS: Lat. 45º 20′ 37.99″ N Long. 7º 1′ 42.52″ E)
Length	1000m
Ascent/Descent	510m
Route grading	technical grade: 1–2; exposure: 1–4; seriousness: B (all stages)
Total time	3hrs 30mins
Highest altitude	2260m
Map	3633ET
Technical notes	total escape points: 0
When to visit	May to October

The Via Ferrata d'Andagne, situated part-way between the picturesque villages of Bessans and Bonneval-sur-Arc and surrounded by soaring glaciated peaks, makes for an ideal introduction to the upper valley of the River Arc. The first stage, which is very short, is suitable for children and beginners. The second stage scales the cliffs overlooking the road at their steepest point. Despite the rather daunting appearance of the cliff-face at this point, which features a massive overhang, the

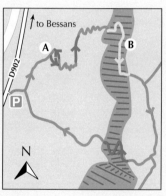

route is relatively straightforward and not noticeably strenuous. The climb affords wonderful views up and down the Arc Valley and of the peaks of the Vanoise National Park, on the other side of the valley.

Access
From Modane take the D1006 and then the **D902** to **Bessans**. Approximately 3km beyond Bessans look out for

The upper Maurienne Valley, from the top of Itinéraire Guy Favre (Stage B)

a via ferrata information panel on the right of the road. Park in the adjacent field.

STAGE A
Itinéraire Pierre Blanc

Length	150m
Ascent/Descent	30m
Route grading	technical grade: 1; exposure: 1; seriousness: B
Time	30mins (approach: 5mins; route: 20mins; return: 5mins)
Technical notes	direction: W; escape points (within stage): 0

Approach
Follow an obvious path that leads across fields to the left. This gains a little height before arriving at the base of some low bluffs.

Route

Leave the path and ascend a series of slabs and short walls. The climb is very simple and well protected throughout. After the cable ends turn left and briefly walk along a path. The cable recommences and crosses an unexposed balance beam before descending to near where you started.

STAGE B

Itinéraire Guy Favre

Length	850m
Ascent/Descent	480m (510m, if combined with Stage A)
Route grading	technical grade: 2; exposure: 4; seriousness: B
Time	3hrs 30mins (approach: 5mins; route: 2hrs 25mins (both stages combined); return: 1hr)
Technical notes	direction: W; escape points (within stage): 0

Route

At the top of the first stage, keep right and continue ascending the steep, grassy slope. The path is briefly cabled, where it overcomes a second bluff via a ledge, the Vire du Greffier. Once the main cliff-face is reached, the cable recommences and the route climbs steeply, via a chimney. At the top of this, a series of short climbs and ledges arrive at a fairly broad ledge, which makes a good place to take a rest. This is followed to the right, until a 6m-long balance beam is crossed. Pass around a corner and ascend, more-or-less directly, to the end of the route. This final climbing section contains a few mildly strenuous moves and is very exposed.

Return

From the grassy balcony at the top of the route, head right. After passing some ruins, descend as indicated by signs and yellow waymarks. Much of the descent path is exposed and slippery and is fitted with a cable, so you should keep your gear on.

The final part of the route is exposed, but well protected

ROUTE 30
Via Ferrata du Col de la Madeleine

Location	Lanslevillard, Savoie
	(GPS: Lat. 45° 18′ 2.48″ N Long. 6° 56′ 19.80″ E)
Length	400m
Ascent/Descent	120m
Route grading	technical grade: 2; exposure: 3; seriousness: A
Total time	1hr 30mins (approach: 10mins; route: 1hr; return: 20mins)
Highest altitude	1820m
Map	3633ET
Technical notes	direction: S; escape points: 0
When to visit	April to October

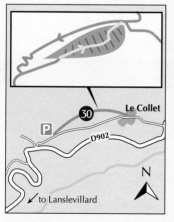

This route has been in existence for some time, but until recently was secured only with pigs' tails pitons for use by roped parties (referred to as a Via Cordata). A fixed cable has now been put in place and the route is a fully fledged via ferrata. Although relatively short and simple by the standards of neighbouring via ferratas, this route is well designed and quite enjoyable. It makes a good complement to the nearby Le Pichet (Route 31), and both routes can be accomplished easily during the course of an afternoon.

Access

From **Lanslevillard** (see Route 31), continue along the **D902** in the direction of Bessans. After a little over 3km, turn left onto a minor road, which heads to **Le Collet**. If you reach a sign for the Rocher d'Escalade de la

The heavily striated rock offers plenty of good handholds, in addition to their artificial counterparts

Madeleine to the right of the main road, you have over-shot the turning by 1km. Once on the minor road, park on the left after 250m.

Approach
Walk briefly uphill until a sign indicates a right turn. The path then traverses between fields and low bluffs until the cable is encountered.

Route
Walk along a ledge until a short, slightly strenuous climb of a few metres up to a higher ledge. (The climb is almost as strenuous as this route gets.) Continue around a corner and then climb for 25m, at a relatively gentle angle, to reach a grassy platform. Walk around a broad, grassy

bay and then climb up to another ledge. By this point the route is becoming a little airy, but the ledge is broad and involves nothing harder than walking. After 40m the ledge disappears as you climb out onto the cliff-face and go straight up for 40m.

At first this is not too steep, but higher up it becomes moderately strenuous in places. Progress is mostly on stemples with some use of the horizontally striated rock for the feet. Once at the top, traverse to the right for 50m. This is on a narrow or occasionally non-existent ledge and feels quite exposed. The final challenge consists of a rising traverse of 35m. There are several slightly strenuous moves, including one moderate overhang of 2m. As throughout the route, the quality of the fixed protection is excellent and the rock offers good footholds. Finish with an easy walk up some slabs and good views of the glaciated peaks across the valley, the highest of which is the Pointe de Ronce (3612m).

Return
Turn left and follow a cairned path that gradually descends to the parking area.

ROUTE 31
Via Ferrata du Pichet

Location	Lanslevillard, Savoie
	(GPS: Lat. 45° 17′ 32.27″ N Long. 6° 55′ 13.53″ E)
Length	350m
Ascent/Descent	100m
Route grading	technical grade: 2 (variant: 1); exposure: 2; seriousness: A
Total time	2hrs (approach: 15mins; route: 1hr 30mins; return: 15mins)
Highest altitude	1600m
Map	3633ET
Technical notes	direction: S; escape points: 1
When to visit	April to October

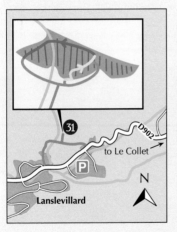

This route, which is short and easy to access, is situated on bluffs overlooking Lanslevillard, one of the larger Haute-Maurienne villages. The via ferrata serves as a good warm-up for the more challenging routes in the vicinity, but it is a fun outing in its own right. It is also a reasonable option when the weather is damp or cloudy. The most notable feature of the route is a large ladder that juts out prominently from the cliff-face. As it is scaled facing outwards, climbing the ladder (which is visible from the village below) is something of a test of nerves.

Access
Lanslevillard can be reached from Modane via the D1006 and then the **D902**. At the top of the village, turn right at a sign 'BALCONS de VAL CENIS – le Haut' and park near a via ferrata information panel.

Approach

Turn right and walk up the main road for 50m. Then turn left as signposted and head along a dirt track for 350m. Turn right up a path running between fields and right again to ascend to the base of the bluffs below the large ladder.

Route

To avoid the ladder (recommended for parties with younger children), follow the walking path to the right to start this route at its escape point and follow the grade 1 section only.

◄ Climb up on weirdly eroded rock for 15m to the foot of the ladder. Although it is well protected, this is probably the hardest part of the route. Ascend the ladder, which feels more stable than it appears, for 12m. At the top, step off onto a broad shelf and traverse just below the top of the cliff until the escape path is met.

Thereafter, a short climb leads to a long, easy traverse to the left and a 15m-long suspension bridge. This is a bit wobbly but not too exposed. A second ladder (easy; climbed facing inwards) follows, beyond which more traversing and a brief down-climb lead to the end of the route.

The outward-facing ladder near the start of the route

Return
Descend for a few minutes to rejoin the approach path.

ROUTE 32
Via Ferrata du Diable

Location	Aussois, Savoie
	(GPS: Lat. 45° 12' 50.59" N Long. 6° 44' 10.60" E)
Length	3.5km
Ascent/Descent	680m approx
Route grading	technical grade: 1–5; exposure: 1–5; seriousness: A
	(all stages)
Total time	A long day
Highest altitude	1310m
Map	3534OT
Technical notes	total escape points: 9 (all stages)
When to visit	March to November
Useful websites	www.aussois.com; www.redoutemarietherese.fr

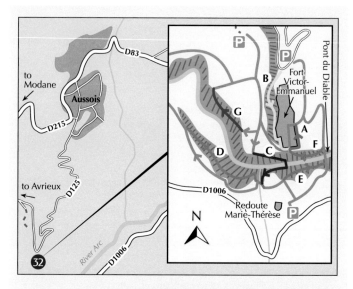

The Via Ferrata du Diable is the largest single collection of via ferratas in France (and perhaps anywhere). Of consistently high quality, the routes make the most of the wonderful high-mountain setting, typical of the Haute-Maurienne. Named for the Pont du Diable, a pedestrian bridge that crosses a huge gorge carved out by the passage of the River Arc, the seven individual routes pass around the sides of the gorge below the Barrière de l'Esseillon. This is the name given to the series of impressive fortifications that dominate the area. Forming an effective blockade across the entire valley, the forts were constructed in the 19th century by the Piedmontese king to defend against French invasion.

Each route can be completed separately or can be linked together as described here, but tackling all seven in one day will be beyond all but the very fittest. The first stage is designed specifically for children and beginners and the second is also suitable for novices. All the others are quite demanding, being both occasionally strenuous and hugely exposed. This is particularly true of Les Rois Mages, which, although short, is one of the hardest and most spectacular routes described in this book. If you intend to spend some time in the Haute-Maurienne consider basing yourself in Aussois. This busy summer resort offers a wide range of accommodation and activities. In addition to paragliding, mountain biking, fishing and canyoning, there is a massive treetop adventure park adjacent to the Redoute Marie-Thérèse. This ends with a gigantic Tyrolean traverse across the gorge.

Access

From Modane, take the **D215** to **Aussois**. From there, follow signs for **Fort Victor-Emmanuel** and park at the rear of the fort. Alternatively, to start from **Redoute Marie-Thérèse**, on the other side of the main valley, follow the **D1006** from Modane until a clearly signposted parking area.

The approach and return times given below are from, and back to, the parking at the rear of Fort Victor-Emmanuel. Note that the approach and return times for Stages D and E, if these stages are being tackled individually, can be reduced considerably by parking at Redoubte Marie-Thérèse.

STAGE A
Les Angelots

Length	400m
Ascent/Descent	30m
Route grading	technical grade: 1; exposure: 1; seriousness: A
Time	1hr (approach: 15mins; route: 30mins; return: 15mins)
Technical notes	direction: E; escape points (within stage): 1

Approach

Follow a track that passes around the eastern flank of Fort Victor-Emmanuel. Cross a drawbridge and enter the fort. Descend through tunnels to the lowest point of the castle.

Route

Exit the fort, by clambering out of the indicated gun port, and turn left. The route then traverses beneath the fortress wall. Descend and briefly walk (escape is possible

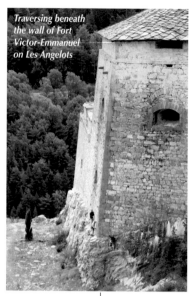

Traversing beneath the wall of Fort Victor-Emmanuel on Les Angelots

here) before climbing back up and again traversing below the wall. Pass underneath the entrance drawbridge for the fortress, cross a small suspension bridge and finish. This is a short introductory route designed principally for smaller children and contains no noticeably strenuous moves. It is exposed by no more than 10m.

Return

Walk up to the drawbridge to pick up the approach path.

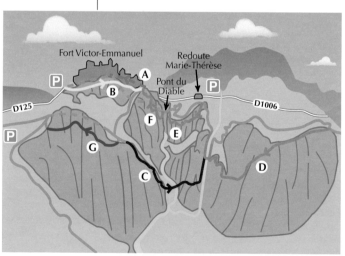

STAGE B
Les Diablotins

Length	500m
Ascent/Descent	20m (50m, if combined with Stage A)
Route grading	technical grade: 2; exposure: 2; seriousness: A
Time	1hr 30mins
	(approach: <1min; route: 1hr 10mins; return: 20mins)
Technical notes	direction: W; escape points (within stage): 0

Approach
The route starts immediately to the west of the car park.

Route
The via ferrata involves a long, more-or-less level, traverse around the western flank of the bluffs not far below the walls of the fort. At first, the cable leads along a narrow path surrounded by trees. Exposure increases as the path

Les Diablotins involves a fairly level traverse, which is only occasionally exposed

183

disappears and the route edges out onto the cliff-face proper. A short balance beam is crossed before the route returns to less vertical terrain. A series of vegetated ledges are then followed, interspersed with more short balance beams and a three-wire bridge, none of which is in a particularly airy position. A straightforward descent arrives at the south face of the fort. Finish by climbing through the specified gun port or, to continue, go straight ahead for Les Angelots (Stage A) or right for La Descente aux Enfers (Stage C) and Les Rois Mages (Stage G).

Return
Follow a succession of large tunnels up through Fort Victor-Emmanuel. Turn left at the entrance to the fort, and take the signposted track back to the car park.

STAGE C
La Descente aux Enfers and La Montée au Purgatoire

Length	450m
Ascent/Descent	160m (210m, if combined with preceding stages)
Route grading	technical grade: 4; exposure: 4; seriousness: A
Time	2hrs 45mins
	(approach: 35mins; route: 1hr 30mins; return: 40mins)
Technical notes	direction: S and N; escape points (within stage): 0

Approach
Follow a track that passes around the eastern flank of Fort Victor-Emmanuel. Cross a drawbridge and enter the fort. Descend through tunnels to the lowest point of the castle. Put your gear on here and exit the fort through the indicated gun port. Turn right and descend into a small valley, keeping left at a junction with the path for Les Rois Mages (Stage G).

Route
Carefully descend along a gravelly ledge for 100m. The ledge is exposed but presents little difficulty, being quite

A large group on La Descente aux Enfers

wide. At the end the cable disappears over the edge of the bluffs and descends the face of the gorge for 25m. The descent is not too strenuous, but involves a few awkward moves. Step off the bluffs and onto the Passerelle des Enfers, a 20m-long bridge. This crosses above the River Arc to the other side of the gorge and, despite appearances, is fairly stable. Beyond the bridge, La Montée au Purgatoire works its way along a system of generally broad ledges to arrive at a section of walking path, which crosses a small bay. This makes a good place to rest before tackling the remainder of the route.

Turn a corner and climb up towards a waterfall, the Cascade du Nant. Although well protected by closely spaced rungs, the climb becomes increasingly strenuous, especially towards the top. Additionally, you will probably get a little wet, depending on the volume of water in the Ruisseau du Nant. Having climbed above the waterfall, either cross a rather unstable 15m-long bridge over the stream to visit Le Chemin de la Vierge (Stage D), or keep left to finish. The left-hand option also leads to La

Crossing the Passerelle des Enfers

Traversée des Anges (Stage E). The cable ends after a little more climbing along the true right bank of the stream.

Return

Briefly walk uphill to the treetop ropes course in the vicinity of Redoute Marie-Thérèse. From here, you can either start La Traversée des Anges (Stage E), or if you have had enough, keep right and walk to the east. Descend and cross the **Pont du Diable**, from where a track heads back to the car park.

STAGE D
Le Chemin de la Vierge

Length	1100m
Ascent/Descent	150m (360m, if combined with preceding stages)
Route grading	technical grade: 3; exposure: 4; seriousness: A
Time	3hrs 30mins (approach: 50mins; route: 2hrs; return: 40mins)
Technical notes	direction: NE; escape points (within stage): 0

Approach
Descend to the Pont du Diable and then walk uphill to
the treetop ropes course. Pass beneath the ropes course
and descend a little to the northwest. Put your gear on
here. A short section of cable leads down by the side of a
stream, the Ruisseau du Nant, to an airy bridge at the top
of La Montée au Purgatoire (Stage C). Beyond the bridge,
the cable ends and a long path, indicated by blue waymarks, is followed along the top of the gorge to a wooden
gate at the start of the via ferrata.

Route
Start with a strenuous 5m down-climb followed by a long
walk on a level path, which is protected by cable. A balance beam is followed by more traversing, now across
the face of some bluffs. Although the bluffs are low, the
long drop to the river, 120m below, results in a fairly airy
experience. Progress is mostly on stemples and there are
several brief sections that are moderately strenuous, but
well spaced apart. Two more balance beams and one short
two-wire bridge lead to the end of bluffs and a short walk.
Cross another balance beam and more bluffs, which are
higher than the previous set, but otherwise similar.

The route then loses height via two ladders, which
are descended facing outwards for 13m and 15m, to a
break in the cable. After another section of walking a
final set of bluffs are climbed. This involves a vertical
climb of 40m, passing through a few small overhangs,
followed by a delicate, exceptionally exposed, traverse
that crosses near the top of the huge sweep of bluffs just
to the west of the Cascade du Nant. Recross the bridge
above the waterfall to finish.

Return
Briefly walk uphill to the treetop ropes course in the
vicinity of Redoute Marie-Thérèse. From here, you can
either start La Traversée des Anges (Stage E), or if you have
had enough, keep right and walk to the east. Descend
and cross the **Pont du Diable**, from where a track heads
back to the car park.

STAGE E
La Traversée des Anges

Length	360m
Ascent/Descent	60m (420m, if combined with preceding stages)
Route grading	technical grade: 3; exposure: 4; seriousness: A
Time	2hrs (approach: 35mins; route: 1hr; return: 25mins)
Technical notes	direction: N; escape points (within stage): 1

Just beyond the escape point on La Traversée des Anges

Approach
Descend to the **Pont du Diable** and then walk uphill to the treetop ropes course. Pass beneath this and head towards the edge of the gorge.

Route
Start with an exposed but easy descent and long traverse, using a series of ledges. The ledges gradually narrow and then disappear altogether as you begin to traverse above a massive overhang. There is an escape point here, which you should use if the first part of the route has been too much, as the second part is more difficult and exposed.

Continue to traverse above the overhang for 30m, mostly on stemples, with a very 'immediate' drop beneath you. This is quite strenuous in places, but there is a reasonable spot to take a rest just beyond the overhang. Pass around a corner to receive temporary relief from the exposure. This does not last for long as a short, delicate, descent leads back out onto the sheer side of the gorge. A couple of brief traverses, between which is a short climb (all slightly strenuous), lead to the final challenge. This consists of a muscular climb of 12m, which returns you to the top of the bluffs.

Return
Recross the **Pont du Diable**, and retrace the approach route.

STAGE F
La Montée au Ciel

Length	450m
Ascent/Descent	140m (560m, if combined with preceding stages)
Route grading	technical grade: 3; exposure: 4; seriousness: A
Time	2hrs (approach: 25mins; route: 1hr 15mins; return: 20mins)
Technical notes	direction: S; escape points (within stage): 0

Pont du Diable and the first part of La Montée au Ciel

Approach

Descend to the **Pont du Diable**. The route starts just before the bridge.

Route

If you have made the full circuit starting with La Descente aux Enfers this final leg should come as something of a relief, being a little less arduous than the previous stages.

After a short descent a broad ledge, which passes beneath the Pont du Diable, is followed. The route then leads across the face of the gorge, generally gaining height at a fairly gradual rate. Although the river is a long way down, the series of broad ledges and terraces encountered mean that the exposure is not too constant and there are plenty of places to rest. There are a number of sections of vertical climbing, which vary in length from 5 to 25m and are well protected. Towards the end of the route, several of these climbs pass through small overhangs and are reasonably strenuous. Having arrived at the top of the bluffs, either crawl through the indicated gun port to finish or go right for Les Angelots (Stage A) or left for La Descente aux Enfers (Stage C) and Les Rois Mages (Stage G).

Return

Follow a succession of large tunnels up through Fort Victor-Emmanuel. Turn left at the entrance to the fort, and take the signposted track back to the car park.

STAGE G
Les Rois Mages

Length	300m
Ascent/Descent	120m (680m, if combined with preceding stages)
Route grading	technical grade: 5; exposure: 5; seriousness: A
Time	2hrs 30mins
	(approach: 30mins; route: 1hr 10mins; return: 50mins)
Technical notes	direction: SW; escape points (within stage): 1

Approach

Take the same path used to approach La Descente aux Enfers (Stage C). At the final junction, turn right. (Note that if doing only this stage, a more rapid approach and return is available: drive 500m down the D125 beyond the parking area at the back of Fort Victor-Emmanuel and take a small road on the left. Park at the end of this road and follow the obvious path until a sign indicates the turn-off for the start of the route.)

Route

Start by crossing a stable three-wire bridge for 25m (Pont Gaspard). This passes above a shallow bay, so does not feel too exposed. The same cannot be said of the 25m level traverse that follows, throughout which one is directly overhanging a drop of 100m or more. This passage is particularly punishing for taller climbers due to the relative closeness of the hand and foot placements. These mostly consist of artificial holds but use is also made of large, sometimes sloping, rock-holds for the feet. Additionally, there is one important rock handhold to look out for, which should be obvious due to polishing. Never wildly strenuous, progress is nevertheless quite tiring, with only a few points where your arms are not under tension.

Having climbed up for a few metres, you are presented with two options:

1   Go right to escape.
2   If you intend to continue, do not hesitate to use the escape point to take a rest before stepping out onto a two-wire bridge to your left.

*The 82m-long
Pont Melchior on
Les Rois Mages*

Pont Balthazar is 20m long and, being quite slack, is fairly tiring to cross. On the other side a second traverse follows. The first 10m of this is similar in nature to the previous traverse, but the next 10m is much easier, making use of a broad ledge. Finish by crossing the third and final bridge, a stable suspension bridge (Pont Melchior). At 82m in length, this is the longest bridge that has been integrated into any via ferrata created to date.

Return
To return to Fort Victor-Emmanuel keep right, passing a path on your left that descends to the nearby village of Avrieux. Once back at Fort Victor-Emmanuel, follow a succession of large tunnels to the entrance to the fort, and take the signposted track back to the car park.

ROUTE 33
Via Ferrata de L'École Buissonnière

Location	Aussois, Savoie
	(GPS: Lat. 45° 14' 3.90" N Long. 6° 45' 22.43" E)
Length	50m
Ascent/Descent	30m
Route grading	technical grade: 1; exposure: 1; seriousness: A
Total time	1hr (approach: <1min; route: 45mins; return: 15mins)
Highest altitude	560m
Map	3534OT
Technical notes	direction: S; escape points: 2
When to visit	March to November

This short, fun, via ferrata makes good use of two of the many large rock pinnacles that protrude from the forested hillside between Aussois and the nearby village of Sardières. Although designed specifically to be accessible by children, adults can also climb the route. However, taller climbers may actually find some parts a little harder. There are two escape points and several short cuts, so any difficulties are easy to avoid. The name of the route is a play on words, as to attend an *école buissonnière* is to play truant. The nearby Monolithe de Sardières, a 93m-tall rock spire with bolted climbing routes, is well worth a visit for serious rock climbers and other admirers of big pointy rocks.

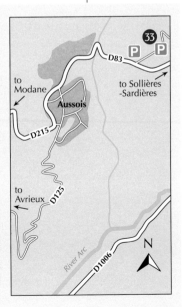

The high point of the route: a two-wire bridge between the two pinnacles on which the via ferrata is constructed

Access
From Aussois, take the **D83** in the direction of Sollières-Sardières. Drive for 1.4km to a parking area with a cross, the Plan de la Croix. Either park here and walk or drive for 500m along a small road signposted for 'Le Monolithe'. The route starts near a sharp bend in the road, with space for two or three cars to park.

Approach
Just beyond a sign marked '1ère comb' pass an information panel for the via ferrata and walk beneath a two-wire bridge crossing between two broad pinnacles.

Route
Scale the back of the right-hand pinnacle until a short balance beam heads out onto a tree. Climb up and around the tree, on pegs driven into the trunk, and return to the rock-face via a second short balance beam. Descend a little to an escape point at the back of the rock and then climb up to the top of the right-hand pinnacle. Cross to the adjacent pinnacle on the two-wire bridge, and then descend along one side of the rock to meet a second escape point.

Continue by descending along the other side of the rock until the end of the route. Part-way along this face there is the option of crossing onto a tree. This is climbed up and around on pegs and branches until a beam is used to reach a second tree. Down-climb the second tree, again on pegs and branches, until the rock-face can be rejoined. This side-route is a little awkward and perhaps best left to lighter people.

ROUTE 34

Via Ferrata du Télégraphe

Location	St-Michel-de-Maurienne, Savoie
	(GPS: Lat. 45° 13′ 2.27″ N Long. 6° 27′ 28.04″ E)
Length	950m
Ascent/Descent	1040m
Route grading	technical grade: 1–2; exposure: 2–4; seriousness: B (all stages)
Total time	4hrs
Highest altitude	1340m
Map	3435ET
Technical notes	total escape points: 0
When to visit	March to November

This route presents you with two options, both of which are quite long. However, only the second option (Stage B) contains any real difficulty and even this is brief. As such, this is a good choice for beginners or when damp weather prevents access to harder via ferratas. Considerable height is gained along the way and the ascent can be quite tiring, particularly in the morning, when the route may be in full sun. The reward for your efforts comes in the form of a good bird's-eye view of St-Michel-de-Maurienne and the surrounding valley, which can be enjoyed throughout the climb.

In addition to the route described below, there is an upper section of via ferrata that runs across bluffs directly beneath the

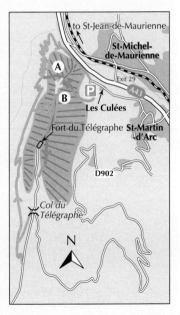

walls of the Fort du Télégraphe. At the time of writing this is closed but, should it reopen, it is reportedly quite easy and arrives at a height of 1612m.

Access

From St-Jean-de-Maurienne, drive south on the **A43** to **St-Michel-de-Maurienne** and take Exit 29 onto the **D1006**. From the centre of St-Michel, head south on the D902 and upon entering **St-Martin-d'Arc**, turn right for **Les Culées**. This turning, which is next to a small bus stop, is easy to miss. Follow signs for the via ferrata through Les Culées to the car park.

STAGE A
Col des Pylônes

Length	500m
Ascent/Descent	400m
Route grading	technical grade: 1; exposure: 2; seriousness: B
Time	2hrs 45mins (approach: 45mins; route: 1hr; return: 1hr)
Technical notes	direction: W and E; escape points (within stage): 0

Approach

Head across a sports field to a large via ferrata information panel. Take a path that heads up forested slopes, with signposts at any junctions. The path then leads up shrub-covered scree slopes, gaining 300m in height.

Route

Ascend a series of low-angle slabs that lead up to the two electricity pylons directly overhead. There is plenty of contact with the rock as the number of stemples is limited, but most progress involves either steep walking or hauling on the cable. The slabs can be a bit of a suntrap in the morning, when the ascent can be quite hard work.

Fort du Télégraphe

Once at the Col des Pylônes, take in the fine views of the Arc Valley and either continue with the first route by descending or go left to tackle Stage B. The descent is initially steep but is well protected with rungs and quickly gives way to easier ground. Having lost a little more height, the cable then leads along a narrow path that was hacked out of the cliff-face to access the pylons in the days before helicopters were an option. The path follows a gradually descending traverse across the face until passing beneath a large water pipe and meeting with a broad track.

Return
Turn right and descend along the track to arrive at a point near an electricity substation. Turn right here and follow the true left bank of the River Arc back to the parking area.

STAGE B
Fort du Télégraphe

Length	450m
Ascent/Descent	640m (1040m, if combined with Stage A)
Route grading	technical grade: 2; exposure: 4; seriousness: B
Time	4hrs (approach: 45mins; route: 1hr 45mins (first part of Stage A combined with Stage B): return: 1hr 30mins)
Technical notes	direction: N; escape points (within stage): 0

Route

From the top of Stage A (where noted above) climb straight up on rungs for 12m. This passage is some-what overhanging and is the most strenuous part of the route. Above this, continue, more-or-less vertically, up the edge of a steep arête for 40m. Progress is quite easy, with lots of stemples and little contact with the pale limestone. However, the climb is quite exposed, especially at one point where the route passes above a heavy overhang. ◄

Compensation comes in the form of wonderful views of the multi-peaked Croix de Têtes (2491m), which once featured a via ferrata of its own.

Above this point, the angle eases and the rest of the route, with one brief exception, involves nothing harder than an easy scramble. Towards the top of the arête, the bunker-like **Fort du Télégraphe** will come into view. Originally the site of an early system of optical telegra-phy, today the fort, which is not open to visitors, contin-ues in a similar role as home to a cluster of communica-tion masts.

Return

Continue uphill, passing a viewpoint and some infor-mation panels, until a signposted junction. Turn right and descend, via a gatehouse, to arrive at the end of Stage A. Follow green waymarks and signs for 'Parking des Culées'.

In the event of the upper part of the route being reo-pened, you would turn left at the junction and continue climbing, passing a gun battery along the way. Above the

The Croix de Têtes and lower Maurienne Valley

upper via ferrata, continue to the **Col du Télégraphe** and descend to the right along a signposted path.

ROUTE 35
Via Ferrata de Poingt Ravier

Location	Valloire, Savoie
	(GPS: Lat. 45° 10′ 0.86″ N Long. 6° 25′ 38.24″ E)
Length	600m
Ascent/Descent	210m
Route grading	technical grade: 1; exposure: 1; seriousness: A
Total time	2hrs (approach: 5mins; route: 1hr 30mins; return: 25mins)
Highest altitude	1650m
Map	3435ET
Technical notes	direction: SE; escape points: 0
When to visit	May to November

Built on bluffs immediately adjacent to the popular resort of Valloire, this is a good via ferrata for complete novices. The angle of ascent rarely approaches vertical and any difficulties are brief and well spaced. It could also be completed as a warm-up before taking on Via Ferrata du Rocher Saint Pierre (Route 36) or when mediocre weather discourages trying anything bolder. Whatever your motivation, you should be

rewarded with a pleasantly trouble-free ascent and a good panorama of the surrounding mountains from the viewpoint above the top of the route.

Access
From St-Jean-de-Maurienne drive south on the A43 and take Exit 29 at St-Michel-de-Maurienne. From there, take the **D902** to **Valloire**. Drive through the town, passing a roundabout with a wooden cow as a centrepiece. Shortly thereafter cross a bridge over the Valloirette Torrent and

A lizard enjoying the midday sun on one of the limestone slabs ascended on the route

turn right. Drive down **Rue de la Bonne Eau** for 450m and park by the side of the road.

Approach
A signposted path leads along the top of a berm to the base of the bluffs situated just to the northwest of the village.

Route
The route, which is quite obvious from below, starts just to the left of a number of low-grade bolted rock-climbing routes. ▶ Follow the cable up a moderately steep slope over broken ground. Progress involves mostly easy scrambling with plenty of contact with good rock-holds. Any steeper sections are quite brief and well protected with closely spaced rungs. At the top of the slope the cable leads up a smooth ramp beneath a broad wall. The ramp, which is the most exposed part of the route, is followed by a sharp turn to the left.

   The angle of ascent eases a little as the route heads up some limestone slabs. At this point, there is a choice.

1   The **Variante La Grotte**, which is the easier option, heads off to the left and involves little more than a steep walk.

There are 95 bolted routes here, graded 3–7.

201

2   The **Variante Directe** continues directly up the slabs, which gradually steepen. At the top of these, there is a final steep climb of 12m on stemples. Above this, the cable continues up the grassy hillside to end next to some telecoms masts.

The other route also ends at this point. Walk a little uphill to reach a good viewpoint, from where the nature of the routes on the Rocher Saint Pierre can be fully appreciated.

Return
Walk off the back of the hillock to a small chapel and then through a collection of rustic Savoyard chalets. This is the hamlet of **Le Poingt Ravier**, from which the route takes its name. In the centre, signs indicate a left turn. Follow the path downhill, passing panels giving information on local plants. Pass through the outskirts of Valloire to arrive at the bridge over the Valloirette Torrent. Turn left down Rue de la Bonne Eau.

ROUTE 36
Via Ferrata du Rocher Saint Pierre

Location	Valloire, Savoie
	(GPS: Lat. 45° 9′ 49.63″ N Long. 6° 25′ 23.88″ E)
Length	900m
Ascent/Descent	180m
Route grading	technical grade: 1–4; exposure: 1–3; seriousness: A
	(all stages)
Total time	3hrs 30mins
Highest altitude	1582m
Map	3435ET
Technical notes	direction: W; total escape points: 4
When to visit	May to November

Constructed on another set of bluffs overlooking Valloire, this classic route is split into two stages, which run consecutively. Although it is possible to do the two routes separately, they are best completed together. The first stage is either very easy or quite challenging, depending on which option you choose, and the second is of average difficulty. Despite the relatively meagre stature of the bluffs, both stages contain a variety of different elements and are fairly exposed. The difficulty of the harder option on Stage A is mainly physical, but should any one part prove to be too much it can be avoided by taking the easier option, which runs alongside the main route. The bluffs will be out of the sun during the morning and, depending on the time of the year, may be rather damp.

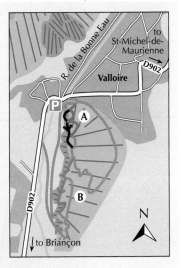

Access

From St-Jean-de-Maurienne drive south on the A43 and take Exit 29 at St-Michel-de-Maurienne. From there, take the **D902** to **Valloire**. Drive through the town, passing a roundabout with a wooden cow as a centrepiece, and shortly thereafter cross a bridge and park on the left.

STAGE A
1ère Partie

Length	450m
Ascent/Descent	160m
Route grading	4 (variant: 1); exposure: 3 (variant: 1); seriousness: A
Time	2hrs 15mins
	(approach: 5mins; route: 1hr 45mins; return: 25mins)
Technical notes	escape points (within stage): 2

Approach

Recross the bridge and take the path directly ahead, passing a small shrine in a cave on your right. An information panel for the via ferrata is on the other side of

Crossing to the detached pillar at the end of Stage A, with Valloire below

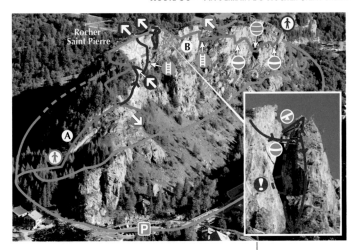

the road. Follow the path for a minute to a junction and turn right, as indicated by a signpost. Shortly thereafter, keep an eye out for a path on the left, which is easy to miss. Just above this point, an information panel indicates the start of the route.

Route
Climb up fairly steeply for 30m, without difficulty or exposure. The angle of ascent eases as a steep walk along a broad ledge leads to the 'Vire du Doute', from where three options are available.

1   If you have already had enough, continue along the ledge and then gradually descend to pick up the return path.

2   To avoid the difficulties of the first passage, climb up for a couple of metres and then follow a partially protected path (Sentier de la Forêt) that climbs the forested hillside. This meets the harder route part-way up then continues to the summit.

3 To carry on with the main route, continue along the ledge and climb up and around a corner. The route then climbs up the bluffs, taking in three short, sharp, overhangs and finishing with a longer overhanging passage of several metres.

Walk uphill (passing the junction with the easier variant on the left), turn right and descend without difficulty to the base of the next set of bluffs. These are climbed, first on rungs and then by a ladder – the Échelle de Tichodrome. ◄ The ladder, which is sturdier than it appears, is topped off by a hefty overhanging passage of a few metres. A little above this an airy traverse to the left on stemples leads to the summit cross of the **Rocher Saint Pierre**.

Tichodrome is a type of small native bird species.

Walk briefly to your right and either finish by keeping left or continue by returning to the cliff-face. Beyond a short, strenuous, traverse, a wobbly 7m-long bridge leads to a detached pillar. Either climb up for 5m to the top of the pillar, which is easy, or down for 15m to its base, which is quite strenuous and a bit awkward. From the base of the pillar, climb back up and into the crevasse between the pillar and the main face and then climb up to the top of the pillar.

The short, strenuous, traverse and bridge that leads to the detached pillar at the end of Stage A

There is a short optional diversion on the left of the crevasse. This involves a very heavily overhanging climb of a few metres followed by a long stretch (or swing for smaller climbers) back across the crevasse.

At the top of the pillar, cross a 5m-long balance beam to finish the stage. To escape, descend to the east. To continue with Stage B, keep right.

STAGE B
2ème Partie

Length	450m
Ascent/Descent	160m (180m, if combined with Stage A)
Route grading	technical grade: 3; exposure: 3; seriousness: A
Time	2hrs 15mins (approach: 35mins; route: 1hr 15mins; return: 25mins) or, combined with Stage A, 3hrs 30mins (approach: 5mins; route: 3hrs; return: 25mins)
Technical notes	escape points (within stage): 1

Route

The start is 20m beyond the end of Stage A. Commence by traversing out onto and across the bluffs, followed by a mildly strenuous down-climb, part of which utilises a ladder. Below this, a protected walk up a fairly broad ledge leads to a good rest point, from where escape is possible.

Cross a somewhat unstable 14m-long suspension bridge, with an airy and strenuous move to get off the end. A steep down-climb leads to more traversing across the face, which gradually loses height until a two-wire bridge is crossed. Regain some height and traverse for a time, passing a small, easy, balance beam. Turn a corner and climb down a little to cross a 40m-long suspension bridge, which is rather wobbly. As before, there is an awkward and strenuous move to get off the end of the bridge, back on to the rock-face. Briefly disappear into a broad crevice and climb out of this to finish.

Return

Traverse around the hillside until arriving at the main path coming off the Rocher Saint Pierre. Turn right, descend and turn right again in front of a chapel. The path then returns north beneath the line of the cliff-face before linking up with your approach path.

ROUTE 37

Via Ferrata de Comborsière

Location	St-Sorlin-d'Arves, Savoie
	(GPS: Lat. 45° 13′ 16.15″ N Long. 6° 12′ 45.42″ E)
Length	260m
Ascent/Descent	110m
Route grading	technical grade: 1 (variant: 2); exposure: 2; seriousness: A
Total time	2hrs (approach: 10mins; route: 1hr 30mins; return: 20mins)
Highest altitude	1870m
Map	3335ET
Technical notes	direction: N; escape points: 0
When to visit	May to October

The small resort of St-Sorlin has constructed this via ferrata on the slopes leading to the Col de la Croix de Fer. The route is a good choice for any beginner in possession of a reasonably strong head for heights. Although somewhat exposed, it is fairly short, quite easy and contains most of the different elements found on modern via ferratas. For more experienced via ferratists, a visit to the route is justified by the exceptional views from the col, in particular, of the three imposing Aiguilles d'Arves (3514m), which dominate the area.

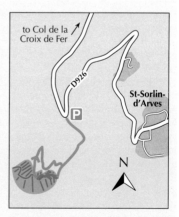

To use the optional Tyrolean traverse at the end of the route, you will need to bring a grey Petzl Tandem Speed pulley.

Approaching the Pont des Chevres

Access
From St-Jean-de-Maurienne, signs for 'Vallee de l'Arvan' lead to the **D926**. Follow this to **St-Sorlin-d'Arves** and continue in the direction of the **Col de la Croix de Fer**. At the third hairpin bend encountered above St-Sorlin (1.3km from the end of the village), turn left and park next to a via ferrata information panel.

Approach
From the end of the car park, walk to the southeast along a level path. The route starts at the eastern end of some bluffs, next to a tree. ▶

There are 12 bolted rock-climbing routes on the wall next to the start of the via ferrata, graded 3–6.

Route
Scale a low-angle wall, on closely spaced rungs, for 25m. Pass around onto the northern face of the bluffs and cross a balance beam. This crosses a gap in the cliffs for 6m and

209

while fairly exposed, feels quite secure. Pass a second balance beam, similar to the first, and continue traversing across the face, gaining a little height along the way. Cross another gap in the bluffs on a wobbly 20m-long bridge, the Passerelle de Comborsière. On the other side of the bridge, climb up a little to a junction and a choice of routes.

1   Keep left and continue climbing (the easier option).

2   Go right, along a third balance beam, the Pont des Chevres, for a slightly harder variant. This involves a slight descent followed by a brief traverse and ascent around a blunt buttress. The stemples are more widely spaced than on the rest of the route and this is reasonably strenuous for a several metres.

The two routes rejoin further up the buttress. From here it is possible to finish by keeping right and continuing to the top of the buttress or go left to cross the Pont des Perrons, a 20m-long two-wire bridge, which is not very stable. Beyond the bridge, more cable leads easily to the top of the bluffs, the end of the route, and the start of an optional Tyrolean traverse. This runs for 120m and is never more than 15m above the ground.

Return
Descend by the obvious path to quickly rejoin the approach path.

ROUTE 38
Via Ferrata de St-Colomban-des-Villards

Location	St-Colomban-des-Villards, Savoie (GPS: Lat. 45° 16′ 46.99″ N Long.6° 12′ 37.53″ E)
Length	730m
Ascent/Descent	280m
Route grading	technical grade: 1–3; exposure: 1–3; seriousness: A (all stages)
Total time	3hrs
Highest altitude	1470m
Map	3433OT
Technical notes	direction: SW; total escape points: 3
When to visit	March to November

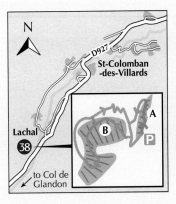

The eastern flank of Mont Rond does not at first appear to be a promising location for a via ferrata. Despite this, the heavily vegetated bluffs above the tranquil village of St-Colomban-des-Villards hold two routes, both of which are well worth visiting. The first route is short and easy, and designed specifically for beginners and children. The second route, which is entirely separate from the first, is a tough mid-grade outing that involves several fairly athletic passages in quite exposed positions.

211

Crossing the Pont des Tânnes (Stage B)

Access

Take Exit 26 off the A43, which runs between Chambéry and Modane, and follow signs for 'Vallée des Villards'. Continue on the **D927**, until **St-Colomban-des-Villards**. From the entrance to the village, continue for around 2.5km in the direction of the **Col de Glandon**. Pass the hamlet of **Lachal** and park to the right of the road, next to a large via ferrata information panel.

Ascending Dalle Noire (Stage B)

STAGE A
Via Ferrata École du Rocher de Capaillan

Length	130m
Ascent/Descent	40m
Route grading	technical grade: 1; exposure: 1; seriousness: A
Time	45mins (approach: <1min; route: 35mins; return: 10mins)
Technical notes	escape points (within stage): 1

Approach
The first stage starts just to the right of the information panel. (To avoid this and head straight to La Chal (Stage B), follow a steep path, which starts just next to the information panel, for 15mins.)

Route
Start with a traverse of 25m, the last 6m of which cross a two-wire bridge. This contains a few mildly strenuous moves (especially for taller climbers) but is not remotely exposed, being only a little above ground level. It is possible to escape from the route after the bridge. To continue, pass through a gate and scale bluffs directly overlooking the river. The bluffs are not too steep and not very airy, making for a fairly gentle ascent. Having gained some 30m in height, pass along the cliff-face and cross a stable 10m-long bridge. Beyond this, the cable gains a little more height before ending on the tree covered southeastern flank of Mont Rond. The route is well protected throughout and passes a number of panels giving instruction in the correct use of via ferratas.

Return
Follow a path to the left. At a junction, keep left to escape from the route or go right to continue with Stage B, which is considerably more challenging.

STAGE B
Via Ferrata de la Chal

Length	600m
Ascent/Descent	280m (280m, if combined with Stage A)
Route grading	technical grade: 3; exposure: 3; seriousness: A
Time	2hrs 45mins (approach: 20mins; route: 2hrs; return: 25mins) or, if combined with Stage A, 3hrs (approach: <1min; route: 2hrs 35mins; return: 25mins)
Technical notes	escape points (within stage): 1

Route
Start with a steeply rising traverse to the left, via the Pilier Jaune, which involves a few awkward or slightly strenuous moves. Progress eases, but exposure increases, as the cable leads along the edge of the Arête des Moulins. A briefly muscular traverse then leads to a 20m-long bridge, the Passerelle des Chèvres.

Beyond this turn right to escape (Sortie de la Croix) or descend to the left to continue. The cable then passes around a broad vegetated bay without gaining or losing much height. Part-way along two two-wire bridges are crossed, both of which are stable and not very exposed. The first, Pont des Tânnes, is 7m long and the second, the Pont des Sarrazins, is 15m long.

Mont Rond

Exposure increases as La Descente sous les Toits is crossed

Pass around a corner and commence a down-climbing traverse beneath a large overhang (La Descente sous les Toits). This is not particularly strenuous but requires some awkward reaches and feels much more airy than anything thus far encountered. More traversing then leads to the crux of the route, the Fissure en Oblique. This consists of a steeply rising traverse using rungs for the hands and a narrow crack for the feet. Although only 10m in length, this is quite strenuous and large boots may have to be jammed into the crack. Above this, continue ascending via a lichen-covered slab (Dalle Noire) and some easy terraces to reach the end of the route.

Return
Briefly head uphill then descend to the right, following signs for 'Pont de Capaillan' and 'Retour par le Reposeu'.

ROUTE 39
Via Ferrata de l'Adret

Location	Pontamafrey-Montpascal, Savoie (GPS: Lat. 45° 18′ 48.83″ N Long. 6° 20′ 33.51″ E)
Length	600m
Ascent/Descent	370m
Route grading	technical grade: 3–4; exposure: 3–4; seriousness: A (all stages)
Total time	3hrs 30mins
Highest altitude	740m
Map	3433ET
Technical notes	direction: S; total escape points: 1
When to visit	March to November

Overlooking the crowded valley of the River Arc, the line of bluffs above Pontamafrey contains two via ferratas, which run consecutively with an escape point between them. The first climbs up alongside an attractive waterfall and, although quite airy, is relatively problem-free. The second, although simpler than the first, is much more exposed and strenuous. The latter route climbs directly up the bluffs and contains a number of overhangs, although there are places to rest between the hardest parts. Despite the semi-industrial setting of the valley, both routes have a surprisingly peaceful atmosphere and, due to the relatively low altitude of the bluffs, are good options during cloudy weather.

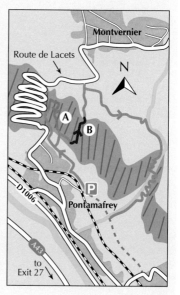

216

Access

The quickest access to Pontamafrey is via Exit 27 of the **A43**, at the northern end of St-Jean-de-Maurienne. Drive through the village, along the **Route de Lacets**, following signs for the via ferrata. Turn right at a sign, cross a railway line and continue up a good gravel road to a large parking area just beyond a via ferrata information panel.

STAGE A
La Passerelle

Length	300m
Ascent/Descent	140m
Route grading	technical grade: 3; exposure: 3; seriousness: A
Time	1hr 45mins
	(approach: 20mins; route: 1hr 10mins; return: 15mins)
Technical notes	escape points (within stage): 0

The suspension bridge from which La Passerelle takes its name

Approach

Follow green arrows on wooden posts, initially back along the gravel road, then by the side of fields until reaching the first bend in the Route de Lacets. From here, the path zigzags up the tree-covered hillside, until an unmarked turning to the right heads into the narrow gully just to your right. If you miss the turning, there is a sign reading 'Retour Parking' by a bend in the road 20m further up the main path.

Route

Once within the gully, start with a brief easy climb up the left-hand side, followed by a 10m walk to the base of a broad rib of rock. This is climbed for 50m. Initially, the climb is a little strenuous, but otherwise the main challenge comes in the form of a massively overhanging roof near the top of the passage. This is overcome with the aid of an odd ladder construction, which, while not physically demanding, is wonderfully exposed and a little wobbly. After a second ladder, which is less dramatic than the first, briefly traverse across to a stable 20m-long

suspension bridge. This crosses the head of the gully, passing close to a verdant waterfall.

From the end of the bridge, both difficulty and exposure reduce, as a generally descending line is followed. At first this crosses the other side of the gully, partly utilising a fairly broad ledge. Once beyond the gully a low-angle arête is down-climbed, followed by a gradually descending traverse across the main cliff-face. One final short easy down-climb brings you to the end of the stage.

Return
Either keep left to continue to Stage B or descend along a partly cabled escape path to the right to rejoin the approach route.

STAGE B
Le Bastion

Length	300m
Ascent/Descent	230m (370m, if combined with Stage A)
Route grading	technical grade: 4; exposure: 4; seriousness: A
Time	2hrs 15mins (approach: 15mins; route: 1hr 15mins; return: 45mins) or, if combined with Stage A, 3hrs 30mins (approach: 20mins; route: 2hrs 25mins; return: 45mins)
Technical notes	escape points (within stage): 0

Route
From the junction with the path from Stage A, head right along the bottom of the cliff-face for a couple of minutes until the cable commences with a short climb up to a broad ledge. This is followed until the first challenge of the stage is encountered. This involves a vertical climb of 20m up a broad chimney. While steep, the chimney is very well protected with numerous large stemples and is consequently not too difficult. Continue gaining height up a series of short climbs over fairly straightforward terrain until arriving at the base of a buttress.

Climb straight up the end of the buttress for 30m, passing through several short, moderately pronounced, overhangs. Move over to the right-hand side of the buttress and climb, more easily, for a further 10m. Once on top of the buttress, the cable heads along a narrow rib of rock leading back to the main cliff-face. While not especially steep, this feels particularly airy. At the top of the rib a small belvedere makes a good, if rather cramped, place to take a breather.

The third and final section of climbing starts immediately beyond the belvedere and involves a series of short climbs and brief traverses for 30m. This is moderately strenuous, with a few moves that are slightly overhanging, but is not as difficult as the previous passage. Once at the top of the main cliff-face, continue climbing at a shallower angle for a few minutes. After overcoming one last short overhang, the cable ends at a grassy platform from which fine views of the surrounding countryside can be enjoyed (if you ignore the motorway and industrial estates below).

Return
Follow a path heading north towards Montvernier and at a signposted junction turn either left or right, as preferred, back to Pontamafrey. Left heads down the Route de Lacets. Turn right for 'Pontamafrey par la Gorge' (recommended), which follows a narrow path by the side of a waterfall down through a picturesque gorge.

GRENOBLE

*Ascending the 25m buttress at the start of
Via Ferrata Cascade de la Pisse (Route 46)*

221

INTRODUCTION

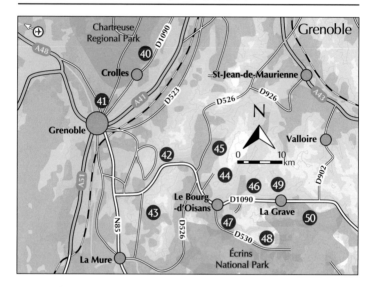

Grenoble is the largest city in the region and, closely hemmed in by mountains, is known as the capital of the Alps. With a population of 160,000 and a metropolitan area of 18 square kilometres, Grenoble has a decidedly big city feel. Most visitors to the Alps will probably prefer to treat Grenoble as a starting point rather than as a place to base themselves. If you do wish to spend some time here, there are plenty of tourist attractions, with La Bastille (see Route 41), being perhaps the most worthwhile.

Only one via ferrata is located in Grenoble itself, with one other to the

north on the edge of the Chartreuse Massif. The remainder are situated to the east, in the region known as L'Oisans, which consists of the valley of the River Romanche and its tributaries. This marvellously scenic corridor runs between the Belledonne, Grandes Rousses and Arves massifs to the north and the Taillefer and Écrins massifs to the south. This latter mountain range contains some of the most impressive peaks and most famous mountaineering routes in the French Alps.

Grenoble has excellent road links to the rest of France, with the A48 motorway to the west leading directly to Lyon, the country's second largest city, and the A41 heading north to Chambéry. It is similarly well served by rail links and can be reached from Paris by train in three hours. Grenoble airport is situated a little to the north of the city (see Getting to the Alps in the Introduction). Within Grenoble, your choice of accommodation is limited to hotels. Further afield, upmarket accommodation is somewhat limited.

Budget options, however (particularly campsites) are abundant.

The nine via ferratas in this chapter include an even mixture of sports routes and mountain routes. They are mostly mid-grade options and, other than the first stage of Via Ferrata de l'Alpe du Grand Serre (Route 43), are not suitable for absolute beginners.

For tourist information see the websites listed in Appendix D.

Although strenuous and sustained, the Grande Diédre is very well protected (Route 40, Stage B)

ROUTE 40

Via Ferrata de la Cascade de l'Oule

Location	Crolles, Isère
	(GPS: Lat. 45° 17′ 59.03″ N Long. 5° 53′ 54.02″ E)
Length	1400m
Ascent/Descent	1340m
Route grading	technical grade: 3–5; exposure: 4–5; seriousness: A
	(all grades)
Total time	4hrs 30mins to 7hrs (if both stages climbed consecutively)
Highest altitude	930m
Map	3334OT
Technical notes	direction: E; total escape points: 4
When to visit	March to mid-November
Useful websites	www.ville-crolles.fr; www.sainthilairedutouvet.com

Located on bluffs overlooking the Grésivaudan Valley and River Isère, this via ferrata is notable both for the difficulty of one of its constituent parts and for the exceptionally fine views it offers. The broad sweep of the valley and the opposing mountain range, the Chaîne de Belledonne, make for a dramatic backdrop as you scale the heavily striated cliffs. The Grand Dièdre is justly renowned for its difficulty, being very strenuous and particularly sustained by the standards of most via ferratas. The adjacent route, the Vire des Lavandières, is longer but quite a bit easier, although it still has its share of

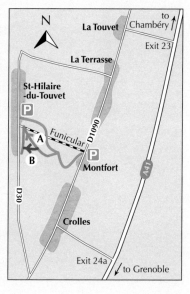

challenges. Gaining access to the route is made simple by a funicular railway that runs up the nearby bluffs between the valley floor and the Plateau des Petites Roches, which sits on the edge of the Chartreuse Massif.

Access

The easiest access to Crolles is via Exit 24a of the **A41**, which runs between Grenoble and Chambéry. From **Crolles**, drive 2km to the north on the **D1090** through **Montfort** and park on the left next to the funicular Lower Station.

It is also possible to approach the route from the top of the bluffs by starting from **St-Hilaire-du-Touvet**. For this alternative, from Montfort, continue on the D1090 to **La Terrasse** and turn left up the **D30**. At St-Hilaire, park near the funicular Upper Station.

STAGE A
Parcours par la Vire des Lavandières

Length	600m
Ascent/Descent	670m
Route grading	technical grade: 3; exposure: 4; seriousness: A
Time	4hrs or 2hrs 50mins (approach: 1hr, 30mins by funicular; route: 2hrs; return: 1hr, 20mins by funicular)
Technical notes	escape points (within stage): 3

Approach

From either the bottom or top **Funicular Station** take a steep but well-signposted path, the **Sentier du Pal de Fer** (starting from the Top Station is considerably less arduous). For even less effort, take the funicular to the **Middle Station** and follow a path, as indicated by a sign, which quickly meets the main approach path. This option currently costs €7.80, including the return trip. The funicular, which is the oldest and steepest in the French Alps, is typically open from 1000 to 1900 during the summer (see www.funiculaire.fr for details).

Route
Climb straight up a broad and heavily striated buttress for 80m. This is not too steep at first but the final 25m is fully vertical and contains a number of short overhanging passages. At the top of the buttress, follow an eroded path steeply uphill to the junction with the harder Stage B (see below), taking care not to dislodge any stones on to climbers below you.

Turn right at the junction to stay on the easier route, and descend a little to a broad balcony, situated directly beneath the Cascade de l'Oule. This makes a pleasant place to take a break and cool off. Beyond the balcony, a vegetated ledge system is followed until a mildly strenuous ascent of 20m and a further narrow ledge meets the first escape path. Climb upwards for 30m, gain some height up a steep and dirty ledge, and then climb for a further 30m until meeting a low-angle ladder. Both sections of climbing contain some short moderate overhangs. Above the ladder, turn right to escape via a short

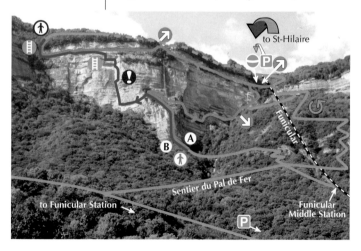

balance beam and suspension bridge over the line of the funicular. To continue, head to the left along a vegetated ledge (Chemin de Ronde).

At times the ledge is quite broad; at other times it narrows considerably to reveal impressive views of the valley below you. This leads to a bizarrely shaped waterfall (Cascade de l'Oule again) and the third escape point, the Échelle des Maquisards. The original Échelle des Maquisards, the remains of which are still visible, was used by resistance fighters during World War II to access a hidden weapons cache. Another ledge (Sangle Chourère) brings you to the junction with the Grand Dièdre (Stage B).

The Grésivaudan Valley from the Chemin de Ronde

STAGE B
Parcours par le Grand Dièdre

Length	800m
Ascent/Descent	670m (1340m, if combined with Stage A)
Route grading	technical grade: 5; exposure: 5; seriousness: A
Time	3hrs 45mins or 2hrs 35mins (approach: 1hr, 30mins by funicular; route: 1hr 45mins; return: 1hr, 20mins by funicular)
Technical notes	escape points (to Stage A): 1

Route

At the top of the first climb on Stage A (as described above), turn left at the junction and walk easily along a broad ledge, the Vire a Vélo. This leads to the base of the obvious dihedral from which the stage takes its name. The cable then heads straight up the cliff-face for 100m, all the while in or near the dihedral. After the first 20m, a couple of ledges are met; otherwise progress is *Ascending the* consistently strenuous with numerous short and not-so-*Grande Dièdre* short overhangs, a few of which are quite pronounced.

Stemples are plentiful throughout the climb, but it will probably still be necessary to use a number of fairly small, sometimes shiny, rock steps. Halfway up, the dihedral narrows, and a difficult move to the right leads to marginally easier ground. From here, ascend straight up a blank wall, still with plenty of demanding moves. At the top of the climb, a small ledge is followed by a much bigger one, above which is a large overhang. This is overcome by ascending an exceptionally exposed outward-facing ladder for 7m.

Given the sustained nature of the climb, you should be prepared to use your rest lanyard to take a break. Additionally, there are three short side cables to assist with passing. The first is on the second ledge near the start, the second is about halfway up and the third is on the penultimate ledge near the top of the climb. Above the outward-facing ladder, a short climbing traverse leads to the junction with the other stage. From here, head left along a ledge until a second, much less exposed, outward-facing ladder of 10m is reached. Above this a steep wall of 20m is climbed before walking to the finish.

Return

A good path heads towards St-Hilaire and the funicular Upper Station. A paragliding take-off area is passed partway along. From St-Hilaire, use either the funicular or the **Sentier du Pal de Fer** to descend to the Lower Station. For those who wish to make their return by rather more ethereal means, it is possible to descend by paraglider (*vol libre*). This can be organised through prior arrangement with a local company (see www.ville-crolles.fr and www.sainthilairedutouvet.com).

ROUTE 41

Via Ferrata Les Prises de la Bastille

Location	Grenoble, Isère
	(GPS: Lat. 45° 11′ 39.50″ N Long. 5° 43′ 7.72″ E)
Length	580m
Ascent/Descent	230m
Route grading	technical grade: 3–4; exposure: 2; seriousness: A (all stages)
Total time	2hrs 30mins
Highest altitude	440m
Map	3335OT
Technical notes	total escape points: 1
When to visit	February to November

This uniquely urban route affords climbers the opportunity to carry out their own (hopefully less bloody) storming of the Bastille. The via ferrata is built on and around the defensive features of a fortified hillside that directly overlooks Grenoble. Given its location the route can be very busy, particularly at weekends. Both stages are quite difficult within their grades and should not be underestimated. A particular challenge of the routes is that, due to the high number of

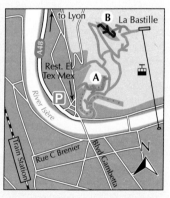

users, some rock-holds have become quite polished. Having reached the top of the via ferrata, further exploration of the fort, which contains a museum and restaurant, is worthwhile. The grounds of the park in which the route is situated are open from 0900 to 1930 in summer and 1730 in winter.

Access

The start of the route is located at the base of the prominent fortified hill that dominates the north of the city centre

(**La Bastille**). If approaching from Lyon along the **A48**, follow signs for 'Grenoble–Bastille' and 'St Martin le V' until, immediately below La Bastille, a rather convoluted roundabout is encountered. Once on the roundabout, following signs for Parking de l'Esplanade (free – closed 16 April–8 May), which is immediately to the left of **restaurant El Tex Mex**. If approaching from the south of the city the easiest option is to stay on the A48 until north of the city centre and then follow signs for St-Martin-le-Vinoux.

STAGE A
Falaises VICAT

Length	250m
Ascent/Descent	40m
Route grading	technical grade: 3; exposure: 2; seriousness: A
Time	1hr 15mins (approach: 5mins; route: 50mins; return: 20mins)
Technical notes	direction: SW; escape points (within stage): 0

Approach
To the right of the restaurant El Tex Mex is Route de Lyon. Follow this for 50m and look for a sign 'Clinique Veterinaire de L'Esplanade' on the right. Go through the gate and continue for 100m to reach the start of the route and a via ferrata information panel. There may be an encampment of homeless people living in the vicinity of the base of the route.

Route
A very small practice via ferrata is located next to the start of the route. This is aimed at children and beginners and is considerably easier than the main route.

Traversing around the Cirque VICAT

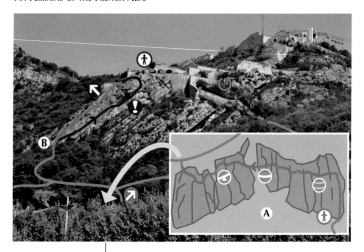

The route climbs steeply up to a height of 25m and then leads around the walls of a natural amphitheatre (Cirque VICAT). In an effort to discourage the unprepared, the initial 3m of climbing is not cabled and has a limited number of holds. Interspersed between a distinctly wobbly 13m-long two-wire bridge, a 25m-long suspension bridge and a 5m-long balance beam are passages of mostly level, but occasionally awkward, traversing. The large volume of traffic on the route has caused considerable polishing of the rock. Although the number of rock-holds is limited, shoes with good grip should be considered obligatory. Shorter climbers might even consider using rock-climbing shoes.

Once above the amphitheatre, the cable ends as you pass through a gate. Close this behind you and turn left (if you have had enough and are ready to stop, turn right after the gate and descend via the Jardin des Dauphins). Follow blue waymarks up through Parc Guy Pape. The way is not very clear, but if you simply keep on the main path, you should arrive at a large defensive wall. Follow the wall uphill until the next section of via ferrata (Stage B) comes into view.

STAGE B
Falaises de la Bastille

Length	330m
Ascent/Descent	190m (230m, if combined with Stage A)
Route grading	technical grade: 4 (variant: 3); exposure: 2; seriousness: A
Time	2hrs 30mins (approach: 5mins; route: 1hr 50mins (both stages combined); return: 35mins)
Technical notes	direction: S; escape points (within stage): 0

Route
Start with a steep and moderately strenuous climb of 15m, which arrives at a small wooden platform. From here, either continue climbing to take a much easier line or go right and follow a long rising traverse up a low bluff running beneath the outer defences of the fort. Part way along the latter, there is a second wooden platform, from which it is possible to escape onto the upper, easier variant. If you found the initial vertical passage difficult, you should certainly choose

Climbers on the final part of the harder variant

233

the higher option, as the lower line, while relatively unexposed, is more challenging than anything else on the route, being noticeably muscular and sustained. Additionally, some of the foot placements are becoming fairly polished, although this is not as noticeable as it is on Stage A.

The only reasonable places to rest without hanging from a rest lanyard are the two small wooden platforms at the junctions with the easier route. Beyond the second junction, the final passage is similar in nature to the previous one, but a little shorter.

◀ After descending into a defensive fosse, the cable ends. Walk along the bottom of the fosse to the base of the final section of via ferrata. This climbs for 20m, with a few mildly strenuous moves, until it terminates through the mouth of a gun emplacement.

Whichever line you take, it is worth stopping occasionally to admire the unfolding views of the city (as well as to catch your breath).

Return
Head out of the casemate, ensuring that you close the gate behind you. Descend via the various levels of the fort and the colourful Jardin des Dauphins to the roundabout and parking. Alternatively, continue ascending to the top of the fort, from where it is possible to take a cable car (€4.95) back to street level (see www.bastille-grenoble.fr).

ROUTE 42
Via Ferrata du Croix de Chamrousse

Location	Chamrousse 1650, Isère (GPS: Lat. 45° 7' 32.05″ N Long. 5° 52' 44.80″ E)
Length	650m
Ascent/Descent	290m
Route grading	technical grade: 2–3; exposure: 2–3; seriousness: B (all stages)
Total time	4hrs
Highest altitude	2253m
Map	3335OT
Technical notes	direction: E; total escape points: 2
When to visit	March to October (but note cable car opening dates below)

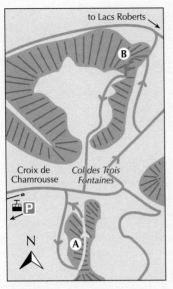

A visit to the two via ferratas of the Croix de Chamrousse is a fine excuse to explore this attractive corner of the Belledonne Massif. Easily accessible by cable car from the ski resort of Chamrousse, this popular day trip for the inhabitants of Grenoble offers great mountain scenery and wide-ranging views of the city and its surrounds. Via Ferrata Les Trois Fontaines (Stage A) is mostly level and rarely strenuous, with only an airy crossing of a two-wire bridge presenting any noticeably physical challenge. Via Ferrata Les Lacs Roberts (Stage B) is a little more arduous, but still relatively straightforward, and affords pleasant views of the eponymous collection of lakes.

Doing both routes within a day should be within the capabilities of most, and if you have any time left over the surrounding area is well worth further investigation. The Telecabine de la Croix, used to approach the routes, is open from 25 June to 28 August, 0900–1700. An adult return costs €7.

Access

Chamrousse 1650 can be accessed from Grenoble by taking the D524 to Uriage and from there, the D111. Park between the Telecabine de la Croix and the tourist office, both of which are located at the entrance to the resort.

STAGE A
Via Ferrata Les Trois Fontaines

Length	350m
Ascent/Descent	80m
Route grading	technical grade: 2; exposure: 3; seriousness: B
Time	2hrs (approach: 15mins; route: 1hr 35mins; return: 10mins)
Technical notes	escape points (within stage): 2

Approach
Tickets for the cable car can be bought at the tourist office (ascending on foot, via a series of signposted paths, adds 2hrs and 600m of height gain). The cable car deposits you at the **Croix de Chamrousse**. From the Upper Station head east over the plateau, passing the tops of two ski lifts on your left. After 10mins you should arrive at the end of the via ferrata and some orientation tables. Continue to the south, keeping a broken ridgeline just to your left. The route starts next to an information panel for the via ferrata.

Crossing the exposed 20m two-wire bridge

Route

A series of increasingly narrow ledges lead out onto the east face of the bluffs. Stemples are present in only a few places, but the rock offers many good holds and progress is fairly straightforward. Pass across a gully containing the first escape point and then gain some height up a series of low-angle slabs. The route then levels off again and traverses across the face, with plenty of exposure, to a two-wire bridge across a second gully. The 20m-long bridge is exposed and not very taut. Consequently, the crossing, which is best undertaken facing outwards, is fairly hard work.

There is a second escape path on the other side of the bridge. To continue, keep right and cross a series of three balance beams, all of which are quite secure. More traversing leads to a 10m-long three-wire bridge, which is slack but not too exposed. Finish with a squeeze through a narrow crevice (backpacks off) and some easy ledges.

Return

Walk to your left and retrace the first part of your approach, heading west over the plateau to the cable car Upper Station.

STAGE B
Via Ferrata Les Lacs Roberts

Length	300m
Ascent/Descent	210m (290m, if combined with Stage A)
Route grading	technical grade: 3; exposure: 2; seriousness: B
Time	2hrs 15mins (approach: 25mins; route: 1hr 30mins; return: 20mins) or, if combined with Stage A, 4hrs (approach: 15mins; route: 3hrs 25mins; return: 20mins)
Technical notes	escape points (within stage): 0

Approach
From the top of the cable car, head east over the plateau and pick up a signed path that descends steeply via **Col des Trois Fontaines** to the **Lacs Roberts**, a collection of several agreeably arranged tarns. Near the col, ignore a sign for the via ferrata on your left (which is for the return path), and descend to the northeast. Once in the vicinity of a small pool, take a narrow path (via ferrata sign) that traverses beneath a series of bluffs.

Passerelle des Lacs Roberts

Route

The start is indicated by an information panel. Climb straight up the bluffs for 50m. This involves a few slightly strenuous moves but is generally well protected with plenty of stemples and good rockholds. The angle of ascent eases and progress changes to a hands-on walk. Continue to gain height and then traverse along the bluffs to a bridge that crosses a broad gully. The 14m-long bridge, Passerelle des Lacs Roberts, does not feel particularly exposed but is fairly wobbly.

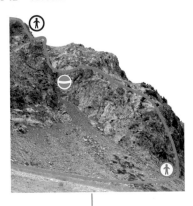

Once on the other side of the gully, an airy climbing traverse leads to the base of a buttress. Climb up the end of the buttress for 25m, encountering a few strenuous moves along the way. Briefly walk along the top of the buttress then scale a final vertical section for 30m. This is less exposed and easier than the previous climb, containing only one small overhang.

Return

Turn left and follow signs and waymarks across a plateau. Descend slightly to meet the approach path in the vicinity of the Col des Trois Fontaines. From here, turn right to return to the cable car Upper Station.

ROUTE 43
Via Ferrata de l'Alpe du Grand Serre

Location	Station de l'Alpe du Grand Serre, Isère
	(GPS: Lat. 45° 1′ 38.90″ N Long. 5° 51′ 36.28″ E)
Length	1250m
Ascent/Descent	1140m
Route grading	technical grade: 1–4; exposure: 1–4; seriousness: A–B
Total time	8hrs 45mins
Highest altitude	2080m
Map	3336OT
Technical notes	direction: SW; total escape points: 4
When to visit	May to October

There are two entirely separate, and quite different, routes accessible from Station de l'Alpe du Grand Serre. The first is fairly short, very easy and lots of fun. The second, although at a relatively low altitude, has a distinctly mountainous feeling. As the name suggests, the first route, Via Ferrata de la Cascade, is built around the course of a small waterfall. This playful route crosses a number of unexposed bridges and

passes several escape points, resulting in a fairly relaxed ascent suitable for children and beginners. While it could be completed as a warm-up for the second route, Via Ferrata du Grand Bec, to do both together would take a full day, and should be considered only by the very keen.

This latter route follows a long ascending line up a steep mountain arête to arrive at the top of the Grand Bec, a prominent 'beak' of rock sticking out from the main ridgeline. Split into two stages, the first is very well protected and suitable for beginners who wish to experience something like a mountain scramble without too much of a challenge. Only the more experienced should continue past the escape point to the summit, as the second stage is considerably more difficult and exposed. The route should be started only with a clear weather forecast. Apart from any safety concerns, this will allow you to enjoy fully the wonderful views on the return journey, which is substantially longer than on most via ferratas.

Access
From Grenoble, take the N85 in the direction of Briançon until Vizille and from there the D1091 to Séchilienne. Turn right onto the **D113/4** and drive up a long series of hairpin bends. Having passed a sign indicating the entrance to **Alpe du Grand Serre**, continue for 600m to a large parking area on your left. Drive for a further 50m and turn left down Route de la Cascade. Either park by the side of this road, or in the large parking area recently passed.

STAGE A
Via Ferrata de la Cascade

Length	500m
Ascent/Descent	270m
Route grading	technical grade: 1; exposure: 1; seriousness: A
Time	2hrs 15mins
	(approach: 5mins; route: 1hr 30mins; return: 40mins)
Technical notes	escape points (within stage): 3

Approach
Walk up Route de la Cascade to a picnic area. There are information panels for both via ferratas here. The route starts near the waterfall at the back of the picnic area.

Route
Scale a wall to the right of the waterfall for 20m. The angle is not too steep and the abundant fixed protection is closely spaced. Once above the waterfall, the route closely follows the stream, which tumbles down the slabby rock-face

Ascending
Le Balcon

Rock
Climbing
area

through a shallow groove. Repeatedly cross the stream, only a little above the water, on a series of short two-wire and three-wire bridges and balance beams. The last bridge leaves you on the true right side of the stream and is followed by a second easy climb up a low-angle slab. A short walk then leads to the first escape path.

Continue gaining height, via a third slab (Le Balade) and the rocky edge of a slight escarpment (Le Balcon). Pass a second escape path and after a little more easy climbing and a brief walk, arrive at Les Costauds. The climb up this 10m-high vertical wall is slightly strenuous at first. Above the wall, the angle eases as another slab is ascended before arriving at a broad platform. There are good views from here of the long escarpment to the west, which overlooks Grenoble (the Montagne de Lans). Above the platform, the third escape path descends to the left on the intersecting GR50. To end the stage, walk down this for a minute until a sign on your right indicates a final easy climb, which leads up some low-angle slabs to the finish.

Return

Turn right along an unpaved vehicle track. At a signpost, turn right again and descend via the GR50. This returns to the picnic area and Route de la Cascade. If parked at the large car park on the main road, a little time can be saved by taking a right turn partway down the GR50, at a junction with a path marked 'Retour Parking'.

STAGE B
Via Ferrata du Grand Bec 1ère Partie

Length	550m
Ascent/Descent	590m (860m, if combined with Stage A)
Route grading	technical grade: 1; exposure: 2; seriousness: B
Time	3hrs 30mins
	(approach: 50mins; route: 1hr 40mins; return: 1hr)
Technical notes	escape points (within stage): 0

Approach
Walk up Route de la Cascade to a picnic area. There are information panels for both via ferratas here. Turn right and follow a broad track and later a path. There are signposts for the via ferrata at all junctions.

Route
Begin with a pleasant climb of 40m. As with most of this stage, this is not strenuous and stemples are closely spaced, making for easy progress. Fine views should

Easy climbing near the start of the stage; the summit of the Grand Bec in the background

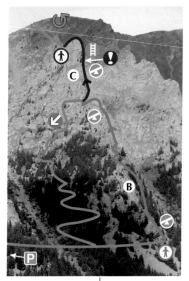

already be in evidence as well as a modicum of exposure. Reach a 5m-long balance beam (La Poutre de Chamois), beyond which is a mildly strenuous move to regain the crest of the broken arête, which is climbed for much of the route.

Continue up the arête to a fat pinnacle, which is traversed around on the right with a mildly strenuous passage of a few metres. Alternatively, take the cable on the left to avoid this. Both options quickly rejoin and continue up the broad crest of the arête without noticeable difficulty or exposure, passing a couple of breaks in the cable. At the second break, keep an eye out for a small arrow on a rock indicating the path. Above this point, the route continues to gain height up straightforward terrain until a second short, easy balance beam is crossed. Beyond this, a short descent leads to the end of Stage B.

Return

Go left via the escape point and descend steeply down a grassy slope to rejoin the approach path. Keep your gear on as the return path has some cable on it.

STAGE C
Via Ferrata du Grand Bec 2ème Partie

Length	200m
Ascent/Descent	280m (1140m, if combined with preceding stages)
Route grading	technical grade: 4; exposure: 4; seriousness: B
Time	6hrs 30mins (approach: 50mins; route: 3hrs 30mins (Stages B and C combined); return: 2hrs 10mins)
Technical notes	escape points (within stage): 0

Route
After a brief walk uphill, the cable heads up a system of broken ledges without difficulty. The route then follows a series of steeply rising traverses interspersed with short vertical climbs. The first of these, which rises for 10m, gives a good indication of the several moderately strenuous sections that follow. Good use is made of large rock-holds and there are plenty of rungs on the steeper parts. Exposure increases rapidly as you progress up and around the south face of the Grand Bec, until arriving at a narrow ledge. This is a good place to take a break and review the next section of the route.

This gains a little height, crosses a short balance beam (La Poutre de l'Aigle), then follows a steeply rising traverse for 12m before climbing up to a ladder. The entire passage between the beam and the ladder is extremely airy and quite challenging. The crux (without which the stage would be of a lower grade) is the overhanging move from the top of the rising traverse. Due to the placement of the fixed protection, this is quite strenuous and you may find it rather awkward. At the end of the traverse, there are some small rungs that should be immediately above your head. These are not altogether obvious and it is worth taking some time to locate them prior to starting the traverse.

Above this point, a short strenuous climb brings you to the 10m ladder (L'Échelle du Thabor), which is climbed facing outwards and feels rather airy. Progress

245

eases from here as a low-angle slab is ascended before more easy climbing brings you to the top of the Grand Bec. Views from here now include much of the city of Grenoble, sprawling across the river plain 20km to the northwest. Descend, without any problems, off the back of the 'beak' to the end of the cable.

Return

Follow a vague, occasionally hands-on path uphill towards a weather gauge. The path then continues to wind uphill until Lac Brouffier comes into view. Having arrived at a large wooden post, take a path on the left, which is marked with a large cairn. This path, along which there are a few arrows and the occasional cairn to indicate the way, descends to **Lac Brouffier**. Just past the mouth of the lake, turn left and descend to **Lac de Prévourey**. From there follow signs for 'Alpe du Grand Serre' down the GR50. This returns to the picnic area and Route de la Cascade.

   If parked at the large car park on the main road, a little time can be saved by taking a right turn part-way down the GR50, at a junction with a path marked 'Retour Parking'.

ROUTE 44
Via Ferrata de l'Alpe d'Huez

Location	L'Alpe d'Huez, Isère
	(GPS: Lat. 45° 5' 4.68" N Long. 6° 6' 2.62" E)
Length	600m
Ascent/Descent	500m
Route grading	technical grade: 2–3; exposure: 3; seriousness: B (all stages)
Total time	4hrs (if both stages climbed consecutively)
Highest altitude	1850m
Map	3335ET
Technical notes	direction: S; total escape points: 0
When to visit	May to October

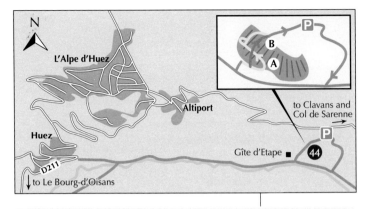

L'Alpe d'Huez is well known in France, both as a ski resort and as one of the principal mountain stages of the Tour de France, but the resort provides plenty of other forms of distraction. In addition to hiking, climbing, fishing and mountain biking a fine via ferrata has been constructed. This has two lines, which cross over part-way along. The first route, which is quite simple, is suitable for beginners. The harder route, which is also simple in design, but nevertheless very enjoyable, is noticeably more challenging due to its relative steepness and the amount of rock contact involved.

Access
From Grenoble, take the N85 in the direction of Briançon until Vizille and from there the D1091 to Bourg-d'Oisans. Turn left onto the **D211** and ascend a long series of hairpin bends to **L'Alpe d'Huez**. Drive through the sprawling ski resort, following signs for the Altiport, Clavans and Col de Sarenne. Keep left at the turning for the **Altiport** (a small airstrip) and drive for a further 1.8km. Park to the right of the road, next to an information panel for the via ferrata.

STAGE A
Itinéraire des Gorges de Sarenne/Découverte

Length	280m
Ascent/Descent	250m
Route grading	technical grade: 2; exposure: 3; seriousness: B
Time	2hrs (approach: 25mins; route: 1hr 30mins; return: 5mins)
Technical notes	escape points (within stage): 0

Approach

There is a gîte d'étape near the base of the route, which may serve refreshments during the summer. ◄

Take the path indicated by a signpost for the via ferrata, which descends to the southeast into the Gorge de Sarenne. Once at the bottom of the slope turn right and walk along the GR54 for 450m. Turn right at a via ferrata information panel and take a narrow path to the foot of the bluffs. ◄

Route

Start with an easy walk to the right along a ledge, passing below the start of the harder route (Stage B). Having gained a little height, the route then steepens considerably as it doubles back to the left. A series of small grassy ledges are ascended without much difficulty until the route levels off and traverses to the left. Cross the harder route and walk along a narrow ledge, which is a good place to take a break.

Towards the end of the ledge, there is a choice of routes:

1   The more interesting option ascends a vertical wall, on the right of the ledge, for 12m. Above this, a steep and exposed climbing traverse, involving a few slightly strenuous and delicate moves, gains a further 15m.

2   This steeper passage can be avoided by continuing to the end of the ledge and following a rather circuitous line around the side of the bluff.

The two routes converge on a grassy shelf. From here, the cable leads to a moderately steep slope, which is ascended via a series of short walls and shelves, to the top of the bluffs. This final passage is not exposed and involves only a few mildly strenuous moves.

Return
Follow a vague path that heads across the plateau at the top of the bluffs in a generally northeast direction. Pass the return path from the top of Stage B on your right. There are good views from the plateau of the Gorge de Sarenne and surrounding mountains. The Oisans (which are the northern peaks of the Écrins Massif) are visible through the Col de Cluy, above the southern side of the gorge.

249

STAGE B
Itinéraire de Pierre-Ronde/Sportif

Length	320m
Ascent/Descent	250m (500m, if combined with Stage A)
Route grading	technical grade: 3; exposure: 3; seriousness: B
Time	2hrs (approach: 25mins; route: 1hr 30mins; return: 5mins)
Technical notes	escape points (to Stage A): 1

Route

Having diverged from Stage A at the first junction encountered (see above), briefly ascend a ramp. This steepens to a more-or-less vertical wall, which is climbed for 30m. The wall is fairly broken, providing plenty of good handholds, and there are also stemples to aid progress. Towards the top of the wall, the angle eases slightly as a series of short slabs are climbed. Arrive at a narrow ledge, which the easier Stage A crosses to the left (take the easier option if you have struggled at all up to this point as the next passage is the most difficult part of the route). The next section involves a strenuous climb of 15m up a pale slab. The slab is fairly well protected but there are also a few moves that make good use of rock-holds. Above this, exposure

The Roche de la Muzelle (3465m) seen through the Col de Cluy

reduces as the route crosses a series of wide shelves, separated by vertical walls of between 10 and 20m. These are ascended via climbing traverses, with only a few brief difficult moves, until the cable ends at the top of the bluffs.

Return
Head across the plateau at the top of the bluffs and join the return path for Stage A.

ROUTE 45
Via Ferrata Cascade de la Fare

Location	Vaujany, Isère
	(GPS: Lat. 45° 9′ 13.57″ N Long. 6° 5′ 20.94″ E)
Length	900m
Ascent/Descent	1060m
Route grading	technical grade: 2–3; exposure: 2–3; seriousness: B (all stages)
Total time	7hrs 30mins (if both stages climbed consecutively)
Highest altitude	1715m
Map	3335ET
Technical notes	direction: NW; total escape points: 1
When to visit	May to October

Opened in the summer of 2012, this new route is built on the western flank of the Grandes Rousses Massif, overlooking the small resort of Vaujany. The route is a little unusual, in that it consists of two different lines running adjacent to each other, which are both of similar difficulty. An upper section, which is a little harder than the rest of the route, can be undertaken after completing whichever of the lower options you prefer. Whatever

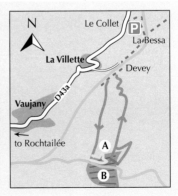

line you take, the entire route is very well protected and involves little contact with the rock. If it is hot and you wish to avoid the sun, climb the route in morning.

Access
From Grenoble, take the N85 in the direction of Briançon until Vizille and from there continue on the D1091 until Rochtailée. Turn left onto the D526 and follow signs for Vaujany for 7.5km. Turn right up the **D43a** and drive through **Vaujany** and **La Villette** to **Le Collet**. Park next to some tennis courts and a via ferrata information panel.

Climbers on the upper, optional, section (shared by both stages)

STAGE A
Les Passerelles

Length	500m
Ascent/Descent	530m
Route grading	technical grade: 2 (variant: 3); exposure: 2; seriousness: B
Time	4hrs 15mins
	(approach: 35mins; route: 2hrs 25mins; return: 1hr 15mins)
Technical notes	escape points (within stage): 1

Approach
Walk to the north of the tennis courts and descend along a broad gravel track. Turn right at **La Bessa** and then left at **Devey**. Continue to Le Moulin, turn left off the track and follow a narrow path that gradually gains height until it terminates next to the Cascade de la Fare. Stage A starts a little further back, on the left; Stage B starts immediately above the end of the path.

Route
Start by climbing up a 10m ladder attached to the side tree. Return to the ground via a 10m two-wire bridge, then climb a couple of short easy rock steps. Continue upwards, taking a fairly direct line up a series of slabs of 10 to 30m in length. The route passes through two tiny overhangs, but otherwise the slabs are not particularly steep. Once the waterfall disappears behind a buttress, the route veers off to the left and arrives at the Passerelle de la Fare, a 40m-long plank bridge crossing above a broad bay. The bridge is only moderately exposed but is a little slack and involves a bit of a stretch to get off the end.

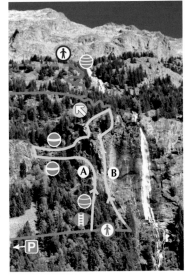

This immediately leads to a 15m vertical climb, which is slightly overhanging in places. Above this, turn around and re-cross the same bay on another bridge, the Passerelle du Berrichon. This is identical to the first bridge, except for being more exposed.

Once on the other side of the bridge, cross an exposed ledge for 10m and pass back onto the main cliff-face. A further 25m of easy climbing brings you to a tree-covered shelf. Walk up through the trees for a few minutes to the junction with the harder route (Stage B) and the end of the cable.

Follow an obvious path uphill for a few minutes. At a signposted junction, either keep left to finish via the escape point, or go right to tackle the upper part of the route. This starts with a steep climb of 30m. Initially, this is fairly trouble-free, but becomes progressively harder towards the top due to the presence of some small overhangs. More climbing, at a gentler angle, then leads to a short traverse across to a 10m-long three-wire bridge, the Pont de Montfrais. This is stable and not at all exposed. Having returned to near the water-fall, ascend some low-angle slabs from where there are excellent views of Vaujany and the Oisans region. An easy traverse along a ledge leads to more slabs and the end of the route.

Return
Walk uphill and turn left at a signpost. Descend a long series of zigzags to arrive between Le Moulin and Devey. Turn right and retrace your approach route.

STAGE B
La Cascade

Length	400m
Ascent/Descent	530m (1060m, if combined with Stage A)
Route grading	technical grade: 2 (variant: 3); exposure: 3; seriousness: B
Time	4hrs
	(approach: 35mins; route: 2hrs 10mins; return: 1hr 15mins)
Technical notes	escape points (within stage): 1

Route

Start with an easy climb up a low-angle slab. Above this, the route briefly steepens, with one mildly strenuous move, before a second low-angle slab is ascended without difficulty. The biggest challenge you are likely to face on these slabs is from the spray coming off the waterfall, which is close to the route for much of its course. Having reached a broad shelf, the route now steepens and a climb of 60m ascends the bluffs just to the left of the waterfall. The climb is fully vertical in only two places, both for a few metres, so it is not too difficult. At the top of the face, a broad shelf leads to a final easy climb of 15m. Above this, the cable continues up the hillside before ending next to the top of Stage A. See above for details of the remainder of the route.

Ascending easy slabs beneath the Cascade de la Fare

ROUTE 46
Via Ferrata Cascade de la Pisse

Location	Near Le Freney-d'Oisans, Isère
	(GPS: Lat. 45° 2′ 20.47″ N Long. 6° 11′ 6.49″ E)
Length	330m (and 200m in descent)
Ascent/Descent	450m
Route grading	technical grade: 3; exposure: 5; seriousness: B
Total time	3hrs 15mins
	(approach: 15mins; route: 1hr 45mins; return: 1hr 15mins)
Highest altitude	1540m
Map	3335ET or 3336ET
Technical notes	direction: S; escape points: 0
When to visit	May to November

This is a simple via ferrata in an awe-inspiring location. The route follows the line of a huge waterfall, the onomatopoeically named Cascade de la Pisse. This 250m-high torrent tumbles down the north side of the Val de Romanche, which is arguably the most impressive of any of the major alpine valleys. The climb is extremely steep and severely exposed for much of its course and also lacks any escape points.

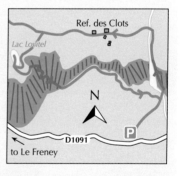

Several physically challenging sections have to be overcome, but these are fairly well spaced out and have good spots to relax between them.

Be aware that this via ferrata is one of the hardest of its technical grade and is not recommended for children, due to the wide spacing between some stemples. The route is south facing and the ascent can be very hot in the summer. Relief from the heat can be enjoyed via the spray coming off the waterfall and a cold drink purchased from the refuge at the top of the route.

Access

From Grenoble, take the N85 in the direction of Briançon until Vizille and from there continue on the D1091 through Le Bourg-d'Oisans and Le Freney-d'Oisans. From **Le Freney**, follow the D1091 to the Barrage du Chambon and drive for a further 4.25km until a graffiti-covered building is visible to the right of the road. Park below a via ferrata information panel, which is to the left of the road.

Approach

Pass the information panel and follow a path marked with red waymarks that climbs at a fairly gentle angle. This leads to the foot of the bluffs, just to the true left of the waterfall. The stream at the base of the waterfall will need to be crossed and, depending on how much water is flowing, could require care. In normal summer conditions the stream should be about 3m wide and 20cm deep, but this will vary widely, depending on recent rainfall and snowmelt. The crossing could be avoided by starting a little further up the road, but you will still have to recross the stream above the waterfall, so this is not recommended.

Approaching the top of the waterfall

257

Route

Climb up and around a squat buttress for 25m. This is moderately strenuous but the angle then eases as the cable leads up straightforward terrain. Progress is mostly on rungs and any rock-holds are large and obvious. The cliff-face gradually becomes steeper and steeper until a 15m-high wall is climbed. It is worth taking a break on the small platform at the top of the wall as the next passage, which is the crux of the route, is fairly sustained. This involves a vertical climb of 30m up a dihedral. The climb makes use of only a few rock-holds, which are easy to find, but stemples are quite widely spaced in places and the whole climb is fairly strenuous.

Above the dihedral, the angle temporarily eases a little and the route gains more height as it gradually approaches the waterfall. Turn a slight corner and climb at a fairly low angle for 25m. This is not particularly strenuous, but involves an awkward sideways movement. It is also massively exposed. Reach a small ledge, which offers excellent side-on views of the waterfall and is a good place to have a rest.

Beyond here continue climbing with lots of exposure and the occasional brief awkward or strenuous move. Depending on wind and how heavily the stream is flowing, you might also be subject to a fair amount of spray from the waterfall. Eventually, as you draw level with the top of the waterfall, the angle eases considerably until the cable ends on a grassy meadow.

Return

Keep your gear on. Follow red waymarks uphill and to the west and carefully recross the stream. There are excellent views of the Écrins Massif from here, with La Meije

(3982m) prominent to the southeast. The upper Cascade de la Pisse, which is extensively coated with calcium deposits, is visible to the north. After a few minutes the path arrives at the **Refuge des Clots**, where food, drink and accommodation can be purchased. Take a signposted path to **Lac Lovitel**. This follows a rather roundabout route, well marked with VF signs, until the top of a section of cable is encountered. Descend carefully down slabs and steep grassy slopes to a ledge, which is followed, with plenty of exposure, to a sharp corner. The cable ends here and a long and circuitous descent follows, utilising a slippery path marked with red waymarks. Eventually, the approach path is rejoined near the base of the waterfall.

A climber reaches the top of the crux pitch

ROUTE 47

Via Ferrata Les Perrons

Location	Venosc or Les Deux Alpes, Isère
	(GPS: Lat. 44º 59' 24.17" N Long. 6º 7' 1.25" E)
Length	900m
Ascent/Descent	770m
Route grading	technical grade: 2; exposure: 2; seriousness: A (all stages)
Total time	3hrs 30mins or 4hrs (approach: 1hr 10mins; route: 2hrs;
	return: 20mins by cable car or 50mins on foot)
Highest altitude	1720m
Map	3336ET
Technical notes	direction: SW; escape points: 0
When to visit	May to November
Useful websites	www.venosc.com; www.guides2alpes.com

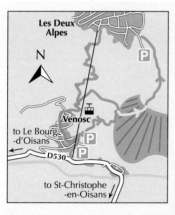

This via ferrata is situated part-way between the charming village of Venosc and Les Deux Alpes ski resort, and can be started from either place. The route is quite simple and follows a long and fairly direct line up a series of bluffs, which are less steep than they appear from below. The ascent is not especially strenuous or technical but it is fairly lengthy and can be tiring, particularly when the sun is shining. That said, it is best when completed in clear weather, to take full advantage of the sublime views of the Vénéon Valley and surrounding mountains.

The approach and return times given above assume a start from Venosc. There is a cable car running between Venosc and Les Deux Alpes that allows for a quick and easy journey to and from the route; if starting from Les Deux Alpes allow 45mins for the approach and 20mins for the return.

Access

From Grenoble, take the N85 in the direction of Briançon until Vizille. From Vizille, follow the D1091 to the hamlet of Le Clapier. Turn right onto the D530 and carry on until the turning for **Venosc**. Continue on the **D530** for a further 250m and park next to the cable car Lower Station. If you do not intend to use the cable car, drive up to Venosc and follow signs for 'Parking Visiteurs'. Alternatively, to start from **Les Deux Alpes**, continue past Le Clapier and drive for a further 2.6km on the D1091. Turn right and follow the D213 to the southern end of the resort.

Approach

A well-signposted path leads up from the cable car station to the parking area at Venosc. From there, the path zigzags uphill to the base of the bluffs situated to the northeast. If starting from Les Deux Alpes, descend on foot from the cable car Upper Station (or by cable car) to Venosc and reascend as described above. During the high season, the cable car runs from 0800 to 2000 and a return ticket costs €5.

The Roche de la Muzelle from the summit of Les Perrons

Route

The entire route consists of a long and more-or-less direct climb straight up the cliff-face. Although the angle varies, the ascent is never fully vertical, and strenuous moves are consequently few and far between. There is a fair amount of rock contact, but holds are abundant. Making use of the knobbly black gneiss in its initial section, rather than climbing on the stemples, can add a little extra challenge if desired. After some initial grassy ledges, two steep walls of 25m and 35m are climbed, with a small vegetated shelf between them.

At the top of the second wall another shelf, shaded by some trees, makes a good place to take a break before continuing to gain height. At a third shelf there is a break in the cable and a path is briefly followed until the cable recommences. Several more walls are climbed, none of which are very steep, until the cable ends on the summit of a rocky knoll. There are fine views to the west of Mont Le Rochail (3022m) as you ascend. From the summit, the principal peaks in view are the glaciated Roche de la Muzelle (3465m) to the south and the Pic du Lac Blanc (3327m) beyond Les Deux Alpes to the north.

Return

The first part of the return path has some short easy cabled sections on it, so you may wish to keep your gear on. The edge of Les Deux Alpes is reached after 10mins. Continue straight ahead through the resort and follow signs for 'Accès Telecabine' to the cable car and descent path (Chemin de Venosc). The latter option, which starts right next to the cable car Upper Station, is well signposted and descends to Venosc and the cable car Lower Station.

ROUTE 48
Via Ferrata de St-Christophe-en-Oisans

Location	St-Christophe-en-Oisans, Isère
	(GPS: Lat. 44° 57′ 47.53″ N Long. 6° 9′ 49.03″ E)
Length	1000m
Ascent/Descent	345m
Route grading	technical grade: 1–3; exposure: 1–3; seriousness: B (all stages)
Total time	3hrs 30mins
Highest altitude	1545m
Map	3336ET
Technical notes	direction: SW; total escape points: 1
When to visit	April to October
Useful websites	www.berarde.com; www.rafting-veneon.com

Located halfway up the Bérarde Valley, this via ferrata is perfectly situated to enjoy the wonderful scenery at the heart of the Écrins Massif. Having wisely eschewed ski resorts and other embellishments, the valley retains a wild and unspoilt atmosphere that can be a pleasant contrast with some areas of the Alps. The route is of middling difficulty and not too arduous as, for most of its course, it follows a fairly level traverse above the tumultuous waters of the River

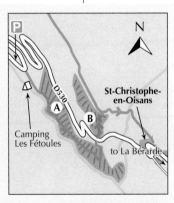

Vénéon. It is also possible to combine the via ferrata with white-water rafting or other watersports as there is a rafting company located at the start of the route. The route is best completed in the morning, when it will be in shade.

Access

From Grenoble, follow the N85 in the direction of Briançon until Vizille. Then take the D1091 to the hamlet of Le Clapier. Turn right onto the **D530** and carry on past Venosc, in the direction of **St-Christophe-en-Oisans** until **Camping Les Fétoules**. Park by the side of the road. If you are doing Stage B only, there are a few parking spaces by the side of the road at the bottom of that stage.

STAGE A
1ère Partie

Length	800m
Ascent/Descent	200m
Route grading	technical grade: 3; exposure: 3; seriousness: B
Time	2hrs 45mins
	(approach: 5mins; route: 2hrs 10mins; return: 30mins)
Technical notes	escape points (within stage): 0

Approach
Walk through the campsite, passing a watersports centre and information panel for the via ferrata.

The route starts with a traverse across bluffs only a few metres above the River Vénéon

Route

Climb out onto a pale bluff, which juts out into the river above some rapids. The cable briefly descends to just above the waterline, before following a climbing traverse around the curve of the bluff for 30m. There is a fair amount of rock contact and progress is moderately strenuous in places. This gives a good indication of the standard of the rest of the stage.

A brief walk along the riverbank is followed by a second, easier, traverse around another bluff. The route then gains 30m in height up the blank face of a third bluff. This is not particularly strenuous but involves the use of some fairly small handholds and feels more exposed than most of the route. At the top of this climb the route eases as a broad ledge is followed. There is some shade here and the ledge makes a good place to rest and take in the view of the prominent peak to the southeast, La Tête des Fétoules (3459m).

The ledge narrows in one or two places and progress is momentarily strenuous for a few metres, but mostly involves nothing harder than walking. A small bay is crossed on a 15m-long bridge, which is fairly exposed

La Tête des Fétoules seen from one of the easier sections of traversing

and very wobbly. Continue traversing around a series of corners and then briefly gain height up a ramp. More traversing, now in a fairly exposed situation, leads out onto the front of a buttress. A strenuous climb of 8m (crux) leads up the slightly overhanging edge of the buttress. The angle then eases and an easy scramble up a bulging strip of rock leads to the end of the cable and the road (D530). To finish here, simply turn left and walk back down the D530.

STAGE B
2ème Partie

Length	145m (345m, if combined with Stage A)
Ascent/Descent	345m
Route grading	technical grade: 1; exposure: 1; seriousness: B
Time	1hr (approach: <1min; route: 30mins; return: 30mins) or, if combined with Stage A, 3hrs 30mins (approach: 5mins; route: 2hrs 35mins; return: 50mins)
Technical notes	escape points (within stage): 0

Route
Cross the road and climb, more-or-less directly, up the broken hillside. Ascend via a series of rock platforms making use of plentiful large rock-holds, with the occasional rung for additional assistance. At one point a vertical wall of 8m is climbed. This involves one or two moderately strenuous moves. Otherwise, the angle of ascent is quite gentle with only a few steeper sections of a few metres. Towards the top the angle further eases and the route ends by a statue of the Virgin Mary, the Vierge du Collet.

Return
Turn right to descend to St-Christophe. From there, turn right to return down the road.

ROUTE 49
Via Ferrata des Mines du Grand Clôt

Location	La Grave la Meije, Hautes-Alpes
	(GPS: Lat. 45° 2′ 29.76″ N Long. 6° 15′ 42.53″ E)
Length	600m
Ascent/Descent	845m
Route grading	technical grade: 2; exposure: 3; seriousness: C
Total time	6hrs
	(approach: 5mins; route: 3hrs 45mins; return: 2hrs 10mins)
Highest altitude	2164m
Map	3435ET
Technical notes	direction: S; escape points: 0
When to visit	April to October

This route could be considered to be one of the oldest via ferratas in France, as the first fixed climbing equipment was put in place here in the early 19th century. This was to facilitate access to a silver mine, which had been worked since the medieval period. The equipment consisted of a perilous 200m-high ladder, a few remains of which are still visible. The current mode of access to the site, in the form of the

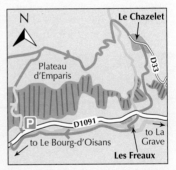

via ferrata, is now considerably safer and affords an interesting opportunity to view the remnants of the extensive mining operation.

Although not very difficult, this is a long outing that could be quite arduous, particularly on a hot day. While the mines will hold most of your attention for the first part of the ascent, the upper section and return path offer wonderful views of the Écrins Massif to the south. The route involves lots of contact with the rock, using plentiful holds. Some care is needed, however, as there is a great deal of loose stone resulting from the mining activity.

Access

From Grenoble, take the N85 in the direction of Briançon until Vizille and from there continue on the **D1091** towards La Grave la Meije. The start of the route, which is easy to miss, is located by the side of the D1091, 3.2km before La Grave and 1.8km before the hamlet of **Les Freaux**. There is a long straight section of road just before Les Freaux, to the side of which are some industrial buildings. Park by the roadside just before these, and near a large via ferrata information panel. If you have use of a second car (or a bike) considerable time can be saved by leaving it at **Le Chazelet** (see Return). This can be accessed via the D33, which leaves the D1091 500m to the east of La Grave, immediately to the right of a tunnel exit.

Cramped climbing up the inside of a massive fissure hewed out of the cliff-face by miners

Approach

A path heads uphill to the base of a massive buttress, which juts out from the cliff-face. The route starts near the bottom of the series of cavities hewn out from the front of the buttress.

Route

Start by climbing adjacent to, and through, a series of mine entrances. The interior of the mine is now extremely unstable and most of the gallery entrances are barred, so do not enter the tunnels, except as directed by the cable. The route passes a number of panels with information on the mining activity written in English. Having gained some height, pass around to the east side of the buttress, and climb steeply up a bare wall for 30m. This is a little more strenuous and exposed than most of the route but is well protected. The angle of ascent eases to a steep scramble and then continues around the east face of the buttress on a narrow path created by the miners.

Having passed much mining debris, and several more mine entrances, arrive at the base of a massive vertical fissure created by the removal of one of the more productive veins of ore. Climb up inside the fissure for 15m, using stemples on both sides. The climb is slightly strenuous and awkward, due to the narrow space between the walls.

Once outside again, follow an ascending traverse across a slab and cross to the west face of the buttress via a long path built by the miners. Having briefly dipped into a large gully, climb back to the east and gain the top of the buttress. From here the cable continues up the hillside for a long time, with progress mostly involving nothing harder than a steep walk, interspersed with a few short easy sections of scrambling. Once the cable ends, continue along the path to arrive at the **Plateau d'Emparis**. The most prominent of the heavily glaciated peaks across the valley are (left to right) La Mieje (3983m), Le Râteau (3809m) and Pic de la Grave (3667m).

Return
Follow signs for Le Chazelet. After the second sign take a path to the northeast, which passes some ruined stone huts and leads to a small col. Descend from the col to Le Chazelet, ignoring a sign to the right reading 'Itinéraire de descente rapide'. Once in Le Chazelet, follow a clearly signed path that descends via a small chapel (Notre Dame de Bon Repos) to Les Freaux. From here, cross the River Romanche and follow a gravel road. Recross the river, turn right, and follow the D1091 to the east for 250m.

ROUTE 50
Via Ferrata d'Arsine

Location	Villar-d'Arêne, Hautes-Alpes
	(GPS: Lat. 45° 1′ 47.89″ N Long. 6° 21′ 33.72″ E)
Length	300m
Ascent/Descent	200m
Route grading	technical grade: 2; exposure: 3; seriousness: A
Total time	1hr 45mins
	(approach: 5mins; route: 1hr 15mins; return: 25mins)
Highest altitude	1850m
Map	3436ET
Technical notes	direction: N; escape points: 1
When to visit	April to October

This brief, simple, route does not take long and could be completed as a warm-up for one of the longer routes in the vicinity: the Via Ferrata des Mines du Grand Clôt (Route 49) or the Via Ferrata l'Aiguillette du Lauzet (Route 51). However, it is a little more strenuous in places than either of those routes and would be a good option for climbers who previously have ascended only easy routes, and want to try something slightly more challenging. In fact, the

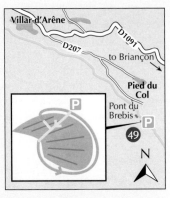

route would probably have earned a higher grade, but for its comparatively short length. For those who are also interested in rock climbing, there are numerous bolted sports routes, of all grades, adjacent to the via ferrata.

Access

From Grenoble, take the N85 in the direction of Briançon until Vizille and from there continue on the **D1091** to the village of **Villar-d'Arêne**. Stay on the D1091 for a further 1km and turn left down the **D207**. Follow signs for the via ferrata across a bridge, the **Pont du Brebis**, and continue until a large parking area near the foot of some crags.

Approach

Follow a path that starts next to a via ferrata information panel up a grassy slope to the base of the bluffs.

Route

Start with an easy ascent up a narrow, muddy, gully. Thereafter, the

From the top of the bluff there are fine views of the Romanche Valley, to the northwest, and of the impressive Montagne des Agneaux (3664m), to the south.

cable climbs more-or-less directly up a broad buttress to reach a platform, where it is possible to escape to the right. Despite the lack of appreciable overhangs, progress is often mildly strenuous and also fairly exposed. The ascent feels quite secure, with short run-outs between sections of cable and numerous stemples, resulting in limited rock contact. Above the escape, the route gains a further 40m in height, via a steep wall of 20m and then a series of low-angle slabs. ◄

Return
Descend to the left, as indicated by a sign on a tree. The return path requires care and is briefly cabled, so you may wish to keep your gear on.

There are fine views of the Romanche Valley from the top of the route

BRIANÇON

*Climbers on the slightly strenuous 10m descent encountered on the
second stage of Via Ferrata de la Falaise (Route 62, Stage B)*

INTRODUCTION

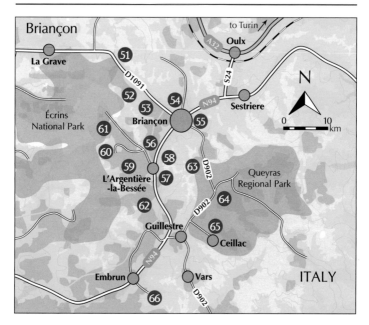

Briançon is the highest city in the European Union, although not the highest in the Alps – Davos, in Switzerland, has that honour. The small city is crammed between the Écrins, Cerces and Queyras mountain ranges at the confluence of the Durance and Guisane rivers. It is very much dominated by a number of fortifications, the most prominent of which protects the atmospheric old town. The more modern lower town has a variety of shops and cafés as well as the train and bus stations.

Briançon has no airport of its own. The most direct access to the city from the UK is via Turin airport (in Italy). From Turin, head west along the A32 motorway to Oulx and then south on the S24/N94 over the Col de Montgenèvre. Note that this route passes through the Susa Valley, which contains a number of fine Italian via ferratas. Alternatively, Briançon can be reached from Grenoble or the Maurienne via the D1091 and Col du Lautaret. If coming from the south, from Marseille or Nice for example, take the N94 along the Durance Valley. The only rail link with the city also comes from the south along the same valley. There is one long-distance bus to Briançon from Marseille via Gap. If travelling by car allow plenty of time for getting around Briançon, as it suffers from bad traffic jams during the summer.

Other than hotels, accommodation choices in the centre of Briançon are limited. You should book well in advance for July and August. If looking for cheaper options, there are campsites a little to the north, east and south. There is also one gîte d'étape within walking distance of the city and several others slightly further out. The wider area contains numerous campsites and plenty of other options.

Of the via ferratas covered in this chapter, two are in Briançon itself,

three are to the north of the city along the Guisane Valley and 11 are located to the south. Of these, seven are situated near L'Argentière-la-Bessée and the Vallouise Valley, three are in the Queyras Massif and one is some way further south in the l'Ubaye Massif. The routes are more densely concentrated than in other chapters, making this a good area to choose if you want to climb lots of via ferratas without driving too far. Although some of them are situated at a relatively high altitude, they still have a fairly long season, being a little further south than other routes in the book. The routes are representative of a good range of difficulties, and quite a few of them involve more rock contact than is typical of French via ferratas. A number are suitable for novices.

For tourist information see the websites listed in Appendix D.

Mont Pelvoux and the Barre des Écrins from the top of Route 51

ROUTE 51
Via Ferrata l'Aiguillette du Lauzet

Location	Monêtier-les-Bains, Hautes-Alpes
	(GPS: Lat. 45° 1′ 5.62″ N Long. 6° 27′ 57.41″ E)
Length	1000m
Ascent/Descent	920m
Route grading	technical grade: 2; exposure: 3; seriousness: C
Total time	5hrs 15mins (approach: 1hr; route: 3hrs; return: 1hr 15mins)
Highest altitude	2611m
Map	3436ET
Technical notes	direction: N and W; escape points: 2
When to visit	June to October

This superb route, the second-oldest via ferrata in France, was strongly influenced by the via ferratas of the Dolomites. In contrast with more modern French via ferratas it takes the form of a long rising traverse. Although it contains very little that is conspicuously strenuous or heavily exposed, the ascent is still challenging, being of considerable length and involving substantial height gain. Those prepared to make the effort will be rewarded with exceptional views of the Écrins Massif, as well as of several other adjacent ranges. Additionally, the climb offers a good opportunity to spot local wildlife such as ibex, choughs, golden eagles and perhaps the rare griffon vulture and

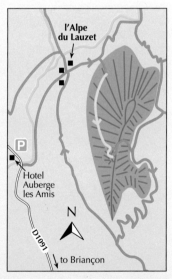

lammergeier (bearded vulture). As with other 'mountain' via ferratas, this route should be undertaken only on a day for which the forecast weather is good.

One of the steeper, more exposed passages encountered above the first escape point

Access
From Briançon, drive north on the **D1091**, passing through Monêtier-les-Bains. Continue to the small hamlet of Le Lauzet and park a little way further on, in the vicinity of the **Hotel Auberge les Amis**.

Approach
Head up the track opposite the hotel and follow the GR50 (red and white waymarks) to some chalets (**l'Alpe du Lauzet**). At a sign for 'Montagne de l'Oule' turn right and, shortly thereafter, at a sign for 'Le Grand Lac', turn left. Walk uphill for 250m to a small sign that reads 'Miege alt 2050m', and turn right. Put on your gear at this point and then take a steep path up a scree slope to locate the first section of cable.

Route
Commence with a straightforward rising traverse, interspersed with a few short climbs, across the northwestern face. Cabling is intermittent and, as with much of the route, frequent use is made of many easy rock-holds. Pass around onto the western face and climb up to a grassy ledge, which makes a good place to stop and admire the now extensive views across the main valley. Gain some height on slabs, assisted by rungs, and then a short ladder to arrive at one of the more challenging passages. This consists of a delicate, downward-sloping traverse across an airy slab followed by a down-climb of 20m on stemples. The cable then passes through a tunnel. This

10m-long passage is narrow in places, so backpacks may need to be taken off before entering.

On the other side, climb up a gully and some slabs, with plenty of rungs for assistance, to arrive at the bottom of a long ramp running up the western face of the mountain. This is followed all the way to the base of the large pinnacle jutting out from the southern end of the mountain. The climb up the ramp involves some sections of mildly strenuous vertical climbing. These are protected by stemples but also make good use of plentiful easy rock-holds. There are several broad grassy ledges between these pitches so, although the ascent of the ramp is long, it is possible to stop and rest in a number of places. However, if you are too tired to continue, it is possible to escape from the ledge at the top of the ramp by turning left and walking up a scree slope to a small col.

The final part of the route is a little more demanding and exposed than anything thus far encountered and may have some snow on it, depending on the time of the year. Follow a steeply rising traverse to the right and then back to the left, briefly squeezing behind a flake of rock. Beyond this, climb more directly upwards until a second escape is passed, immediately to your left. Assuming you are not put off by the exposed position, head right and traverse across and up a series of fine slabs to arrive at the end of the cable and top of the pinnacle. ▶ The views are magnificent. To the west, Mont Pelvoux (3946m) and the Barre des Écrins (4102m) – which is the highest point in France other than the peaks of the Mont Blanc Massif – are the two most prominent of the heavily glaciated peaks of the Écrins Massif. To the south Mont Viso (3841m) in Italy can be seen in the far distance, and the three sharply defined peaks to the north are the Aiguilles d'Arves (3514m).

This peak, surmounted by a large cross, is not the true summit, which is situated to the northeast and is not accessible to walkers.

Return

Carefully descend to a small col between the top of the route and the main summit and pick up an obvious path, which descends in a generally easterly direction. A little below the col, ignore an unmarked path that leads northeast to Col de l'Aiguillette. Continue on the main path, which gradually turns to the south and then descends steeply via a series of zigzags. Once you have levelled out, traverse to the northwest, now on the

Mont Pelvoux (3946m), seen from the first part of the route

GR50, beneath the face that you have just climbed. This brings you back to l'Alpe du Lauzet, from where you can retrace your approach path.

ROUTE 52
Via Ferrata du Rocher du Bez

Location	La Salle-les-Alpes Hautes-Alpes (GPS: Lat. 44° 57' 0.49" N Long. 6° 32' 46.32" E)
Length	550m (350m and 200m)
Ascent/Descent	250m (150m and 100m)
Route grading	technical grade: 1; exposure: 1; seriousness: A
Total time	both routes: 2hrs 30mins (approach: 20mins; route: 1hr 45mins; return: 25mins)
Highest altitude	1620m
Map	3536OT
Technical notes	direction: E; escape points: 1 each
When to visit	May to November

There are two separate via ferratas on the Rocher du Bez. Each is short, easy, and ideal for beginners and children or as a damp-weather alternative to more demanding routes. Both routes are well protected, with closely spaced stemples, and have escape paths at their mid-points. Note that, until recently, there was another via ferrata on the nearby Pointe des Neyzets. It is likely that this has been permanently closed, but it may be worth checking with the

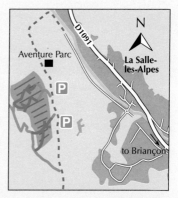

tourist office at Monêtier-les-Bains to see if it has reopened. It was a simple, high-altitude, route and reportedly quite easy.

The steep climb near the start of the right-hand route

Access

From Briançon drive north on the D1091 to **La Salle-les-Alpes** (also called Serre-Chevalier 1400). Near the north end of the village follow signs for 'Aventure Parc'. Cross the river and, at a roundabout, turn right and follow a road along the west bank, still following signs for the Aventure Parc. The road loses its tarmac surface and bends around to the left. Continue past the **Aventure Parc** until a via ferrata information panel to the right of the road is met. Park next to this or, alternatively, 100m further up the road, opposite a rock-climbing area. ▸

In addition to the via ferratas, there are numerous bolted rock-climbing routes (mostly easy) on the Rocher du Bez.

Approach

For the right-hand route, put on your gear on before starting, as there is a short section of cable on the approach path. Follow a path to the northeast and then steeply uphill to a junction. Turn right and continue to ascend to the base of the bluffs. The left-hand route starts further up the road, near the rock-climbing area. Follow a path that starts near a sign for the rock-climbing area for a few minutes. Keep the bolted rock-climbing routes on your right until the far left edge of the bluff, where the via ferrata commences.

Route

The right-hand route starts with a climb onto a boulder. Traverse along the top of this for 10m then move onto the cliff-face and climb for 20m. After traversing around to the right the angle eases until the top of the bluff is achieved. Continue up gradually shelving slabs until, rather unexpectedly, the route drops into a narrow crevice. Briefly follow this until re-emerging at the halfway point. Either turn right to take the escape path or continue by descending to the left along shelving and (possibly slippery) slabs. Once at the edge of the bluffs, descend for 20m and follow a gently descending traverse to the finish. There are a couple of mildly strenuous moves on this final section.

The left-hand route climbs up a broken rock-face near the edge of the bluffs. This is rarely steep and there are no strenuous passages. Part-way up, a short suspension bridge is crossed just before meeting an escape path, which traverses around to the left to meet the descent path. Beyond the escape path, the route continues up the mostly broken rock until reaching the top of the bluffs. The difficulty of the route beyond the escape point increases very marginally.

Return

For the right-hand route, simply descend for a minute to meet the approach path. For the left-hand route, ascend a little to meet the Sentier Botanique, a nature trail, and turn left to descend to the gravel road.

ROUTE 53

Via Ferrata du Rocher Blanc

Location	Chantemerle, Hautes-Alpes (GPS: Lat. 44° 55′ 58.97″ N Long. 6° 35′ 16.28″ E)
Length	350m
Ascent/Descent	570m
Route grading	technical grade: 2–4; exposure: 3–4; seriousness: C (all stages)
Total time	3hrs (if both stages climbed consecutively)
Highest altitude	2550m
Map	3536OT
Technical notes	direction: NE; total escape points: 0
When to visit	June to October (but note cable car opening dates below)

Both of the via ferratas on the Rocher Blanc are short, simple and satisfying. The Voie Facile (Stage A) is quite easy and gives straightforward access to the summit of the peak, from where extensive views of the Écrins Massif can be enjoyed. The Voie Sportive (Stage B) is well designed, arduous and consistently exposed, with the latter element being very 'immediate'. Although stemples are generally plentiful, Stage B involves a little thought-provoking foot and hand rock contact as well. Additionally, while none of the overhangs through which you pass are too long or acute, their cumulative effect creates a reasonably

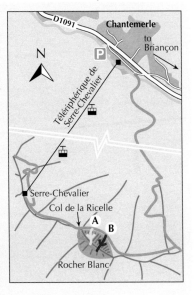

committing route. The C grade for seriousness reflects the relative altitude of the outing as well as the presence of some loose rock, particularly on Stage A. To do both stages, climb the easier route first, then descend and reascend via the harder route. The route is most easily accessed by cable car.

Access
From Briançon, drive north on the **D1091** to **Chantemerle** (also called Serre-Chevalier 1350). Follow signs for **Téléphérique de Serre-Chevalier** (cable car) and park near the Lower Station. The *téléphérique* is located near the tourist office.

STAGE A
Voie Facile

Length	190m
Ascent/Descent	280m
Route grading	technical grade: 2; exposure: 3; seriousness: C
Time	1hr 45mins
	(approach: 20mins; route: 50mins; return: 35mins)
Technical notes	escape points (within stage): 0

Approach
Take the two-stage cable car to the summit of Serre-Chevalier. This is open from 26 June to 29 August between 0900 and 1730 and a return ticket costs €12.20. The unappealing alternative is a steep walk taking 3–4hrs and an additional height gain of 1300m.

From the cable car Upper Station (near which is a useful orientation table), head downhill to your left (south-east). Follow a ski piste to the Col de la Ricelle. From here, ascend for 60m, aiming for the base of the first crag in front of you (Rocher Blanc). Just before reaching the crag, leave the ski piste and follow a level path to the left of the cliff-face. After 100m, the path arrives at the base of the

The off-vertical wall climbed near the start of the Voie Facile

first route, marked 'Voie facile (2)'. A further 100m brings you to the second route, marked 'Voie Sportive (1)'.

Route

An easy 10m rising scramble brings you to a grassy shelf. Turn a corner and climb a somewhat off-vertical wall for 25m. This is well protected with lots of stemples and is not strenuous. Scramble and climb on stemples for 40m up a broken arête. At the top of the arête join a fairly broad ledge that heads left. The ledge, which is quite steep, is followed for 60m. At times it is narrow and

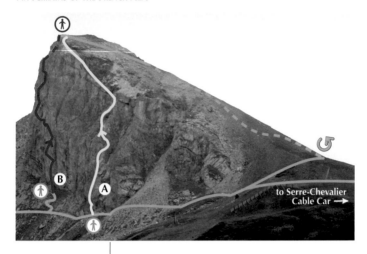

involves an awkward squeeze, at other times it briefly
disappears and is replaced by traversing on stemples.
Rock quality along the whole ledge is poor so take care
if there are climbers or walkers below you. A short climb
leads to some smooth low-angle slabs and the end of the
cable. To descend, turn right; for the summit, turn left.

Return
Follow a vague path, marked by cairns, to the west. This
descends to near the start of the routes and the approach
path.

STAGE B
Voie Sportive

Length	160m
Ascent/Descent	290m (570m, if combined with Stage A)
Route grading	technical grade: 4; exposure: 4; seriousness: C
Time	2hrs (approach: 25mins; route: 1hr; return: 35mins)
Technical notes	escape points (within stage): 0

Route

Start with a 10m climb followed by a 10m traverse to the left. This leads to a climb of 20m that involves a moderately overhanging passage of 3m. Above the climb, a 20m rising traverse to the left contains one small spot where a rest may be had. At the end of the traverse, a further climb of 25m begins with another moderate overhang of 3m. The angle then eases for 20m as straightforward scrambling brings you to a final moderately overhanging wall of 4m.

The cable ends near the summit cairn of the Rocher Blanc, from where a fine 360° panorama may be enjoyed. To the west many of the principal peaks of the Écrins Range are visible. The lower peaks of the Queyras Range can also be seen to the southeast. The long ridgeline across the valley to the northeast is the Crête de Peyrolle. The GR5 trail runs along its summit.

Return

Turn left (north) and walk a little downhill to the top of Stage A.

The Rocher Bouchard (2900m) and Cime de la Condamine (2940m) from the top of the Rocher Blanc

ROUTE 54

Via Ferrata de la Croix de Toulouse

Location	Briançon, Hautes-Alpes
	(GPS: Lat. 44° 54′ 4.75″ N Long. 6° 38′ 41.79″ E)
Length	500m
Ascent/Descent	640m
Route grading	technical grade: 2; exposure: 2; seriousness: B
Total time	3hrs 45mins
	(approach: 40mins; route: 2hrs 20mins; return 45mins)
Highest altitude	1970m
Map	3536OT
Technical notes	direction: S; escape points: 0
When to visit	March to November

This was one of the first via ferratas to be built in France and, although relatively 'plain' by the standards of more modern routes, it still has a lot of merit. The route offers outstanding views of Briançon and of the surrounding mountains. It is also well constructed, with a good balance struck between climbing on stemples and sections of easy scrambling. One word of warning: the route is south facing and fairly long.

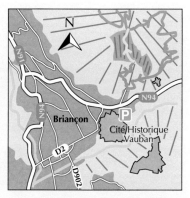

It can be hard work on a hot day and it is best to start early or late during high summer.

Access

From the centre of **Briançon** follow signs for '**Cité Historique Vauban**'. Park in Parking Champ du Mars, which is adjacent to the old city.

Approach

Cross the main road and head up a small lane by the side of Hotel Les Trois Chamois. Follow this until arriving at a via ferrata information panel and a small parking area. Ten minutes can be saved by parking here, but it fills up early. Turn right up a broad track (the GR5) as signed, then, shortly thereafter, left (leaving the GR5) onto a narrow, steep path. The path winds up the tree-covered slope to the start of the route, just to the left of the obvious large gully. The path is fairly clear, but beware of going too far to the right (east).

Le Pas is one of the steeper passages encountered on this relatively easy route

Route

The route follows a fairly direct line up the centre of the cliff-face, not far to the left of the major gully running the length of the bluffs. For the most part this is an easy climb up an off-vertical face of broken rock, with plenty of stemples and short run-outs between sections of cable. The angle eases after Le Pas, a brief vertical climb with a very small overhang, until Passerelle du President, a 3m suspension bridge, which is stable.

Beyond the bridge an off-vertical climb of 25m leads to a long section of easy scrambling interspersed with short stemple pitches. The angle eases and the cable ends as you move away from the large gully. Follow an obvious path uphill for 15mins or so until a cable leads you up a blunt, low-angle arête, which feels quite exposed. This lacks stemples, but there are numerous good rock-holds that make for pleasant climbing. Above the arête, the cable ends again and, after 10mins of walking steeply uphill, recommences for a final section of easy climbing. This follows a broken gully and then crosses some slabs before ending next to a viewing platform. There are wide-ranging views from here of the many fortifications surrounding

Briançon and across the city to the mountains of the Écrins and Queyras ranges, to the west and south respectively.

Return
Continue uphill from the viewing platform for a minute, then follow a path to the right marked 'Briançon par le Fort des Sallettes' (also the GR5), before rejoining the ascent path.

ROUTE 55
Via Ferrata de la Schappe

Location	Briançon, Hautes-Alpes (GPS: Lat. 44º 53′ 43.71″ N Long. 6º 38′ 15.39″ E)
Length	175m
Ascent/Descent	70m
Route grading	technical grade: 1; exposure: 1; seriousness: A
Total time	1hr 15mins (approach: 10mins; route: 45mins; return: 20mins)
Highest altitude	1297m
Map	3536OT
Technical notes	direction: N; escape points: 0
When to visit	Closed 1 November–31 March
Useful websites	www.grimpinforest.com; www.ot-briancon.fr

This small route, located within the grounds of a public park (Parc de la Schappe), is designed specifically for children, but would make a good initiation for adults. It is also a decent option when rain or heat prevents an outing on one of the longer routes in the vicinity. There is an extensive ropes course in the trees just beyond the start of the route, access to which can be arranged

at the Grimp'in Forest kiosk. Access to this route is also arranged at the kiosk (a fee of €3 must be paid), which is open between 1000 and 1800. Via ferrata gear can be hired there.

Access
From the centre of **Briançon** follow green signs for Parc de la Schappe (and also for the Col d'Izoard). There is parking at the entrance to the park, immediately beyond a roundabout.

Approach
Walk through the park, keeping the river on your left. Pass through a tunnel to reach the Grimp'in Forest kiosk. The route starts just before the kiosk, by the side of the tunnel.

Route
Traverse around a small bluff just above the River Durance and pass above the mouth of the tunnel on a sturdy wooden platform. Scale the side of the bluff on closely spaced stemples for 15m. This climb contains the one slightly strenuous move to be found on the route, in the form of a minimal overhang near the top. The rest of the route climbs up on or near the crest of a low-angle arête, with one short and very easy bridge crossed part-way up.

From the top of the route, there are good views of the bluffs up which Route 54 climbs. Directly across the gorge are the walls of the **Cité Historique Vauban**, the fortified old town that dominates Briançon. This was built in the 1690s by the famous military architect, the Marquis de Vauban, and is now a UNESCO World Heritage Site.

Return
A path to the right of the arête quickly returns to the Parc de la Schappe and the approach path.

ROUTE 56
Via Ferrata Les Vigneaux

Location	Les Vigneaux, Hautes-Alpes (GPS: Lat. 46° 7′ 11.92″ N Long. 5° 53′ 24.78″ E)
Length	950m
Ascent/Descent	780m
Route grading	technical grade: 2–4; exposure: 4; seriousness: A (all stages)
Total time	6hrs 15mins (if both stages climbed consecutively)
Highest altitude	1500m
Map	3536OT
Technical notes	direction: S; total escape points: 0
When to visit	March to November

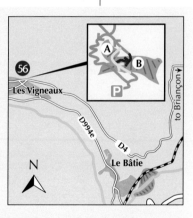

This is one of the earliest via ferratas to be built in France, and it is still one of the best. The route is typically very busy, owing its popularity to a fine location on pale bluffs overlooking the scenic Vallouise Valley as well as to the quality of the construction. The easier option (Stage A) compensates for a lack of physical difficulty by the presence of much exposure, and makes an ideal introduction to via ferratas. The harder option (Stage B) shows the dolomitic origins of French via ferratas, with a number of passages involving delicate hand and foot rock contact. In fact, these sections are about as near to rock climbing as French via ferratas come. To tackle Stage B, you probably should have some rock-climbing experience or be prepared to haul strenuously on the cable for short periods. An additional difficulty comes in the form of a heavily overhanging climb of 10m, which will be most challenging for shorter climbers.

Another factor to be aware of is that the bluffs are south facing and the ascent can be extremely hard work when in full sun.

Access
From Briançon, drive south on the N94 to L'Argentière-la-Bessée and then take the D994e to **Les Vigneaux**. From the centre of the village head east for 500m on the **D4** and turn left onto a gravel road. There is a wooden cross opposite the turning. Park next to a via ferrata information panel.

STAGE A
La Voie du Colombier

Length	450m
Ascent/Descent	390m
Route grading	technical grade: 2; exposure: 4; seriousness: A
Time	3hrs (approach: 20mins; route: 2hrs; return: 40mins)
Technical notes	escape points (within stage): 0

Approach
Take a small path just to the right of the information panel. Keep right at the only junction along the path and continue to the base of the bluffs.

Route
Follow a broad ledge that traverses steeply to the left. Exposure comes on quickly as you make your way up the narrowing ledge. There is plenty of contact with the rock, with only a few metal footplates where the ledge temporarily disappears. Eventually, the ledge ends and is followed by a climb on stemples of 20m up a just off-vertical wall. The angle eases a little and more height is gained, mostly on rock-holds, until a second ledge is reached. The ledge, which is much shorter and narrower

than the last, again traverses steeply to the left. Turn a corner and arrive at a small, shady, platform in a narrow gully. It is at this point that the two routes diverge.

The first steep passage of La Voie du Colombier

To continue with the easier Stage A, follow a gently rising traverse to the left across an off-vertical wall. This has little in the way of protection, beyond the cable, but the rock offers good grip and holds are large. At the end of the traverse, a brief climb leads to a small overhang, which is overcome with the aid of a short ladder. Above the ladder, ascend a wonderfully airy slab for 20m. Then scale an off-vertical wall for 15m to reach the top of the bluffs. The cable continues up a slippery path for a further 20m.

Return

You may wish to keep your gear on as the return path has some easy cabled sections. Follow a path uphill to a junction with a larger path. Turn left and immediately arrive at a clearing with a path ascending to the right, which is marked with red and white waymarks (GR50). From the clearing, do not take the GR50 but descend steeply to the left along a narrow unmarked path. Having passed through a set of low bluffs, the path rejoins the approach route a little above the car park.

STAGE B
La Voie de la Balme

Length	500m
Ascent/Descent	390m (780m, if combined with Stage A)
Route grading	technical grade: 4; exposure: 4; seriousness: A
Time	3hrs 15mins (approach: 20mins; route: 2hrs 10mins (first part of Stage A combined with Stage B); return: 45mins)
Technical notes	escape points (within stage): 0

Route

From the point where Stage B splits off from Stage A (see above), the route initially follows a fairly direct line up the bluffs, gaining 50m. This is almost vertical for the first 20m, but eases a little thereafter. Although there are no

The final steep climb on La Voie de la Balme

overhangs along this climb, there are several passages of a few metres each that lack stemples, requiring you either to haul up on the cable, or use small, but good, rock-holds. Above this, a short walk then leads to the bottom of a chimney.

This point, which has some shade, is a good place to take a rest before tackling the climb up a chimney, which is the crux of the route. The first 10m of the chimney are overhanging, with an initial move that will probably require you to swing your feet up to reach the lowest stemple. The upper 5m are a little less muscular, but involve some fairly tricky moves using the rock. Above this, an easy traverse and brief descent are followed by a final steep wall, which is climbed on stemples for 30m. Above the wall, a traverse to the right across slabs and a few short sections of climbing lead to the top of the bluffs and the end of the cable.

Return
Head uphill then follow a level path to your left, which soon joins with the return path from Stage A.

ROUTE 57
Via Ferrata de l'Horloge

Location	L'Argentière-la-Bessée, Hautes-Alpes
	(GPS: Lat. 44° 47′ 39.42″ N Long. 6° 33′ 19.49″ E)
Length	150m
Ascent/Descent	70m
Route grading	technical grade: 1; exposure: 1; seriousness: A
Total time	1hr (approach: 10mins; route: 45mins; return: 5mins)
Highest altitude	1070m
Map	3437ET
Technical notes	direction: E; escape points: 0
When to visit	March to November

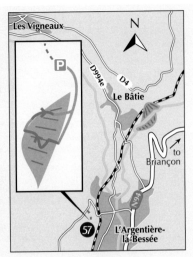

Named for the prominent clock tower that overlooks the route, this small, easy via ferrata makes a good warm-up prior to attempting one of the longer routes in the area. It will not occupy much of your time but is ideal for children, and is also an acceptable option in poor weather. The stemples are closely spaced and the one brief overhang will give an idea of what is involved on more demanding routes. There are a number of easy bolted climbing routes on the small bluffs next to the route.

Access
Take the N94 from Briançon to **L'Argentière-la-Bessée** and then take the **D994e**, following signs for 'Centre Ville'. Immediately beyond a bridge over the River Durance, do not turn left or right, but drive straight ahead, down a narrow road, with a bandstand on your left. Cross the rail tracks and continue round two bends until you come to a sign indicating that camping and caravans are forbidden. Turn left down an unpaved road and drive a short way to the car park.

Approach
Walk past a ruined building and continue to an information panel for the via ferrata. Descend a little, with the line of bluffs on your right, until you reach the base of a squat buttress.

Route
Scale the buttress, then traverse to your left out onto the cliff-face for 10m. Ascend for 10m and cross back to the

right for 10m. A further 10m of ascent has you at the top, with one small overhang near the top being the only difficulty. Keep your gear on and walk to your right for a couple of minutes until a second section of cable is met. This follows a descending traverse without any noticeable difficulty.

Return
The approach path is rejoined just next to the rock-climbing area.

ROUTE 58
Via Ferrata des Gorges de la Durance

Location	L'Argentière-la-Bessée, Hautes-Alpes (GPS: Lat. 44° 48′ 18.69″ N Long. 6° 33′ 44.62″ E)
Length	1800m
Ascent/Descent	315m
Route grading	technical grade: 2–4; exposure: 1–5; seriousness: A (all stages)
Total time	5hrs 45mins
Highest altitude	1140m
Map	3437ET
Technical notes	total escape points: 6
When to visit	April to October (open 0800 to 1800 during the summer)

These via ferratas are quite different in nature to most of the neighbouring routes. As the name suggests, rather than scaling a bluff or mountain, they have been built in the depths of a narrow, steep-sided gorge carved out by the River Durance. The routes make good use of the wonderfully evocative setting, passing across the manically twisted rock-face on both sides of the gorge and crossing back and forth over the river several times. The via ferratas present a wide range of difficulties, with the first stage serving as a good warm-up for the others or as a pleasant short outing in its own right. At the other end of the scale, the Via Ferrata Sportive/Noire is long, very exposed, and quite physical, particularly during its first stage. The

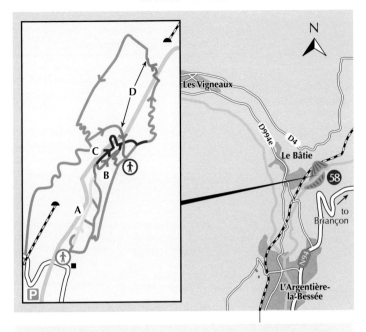

Via Ferrata du Siphon/Rouge, by which the hardest part of the Via Ferrata Sportive can be avoided, provides a good compromise between the two, but is still fairly challenging.

These routes can be a good option on a hot day, as except for the final section of the Via Ferrata Sportive/Noire (Stage D), they are out of the sun. Note that a fee of €6 is charged to access them. In conjunction with these via ferratas it is possible to use two massive Tyrolean traverses, for which an extra fee is charged; this may have to be arranged in advance. The larger of the traverses is 500m long and 200m high.

Access
From Briançon, drive south on the **N94** to **L'Argentière-la-Bessée** and then east on the **D994e** for 2km. Turn right at the entrance to **La Bâtie**, as indicated by a signpost for the via ferrata, and descend to the car park.

STAGE A
Via Ferrata Initiation/Verte

Length	300m
Ascent/Descent	30m
Route grading	technical grade: 2; exposure: 1; seriousness: A
Time	1hr (approach: 5mins; route: 45mins; return: 10mins)
Technical notes	direction: W; escape points (within stage): 3

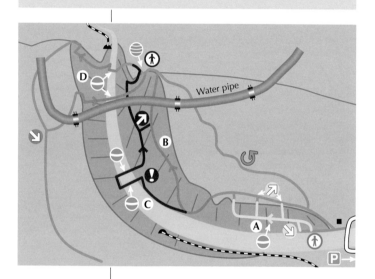

Approach
Walk down the road and cross the river to reach a café, from where tickets can be purchased. Via ferrata equipment can be hired here (€11) and they will also check your own gear and give an explanation of the route in English. Beyond the café, follow the river upstream for a couple of minutes.

Route

Climb up the heavily striated bluffs for 10m to a narrow ledge. This ledge is then followed along the whole length of the stage, with the river 10 to 15m directly below you. There are three escapes along the way: the first, which is not far from the start, descends to the river via a wire ladder. The other two climb up for 15m to the top of the bluffs. A stable 10m-long bridge is crossed at one point, but otherwise the stage involves a straightforward traverse with only a few mildly strenuous passages. The river is normally quite tranquil at this point, lending a relaxed atmosphere to this highly picturesque route.

The ruined defensive walls on the other side of the river are known as Le Barry de la Bâtie and were built in 1376 to defend Briançon against the inhabitants of Embrun.

STAGE B
Via Ferrata du Siphon/Rouge

Length	300m
Ascent/Descent	100m (130m, if combined with Stage A)
Route grading	technical grade: 3; exposure: 4; seriousness: A
Time	2hrs 30mins (approach: 5mins; route: 2hrs (Stages A and B combined); return: 25mins)
Technical notes	direction: NW; escape points (within stage): 0
Note	This stage is shorter and easier than the Via Ferrata Sportive, but still contains a few quite strenuous passages and is almost as exposed.

Route

Having followed signs along a short path from the end of Stage A, arrive at the top of a small bluff. A few minutes' easy down-climbing leads back to the side of the river, now enclosed by a steep-sided gorge, and a choice of routes (see also Stage C). To follow the easier Via Ferrata du Siphon, go right and climb straight up the side of

A via ferratist at the top of the first steep climb

the gorge for 30m. As with most of the route, progress is made principally on stemples with only occasional use of the rock. A strenuous traverse to the left around a corner is followed by a further climb of 10m. Then traverse for 30m to reach a low-angle ramp. The route is extremely airy to this point, with the river directly below your feet, but beyond the ramp exposure eases a little, as does difficulty.

Once above the ramp, traverse around a corner and arrive at a wide ledge, which makes a good place to rest. Pass the escape point from the harder route (Stage C) and climb up and around a corner. This is slightly over-hanging and a bit strenuous for a few metres. Finish by ascending easier ground to reach the top of the gorge.

STAGE C
Via Ferrata Sportive/Noire (First part)

Length	550m
Ascent/Descent	100m (130m, if combined with preceding stages)
Route grading	technical grade: 4; exposure: 4; seriousness: A
Time	3hrs (approach: 5mins; route: 2hrs 30mins (Stages A and C combined); return: 25mins)
Technical notes	direction: NW; escape points (to Stage B): 1
Note	To avoid the most strenuous parts of this stage (which are near the beginning), take the Via Ferrata du Siphon but leave it to join this one via the first escape point of Stage B. The remaining part of the route beyond this escape point is a little easier (grade 3).

Climbers on the first strenuous passage

305

Route

At the junction with Stage B, keep left and walk easily along a broad ledge carved into the side of the gorge. At the end of the ledge, traverse on stemples for 20m and climb up for 10m. This passage is slightly overhanging throughout and fairly strenuous. Cross a stable 15m-long bridge to the other side of the gorge and climb vertically for 15m. This is also slightly overhanging and reasonably strenuous. Cross a second bridge, similar to the first, back to the other side of the river.

A climbing traverse then leads easily up a strikingly patterned rockface to an escape point. To finish here or take a rest go right; otherwise continue to the left with a long traverse. This crosses the face of the gorge, gradually losing a little height, with plenty of exposure but only a few strenuous moves. Having passed around a broad corner, climb up a little further to arrive at the end of the stage and the start of Stage D.

STAGE D
Via Ferrata Sportive/Noire (Second part)

Length	650m
Ascent/Descent	185m (315m, if combined with preceding stages)
Route grading	technical grade: 3; exposure: 5; seriousness: A
Time	4hrs 45mins (approach: 5mins; route: 4hrs 20mins (Stages A, B and D or Stages A, C and D combined); return: 20mins)
Technical notes	direction: SE; escape points (within stage): 1

Route

If you are approaching from the top of Stage B, head downhill to the east.

This stage begins immediately beyond the end of Stage C. ◄ Cross a 20m-long three-wire bridge, which is stable and not exposed. On the other side the cable ends and a path descends to the river. Cross the river on another stable bridge and climb up a broad pillar for 120m. The ascent is mostly just off-vertical and more use is made of the rock

than on the previous stages. While this is not especially strenuous, the climb is long and lacks shade. Consequently it can be hard work on a hot summer afternoon.

At the top of the climb, follow a long traverse to the right. This is airy but quite straightforward, with the exception of one delicate passage of 4m across a low-angle slab on down-sloping foot holds. A further climb of 10m brings you to the top of the pillar. Take in the views of the surrounding mountains and descend off the back of the pillar to the end of the cable. Follow a signposted path, passing an escape point on your right (which returns directly to the car park), and walk beneath the huge water pipe that has been overhead for much of the route. The path leads back to the edge of the gorge, where the cable recommences. Descend for 10m and cross a 55m-long bridge. This is very stable but, with the full height of the gorge beneath you, massively exposed.

Crossing the short delicate passage at the top of the large pillar

Return

Turn right, and descend along well signposted paths to the café.

ROUTE 59
Via Ferrata de Tournoux

Location	Puy-St-Vincent, Hautes-Alpes
	(GPS: Lat. 44° 49′ 29.54″ N Long. 6° 32′ 49.19″ E)
Length	450m
Ascent/Descent	190m
Route grading	technical grade: 3; exposure: 3; seriousness: B
Total time	2hrs 15mins
	(approach: 15mins; route: 1hr 40mins; return: 20mins)
Highest altitude	1930m
Map	3536OT
Technical notes	direction: N; escape points: 1
When to visit	May to October

Located on the other side of the Vallouise Valley from Via Ferrata les Vigneaux (Route 56), this route, while less spectacular than its neighbour, still provides a decent challenge. There are two parts to the route. The first section involves a fairly direct climb up steep bluffs, which is initially strenuous but becomes progressively easier towards the top. The second section descends the same bluffs by an easier line and allows for a round trip to be made. There are good views from the top of the bluffs of the more prominent peaks of the Écrins Massif, in particular Mont Pelvoux (3943m), which lies at the head of the valley, and La Tête d'Amont (2815m), which is directly across the valley.

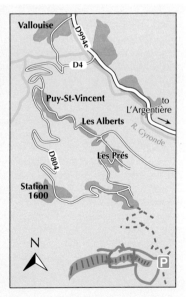

Access

From Briançon, drive south on the N94 to L'Argentière-la-Bessée and then east on the **D994e**. Around 1km before **Vallouise**, turn left and follow the **D4** to **Puy-St-Vincent**. A little beyond the village, at **Les Alberts**, turn right and drive through **Les Prés** in the direction of the Col de la Pousterle. Park just before the col, at Plateau de la Pousterle. The final 2.4km of road is unsurfaced. This should be passable in low-clearance cars, but if you choose to walk add 30mins and 200m of height gain.

Approach

From the car park head northwest to a signpost and follow the indicated path, which leads to a vehicle track. Continue in the same direction and pass through a gate. Look out for a small sign 50m beyond the gate, for the via ferrata on your left. From here, a rough path heads up a tree-covered slope towards the cliff-face.

Route

The first part of the route consists of a straightforward climb up the cliff-face, split into three sections. The initial section, which is the hardest, involves an ascent of 50m. While it contains no big overhangs the climb is reasonably strenuous throughout. At the top of this section there is a small platform, which makes a good rest spot. The next section is similar to the first but shorter and less direct. It is also a bit less strenuous but includes a few awkward sideways moves. Beyond this, a broad sloping tree-covered ledge is ascended to arrive at the final section. This meanders a little more than the previous part and is generally easier, but still contains a few strenuous moves. Stemples are readily available throughout the climb and there is only limited contact with the rock.

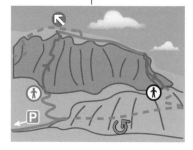

Follow a path to the right for 50m and either go left to escape (a path returns to the parking area) or keep right for the second section of via ferrata. After a few minutes' walking, the cable recommences and the route drops into the back of a narrow gully. A descending traverse leads out of the gully onto the cliff-face, where a series of ledges and short stemple pitches are down-climbed. This descent is not the most pleasant of passages, as there may be a lot of mud after rain and the rock quality is fairly poor in places. The cable run-outs are rather long, so care is required. For these reasons, the section should not be underestimated, although it is not particularly strenuous.

Return
Descend a little via a narrow path, which quickly rejoins the approach route.

ROUTE 60
Via Ferrata du Torrent de la Combe

Location	Puy-St-Vincent, Hautes-Alpes (GPS: Lat. 44° 50′ 1.64″ N Long. 6° 28′ 46.88″ E)
Length	600m
Ascent/Descent	180m
Route grading	technical grade: 1 (variant: 2); exposure: 1; seriousness: B
Total time	2hrs (approach: 10mins; route: 1hr 20mins; return: 30mins)
Highest altitude	1555m
Map	3536OT
When to visit	March to November
Technical notes	direction: all (in shade all day); escape points: 1

This entertaining little route, located on the banks of a woodland stream, makes for a pleasant change from mountaintops and towering cliff-faces. The route consists of a series of short sections of via ferrata and bridges, interlinked by a path running alongside the Torrent de la Combe. It is well suited for children, and adults may actually find some sections a little tricky, due to the close spacing between hand and foot placements on traverses. The route serves as a useful back-up when uncertain weather prevents an outing on one of the more adventurous routes in the neighbourhood. However, this is not a sensible option if heavy rainfall is anticipated or has just occurred, as the stream may be in spate.

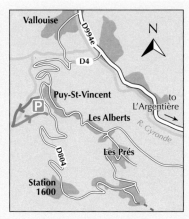

Access
From Briançon, drive south on the N94 to L'Argentière-la-Bessée and then east on the **D994e**. Around 1km before **Vallouise**, turn left onto the **D4** and continue to **Puy-St-Vincent**. Just before the village, turn right onto the **D804** (signposted for **Station 1600**), and continue for 500m. Park on the right in a lay-by.

Approach
From the lay-by, walk downhill for 20m and take the path indicated by an information panel for the via ferrata. The route starts next to a second via ferrata information panel.

Route
Start with an easy ascent of 10m up a ramp on the true right of the stream. This gives a good indication of the nature of the terrain, which is damp and somewhat slippery. Descend back to the streambed and immediately reascend, via two odd 45° 'bridge ladders', to meet an escape path. (Note that this escape path – which starts a little before the information panel on the main path – can also be used to avoid this first part of the route.) Cross

*One of the 45°
ladders at the start
of the route*

a bridge over the stream to the true left side and follow
a path, which is not cabled, for 20mins. Part-way along
the path there is an option of a short cabled climb over a
boulder and later on for a short detour across a series of
wobbly bridges.

At the end of the path, you are presented with two
choices:

1   The easiest option is to stay on the true left bank, just
    above the stream, where a short section of via ferrata
    overcomes a brief rock step.

2   Alternatively, climb the buttress on the true left
    side. This involves an ascent of 15m followed by a
    traverse of 20m, and is the only part of the route that
    is slightly strenuous (grade 2) or exposed.

Just beyond the buttress is another optional diversion.
This involves crossing the stream on a slack, 10m-long,
bridge. Once on the true right side, gain a little height
and follow a traverse for 10m to recross the stream on a
second bridge, which is also wobbly.

Once back on the main path continue up the true left bank for a few minutes and cross the stream again on a final, easy, bridge. The path continues on the true right bank for a little while before leaving the stream to arrive at Combe de Narreyroux.

Return

From Combe de Narreyroux, turn left at a sign for Le Puy and follow a descending path to return to the D804 a little above the parking. Turn left and walk down the road for 250m.

ROUTE 61
Via Ferrata des Gorges d'Ailefroide

Location	Pelvoux, Hautes-Alpes (GPS: Lat. 44° 52′ 38.43″ N Long. 6° 28′ 38.95″ E)
Length	380m
Ascent/Descent	90m
Route grading	technical grade: 2–4; exposure: 2–3; seriousness: A (all stages)
Total time	2hrs
Highest altitude	1300m
Map	3536OT
Technical notes	direction: S; total escape points: 2
When to visit	May to October
Useful websites	www.vallouise.info; www.paysdesecrins.com

Opened in 2011, this route makes for an enjoyable and trouble-free option that can fit into a short half-day. The first stage is quite easy and well suited to families with children. The addition of a second stage, much harder than the first, in 2012, has extended the appeal of the route to more serious fans of via ferratas. That said, neither stage is very long, and the whole route should not take more than two hours to complete. Although specifically designed to be accessible to children, there is a posted minimum height of 1.3m.

Having penetrated this far up the Ailefroide Valley, a trip to Pré de Madame Carle, situated at the head of the valley, is well worth the extra effort. Surrounded by the highest peaks of the Écrins Massif, the upper valley is widely considered to be one of the scenic highlights of the Écrins National Park.

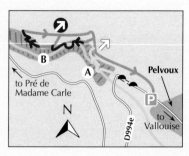

Access

From Briançon, drive south on the N94 to L'Argentière-la-Bessée and then east on the **D994e**, passing through Vallouise and **Pelvoux**. Park immediately beyond Pelvoux, by the side of the road.

STAGE A
Via Facile

Length	200m
Ascent/Descent	30m
Route grading	technical grade: 2; exposure: 2; seriousness: A
Time	1hr (approach: <1min; route: 45mins; return: 15mins)
Technical notes	escape points (within stage): 0

Approach

Walk up the road for 50m, passing through a short tunnel. The route begins just beyond the end of the tunnel, on the right.

Route

A climb of 5m leads to a long traverse above the true left side of the river. The traverse is not strenuous and only

becomes mildly exposed once directly above the river. Progress is mostly on stemples, with occasional footholds on large flat granite steps. Cross a stable bridge for 8m over to the other side of the river, quickly followed by a second bridge between two huge boulders. A third bridge, similar to the last two, crosses back to the true left bank. Continue to traverse, much as before but now gaining a little height. At its highest point the route curves up around a protruding nose of rock for 4m. This is the only part of Stage A that is appreciably strenuous. The route then continues to traverse above the river without any particular challenges until a steep climb of 10m leads to the top of the bluffs and the end of the stage. Turn right to return to the parking or left to continue.

Crossing the first bridge over the Torrent d'Ailefroide

STAGE B
Via Sport

Length	180m
Ascent/Descent	60m (90m, if combined with Stage A)
Route grading	technical grade: 4; exposure: 3; seriousness: A
Time	2hrs (approach: <1min; route: 1hr 35mins (both stages combined); return: 25mins)
Technical notes	escape points (within stage): 1

Route

Carefully descend along a slippery but unprotected path until nearly level with the river. The cabled route starts with an easy traverse along the true left bank. Gain a little height as you enter a narrow slot gorge and cross above the water for 5m to the true right wall, via a two-wire bridge, which is stable. A level traverse of 40m then follows. The walls of the gorge are perfectly smooth so all progress is on stemples. This passage is not strenuous except for one stretch of a few metres, which passes around a bulge.

At the end of the traverse, now with 25m of drop below you, climb up for 8m to a boulder choked between the walls of the gorge. This climb is moderately overhanging and somewhat strenuous. The boulder choke is the first place on this stage where it is possible to rest, other than with a rest lanyard. Cross over the top of the boulder, returning to the true left wall, and follow a rising traverse for 30m. From the end of this, climb up easily to reach the top of the gorge.

From here, either go right to escape, or to continue, keep left and walk along a level path for a minute. Re-enter the gorge, which is now much wider than before, and follow an easy descending traverse. Turn a corner and follow a pleasant traverse along the top of a smooth low-angle wall. At the end of the traverse, overcome a bulging overhang of 3m (crux) and traverse back to your right, now with good views of the Tête de Lauzières (2928m) to the east. Climb up for a few metres and traverse to your left. Climb up for 8m, passing through two small overhangs, the second of which is quite strenuous. This brings you to a broad ledge, above which a few more minutes of easy scrambling leads to the end of the cable.

Return

Having taken in the view to the west of Le Petit Pelvoux (3753m), turn right and follow a well-signposted path back to the car park.

ROUTE 62
Via Ferrata de la Falaise

Location	Freissinières, Hautes-Alpes
	(GPS: Lat. 44° 45′ 27.67″ N Long. 6° 32′ 18.25″ E)
Length	1000m
Ascent/Descent	350m
Route grading	technical grade: 2–3; exposure: 3; seriousness: B (all stages)
Total time	4hrs 30mins
Highest altitude	1650m
Map	3437ET
Technical notes	direction: S; total escape points: 1
When to visit	Closed 16 November–31 March

This is the oldest via ferrata in France, created in 1988. The route was conceived by local guides who were influenced by the via ferratas of the Dolomites, and it is closer in nature to those Italian routes than some more modern French via ferratas. Although it lacks bridges or other 'fancy'

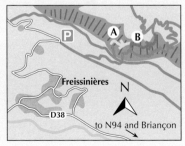

elements and follows a fairly simple line, the route is no less enjoyable for that. It makes excellent use of a series of ledges that pass across the impressive limestone bluffs overlooking Freissinières. This pretty little village, situated in the centre of the southern Écrins Massif, is an ideal base from which to explore this sector of the Écrins National Park. The bluffs are south facing and are likely to be very hot during summer, so take plenty of water with you.

Access

From Briançon, drive south on the N94 for 19km. Turn right onto the **D38** and follow signs to **Freissinières**. At the entrance to the village, turn right, and at a T-junction, right again. Follow the narrow road up beyond the village for a little more than 1km to a hairpin bend. Park to the right of the road, next to a via ferrata information panel.

STAGE A
1ère Partie

Length	500m
Ascent/Descent	170m
Route grading	technical grade: 2; exposure: 3; seriousness: B
Time	2hrs 30mins
	(approach: 30mins; route: 1hr 20mins; return: 40mins)
Technical notes	escape points (within stage): 0

Approach

Head along a level path to the east. Any junctions are clearly signposted, except for one next to a sign 'Forêt Domaniale de Fournel', where you should keep left.

Route

The cable initially gains height up a series of platforms before levelling off and moving around to the south face. This first climb is quite straightforward with a fair amount

Looking towards the Durance Valley and Queyras Massif from one of the broad ledges on the 1ère Partie

of rock contact. Once on the main cliff-face, the route leads along a broad, down-sloping, ledge, which gradually narrows. Although now quite high up, exposure is generally not too 'immediate', and there are plenty of good holds on the limestone. Cross a smooth, off-vertical, slab, via a narrow horizontal weakness and then pass beneath a massive overhang. A short, slightly awkward, descent leads down to a tree-covered shelf and the end of the stage. It is possible to escape from here by descending

along a cabled path. This point also offers some shade and makes a good place to take a rest.

STAGE B
2ème Partie

Length	500m
Ascent/Descent	180m (350m, if combined with Stage A)
Route grading	technical grade: 3; exposure: 3; seriousness: B
Time	4hrs 30mins (approach: 30mins; route: 3hrs (both stages combined); return: 1hr)
Technical notes	escape points (within stage): 0

Route

With the upper Freissinières Valley in the background, a climber approaches the Grotte Ogive

Head up to the right to locate the start of the cable. The route then follows a gradually rising traverse along ochre-coloured bluffs, using an occasionally disappearing ledge system. Having gained the top of a broad buttress, climb down for 10m, passing through a slight overhang. This

feels quite exposed and is a little strenuous. Continue along a fairly broad ledge until the cable dips into a cave, the Grotte Ogive. Leave the cave, via a squeeze through a 'boite aux lettres', and continue around the cliff-face. Finish by climbing up smooth slabs for 40m. Metal aids are not abundant on this final section but the limestone offers excellent grip.

Return
Follow a path that leads to the right. This is rather vague at first but is marked with cairns. Having arrived at **Clot du Puy** (signpost), turn right and descend via a precipitous path to rejoin the approach route near the start of the via ferrata.

ROUTE 63
Via Ferrata d'Arvieux

Location	Arvieux, Hautes-Alpes
	(GPS: Lat. 44° 48' 20.22" N Long. 6° 42' 23.01" E)
Length	1000m
Ascent/Descent	470m
Route grading	technical grade: 2–4; exposure: 3; seriousness: B (all stages)
Total time	4hrs 45mins
Highest altitude	2279m
Map	3537ET
Technical notes	total escape points: 1
When to visit	May to October

Approaching these routes from the south, the first thing that will strike you is the long line of steep bluffs towering above to your left. These bluffs are home to the first of the two routes located near Arvieux. The Via Ferrata des Crêtes de Combe la Roche (Stage A) follows a fairly direct line that climbs straight up the bluffs. The route contains more rock contact than is typical of French routes but lacks any bridges or other such elements. The other route, the Via Ferrata de Pra Premier (Stage B), is normally much busier, being shorter and including an easier option. As such it is a better choice for the less experienced than the first route, which lacks any escape path and can feel like a relatively serious undertaking. There is quite a lot of small loose stone on both routes, which you should be careful not to dislodge.

Although entirely separate, these routes are approached from the same starting place and can be completed in sequence. If you intend to do this, it is easier to start with Crêtes de Combe la Roche and then do the second route, although the first is the harder of the two.

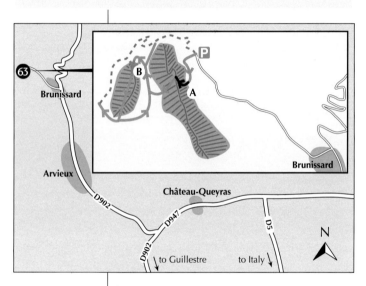

Access

From Briançon, drive south on the N94 to **Guillestre** and then follow the **D902** to **Arvieux**. Continue on the same road to **Brunissard**, and turn left at a sign for the via ferrata. Follow a narrow road to a large car park, beyond which only local traffic may progress.

STAGE A
Via Ferrata des Crêtes de Combe la Roche

Length	600m
Ascent/Descent	240m
Route grading	technical grade: 4; exposure: 3; seriousness: B
Time	3hrs (approach: 15mins; route: 2hrs; return: 45mins)
Technical notes	direction: E; escape points (within stage): 0

Approach
From the car park, descend to the southwest and cross the valley to arrive at an information panel for the via ferrata. The path then climbs to the base of the long line of bluffs. Take care to follow signs as there are a number of different paths below the bluffs.

Route
Start with a vertical climb of 45m. This is fairly well protected by stemples with only limited rock contact and passes through a few minor overhangs. The angle then

Approaching the top of the crux pitch

gradually eases until a belvedere is reached. Beyond the belvedere (a good place for a break) the route follows a long slowly rising traverse to the left. Progress along this section is quite easy, consisting mostly of a steep scramble, with only a handful of harder moves required.

Having turned a corner and passed a small platform (good rest spot), difficulty increases considerably. Scale a steep slab for 25m and then traverse round a corner into a wide chimney. Climb up the side of the chimney for 15m (crux). This is reasonably strenuous and may require the use of several fairly small but obvious rock-holds. Continue gaining height until a broad ledge is achieved. This leads back to the right and the top of the cliff, where the cable ends. The 50m sections below and above the crux are all relatively challenging. There are no large overhangs to be overcome but progress is generally quite strenuous and involves plenty of rock contact.

Return

Take a path marked with cairns, which descend to the northwest. Head down a small valley to arrive at a grassy meadow, which is overlooked to the southwest by the Via Ferrata de Pra Premier. Turn right along the side of the meadow and then descend via a vehicle track to the car park. An optional short-cut path can be taken part-way down the track.

STAGE B
Via Ferrata de Pra Premier

Length	400m
Ascent/Descent	320m (470m, if combined with Stage A)
Route grading	technical grade: 3 (variant: 2); exposure: 3; seriousness: B
Time	2hrs 45mins (approach: 30mins; route: 1hr 30mins; return: 45mins) or, if combined with Stage A, 4hrs 45mins (approach: 15mins; route: 3hrs 45mins; return: 45mins)
Technical notes	direction: NE; escape points (within stage): 1

Approach
From the car park, head uphill on a vehicle track, with the option of a short-cut part-way up, until an information panel for the via ferrata is reached. Cross a grassy meadow and pass around the back of an artificial pond. A path then leads up a scree slope to the base of the bluffs.

A large group passing the escape point

Route

There is a choice of routes to begin with.

1   The easier variant (on the left) continues up along the bottom edge of the bluffs until a steep climb of 30m leads to the junction with the other route. Initially this involves only steep walking. The vertical climb, which makes use of a short ladder part-way up, is also fairly straightforward.

2   The harder route (on the right) starts with a steep 20m traverse to the left. This is mildly strenuous in places but well protected with plenty of rungs, which is fairly typical of most of the route. Above this first climb, the cable leads up a broad shelf to the main cliff-face. A long, steeply climbing traverse to the left then leads up the cliffs. This feels fairly exposed as it crosses several smooth limestone slabs on stemples and large rock-holds, before joining with the easier route. Continue to gain height until the angle eases a bit as you enter a broad depression in the face.

Towards the top of the depression, there is an escape path on the right, which leads easily to the summit. Take this if you are tired but, otherwise, continue with the remainder of the route, which is of similar difficulty to the lower sections. This involves a slightly delicate climb of 20m followed by a traverse of 10m, all with plenty of exposure. Above this the angle again eases and more climbing up steep limestone slabs leads to the summit of Pra Premier (2279m) and the end of the cable.

In case you are feeling too pleased with yourself, take a look at the vast south face of the Crête de l'Alpaliar, just to your north. You will probably see climbers on one of the bolted routes that lead straight up the smooth pink face, overcoming a number of massive overhangs along the way.

Return
Descend to the south until arriving at a junction. Turn left to return, via a small valley, to the grassy meadow below the route. For a more scenic route, turn right and head downhill in the direction of the Chalets de Clapeyto. Having arrived at a vehicle track, turn right and descend to the car park.

ROUTE 64
Via Ferrata de Fort Queyras

Location	Château-Queyras, Hautes-Alpes (GPS: Lat. 44º 45′ 22.19″ N Long. 6º 47′ 32.37″ E)
Length	800m
Ascent/Descent	50m
Route grading	technical grade: 1; exposure: 1; seriousness: A
Total time	2hrs (approach: <1min; route: 1hr 45mins; return: 15mins)
Highest altitude	1400m
Map	3537ET
Technical notes	direction: All; escape points: 1
When to visit	Closed 31 October–30 March

The village of Château-Queyras is named for the castle that dominates it. In addition to its high walls, this fairytale construction is defended by narrow slot gorges on two sides. It is along the sides of one of these gorges that a new via ferrata has been built. The route contains very few strenuous moments, is mostly level and should be in shade other than around midday. Therefore, it is a good option when the weather is too hot for some of the nearby routes. It can be very popular with large groups and tends to be extremely busy

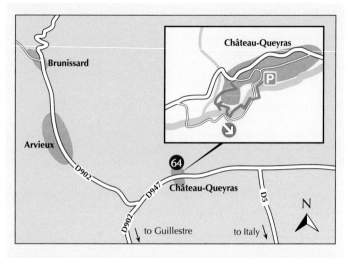

during the summer. The gorge is also popular with watersports enthusiasts, so do not be surprised to see kayakers shooting the rapids just beneath your feet. A visit to the fort, built in the 13th century and much altered in the 17th century, is recommended for those with any interest in the history of the region.

Access
From Briançon, drive south on the N94 to **Guillestre**, and follow the **D902** and then the **D947** to **Château-Queyras** (also called Château Ville-Vieille). Drive into the centre of the village and park by the side of the river, below the castle.

Approach
Cross the bridge at the end of the car park. Turn right and walk along the road for 20m.

Route
Traverse along the true left side of the slot gorge on stem-ples, only a few metres above the water. This is quite

straightforward, as the stemples are closely spaced and the only difficulty is likely to come in the form of traffic jams, at times of high usage. After 100m, cross to the other bank over a stable suspension bridge and continue traversing, occasionally gaining or losing a few metres. Recross the river on a second bridge, similar in nature to the first, and either take the escape path up to the road or continue on the true left bank. After a slight descent, cross back to the true right of the river on a third bridge and climb easily for 30m. Beyond this point the route leaves the slot gorge and follows a narrow path that gradually gains height as it ascends to the fort. After a brief break in the cable, a final section climbs steeply, but without difficulty, to the castle walls.

Via Ferrata de Fort Queyras traverses above the fast-flowing waters of the Guil Torrent

Return
Descend past the castle and through the village, as indicated by signs, to return to the parking area.

ROUTE 65
Via Ferrata des Rochers de la Clapière

Location	Ceillac, Hautes-Alpes
	(GPS: Lat. 44° 40′ 17.60″ N Long. 6° 45′ 46.38″ E)
Length	925m
Ascent/Descent	680m
Route grading	technical grade: 1–2; exposure: 2; seriousness: B (all stages)
Total time	4hrs 30mins (if both stages climbed consecutively)
Highest altitude	2030m
Map	3537ET
Technical notes	direction: S; total escape points: 0
When to visit	April to October

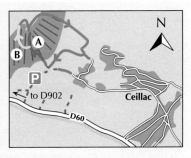

A visit to this pleasant and unpretentious via ferrata is a perfect excuse to discover Ceillac. This rustic village, entirely surrounded by high mountains, is truly a hidden gem of the French Alps. In fact, while the climb should provide a few hours' enjoyment, the principal attraction has to be the view from the route of Ceillac and the wonderful cirque of mountains at the head of the Vallon du Mélezet.

The route splits part-way up with the easier option providing a very straightforward ascent that is suitable for beginners. The more challenging option is a little longer and more involved, but still only briefly strenuous. During the summer, the route is best left until later in the day, when it should be in shade. Take care not to dislodge any loose rock, which is relatively common throughout the route.

Access
From Briançon, drive south on the N94 to Guillestre, and then east on D902. After 9km, turn right onto the

D60, and continue until 1km before **Ceillac**, where a sign for the via ferrata indicates a left turn. Follow a gravel road for 300m and park on a grassy area by the side of the road.

STAGE A
1ère Partie

Length	425m
Ascent/Descent	340m
Route grading	technical grade: 1; exposure: 2; seriousness: B
Time	2hrs (approach: 10mins; route: 1hr 20mins; return: 30mins)
Technical notes	escape points (within stage): 0

Approach
A via ferrata information panel should be visible 100m ahead. Continue past this and follow a path that zigzags uphill to the base of the bluffs.

The Vallon du Mélezet from the top of the route

Route

A smooth wall is climbed for 35m. This makes for a fairly airy start, but is well supplied with stemples and just off-vertical, so not strenuous. Above this, a broad ledge quickly gives way to a second climb of 40m. Once again, there are plenty of stemples and the rock is more broken than the first wall. There is also one very small overhang and the climb is a bit more demanding than the previous one.

From the top of the second climb, difficulty and exposure diminish as the route gains height at a relatively gentle angle up the broken hillside. The limestone under foot makes for enjoyable easy scrambling and any brief steeper sections are well protected. Part-way up the hillside, the junction with Stage B is passed. If you have not struggled with progress so far, it is recommended that you consider joining it, as it involves a more dramatic finale to the route. To continue with the easier route, keep right.

Return

Head uphill and follow a clear path to the right. There is a section of cable on the path so keep your gear on. Go right at a signposted junction located a little above some houses.

STAGE B
2ème Partie

Length	500m
Ascent/Descent	340m (680m, if combined with Stage A)
Route grading	technical grade: 2; exposure: 2; seriousness: B
Time	2hrs 30mins (approach: 10mins; route: 1hr 45mins (first part of Stage A combined with Stage B); return: 35mins)
Technical notes	escape points (within stage): 0

Route
From the junction noted on Stage A a rising traverse to the left is followed by a straightforward climb of 10m. A level walk then leads to the top of a belvedere. On the other side of the belvedere, a bridge crosses a broad bay near the base of a shallow scoop in the cliff-face. The 16m-long bridge does not feel too exposed, and is reasonably stable.

Beyond the bridge, the route then climbs fairly steeply up the scoop for 50m. Stemples are a little less abundant than on the previous steep sections but the rock is quite broken so progress is not too challenging. Near the top of the scoop, traverse to the left for 40m. This is fairly exposed in places and contains a few moderately strenuous or technical moves, particularly for the last 10m. This is followed by a steep climb of 20m to the top of the bluffs and the end of the cable.

Return
Having gained a little height, the path heads to the right and soon joins with the return path from Stage A.

ROUTE 66
Via Ferrata des Orres

Location	Les Orres, Hautes-Alpes
	(GPS: Lat. 44° 29′ 4.17″ N Long. 6° 33′ 0.65″ E)
Length	1000m
Ascent/Descent	430m
Route grading	technical grade: 3–5; exposure: 2–3; seriousness: B (all stages)
Total time	4hrs 30mins
Highest altitude	1840m
Map	3438ET
Technical notes	direction: E; total escape points: 2
When to visit	Closed 31 October–30 March

Despite being relatively isolated from the other routes in this book, this via ferrata is well worth the extra effort required to visit it. There are two stages, which are next to each other but cannot be directly linked into one route. The first is a good mid-grade ferrata suitable for most people; however, the second is considerably more challenging, being both strenuous and requiring a fair amount of rock contact (some experience of rock climbing would be useful). Neither contains any bridges or similar adornments but both are cleverly designed and provide satisfying climbing.

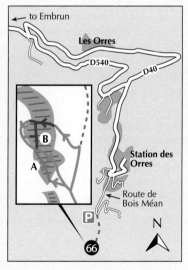

Les Orres is situated above the historic cliff-top town of Embrun and the impressive sweep of Lac Serre-Ponçon, Europe's largest artificial lake. The area is a popular holiday destination due to its pleasant climate and the wide range of summer activities on offer at the Station des Orres, details of which can be found on the station's website, as listed above.

Access
From Briançon, drive south on the N94 until just past Embrun, and then turn left at a roundabout onto the **D40**. Follow this to **Les Orres**, and continue in the direction of **Station des Orres**. A few 100m before the centre of the station turn right at a roundabout onto **Route de Bois Méan** and continue until the first hairpin bend. Park by the side of the road, next to a via ferrata information panel.

STAGE A
Itinéraire du Rocher Marcelinas

Length	500m
Ascent/Descent	200m
Route grading	technical grade: 3; exposure: 2; seriousness: B
Time	2hrs 30mins
	(approach: 30mins; route: 1hr 15mins; return: 45mins)
Technical notes	escape points (within stage): 0

Approach
Follow signs to the south along a dirt track for 800m to arrive at a picnic area. Continue along the same track, in the same direction, for a further 500m, until arriving at a sign indicating the start of the 'Via Ferrata facile'. Take that path, which crosses the valley to the right and then climbs up to the base of some low bluffs.

Route
Start with a moderately strenuous climb of 8m, followed by a climbing traverse to the left. This is the most ardu-ous part of the stage and can be avoided by an easier

Climbers admiring the Vallon de l'Eissalete from the Itinéraire du Rocher Marcelinas

alternative start, a short way to the left. The route then traverses along the bluffs to the right for 100m, occasionally gaining or losing a little height. There may be a number of mildly awkward or delicate moves, depending on your height, but progress is mostly straightforward. After emerging onto a vegetated slope, both difficulty and exposure diminish. Continue traversing, this time on a series of narrow ledges, with occasional climbs of 10 or 20m, until a final steep climb of 10m.

Return

Follow a path out onto a belvedere. There are good views from here of the bluffs you have just climbed as well as of the surrounding valley. The path then descends back beneath the bluffs before rejoining the approach path.

STAGE B
Itinéraire de la Cascade

Length	500m
Ascent/Descent	230m (430m, if combined with Stage A)
Route grading	technical grade: 5; exposure: 3; seriousness: B
Time	2hrs 45mins (approach: 25mins; route: 1hr 35mins; return: 45mins) or, if combined with Stage A, 4hrs 30mins (approach: 30mins; route: 3hrs 15mins; return: 45mins)
Technical notes	escape points (within stage): 2

Approach

From the picnic area, a sign for the 'Via Ferrata difficile' indicates the appropriate path. This descends directly to the bottom of the valley and then briefly gains some height up the other side to arrive at the base of the bluffs.

Route

The first few minutes of easy climbing give little indication of what is to come, as the angle of ascent increases quite gradually. Once clear of the trees the cliff-face steepens to nearly vertical and is climbed for 100m, adjacent to the rather desultory waterfall from which the route takes its name. Although not especially strenuous, progress is harder than it may at first appear. There is a considerable amount of rock contact, and a greater degree of thought is required as to where to place hands and feet than is typical of most via ferratas.

From the small belvedere at the top of the climb it is possible to escape by continuing up the bluffs. This first escape route, which gains a further 50m in height,

Approaching the end of the Itinéraire de la Cascade

is mostly quite easy, but contains one vertical section of 15m that involves some challenging moves as hard as anything found below.

If continuing with the second half of Stage B, which is quite different to the first, keep left at the belvedere. This involves a long and highly strenuous traverse. Little height is gained or lost and it is fairly well protected with stemples, although use is also made of some rather minimalist rock-holds. There is a second escape point part-way along. The crux, however, in the form of a heavily overhanging traverse of several metres, is found before the escape, near the beginning of the section. If you can get past this, the rest of the route should be manageable. Taller climbers will find the traversing generally more strenuous, although shorter climbers will also be challenged towards the end, where some stemples are widely spaced. Note that, if you wish to avoid the crux, it is possible to take the first escape then rejoin the route by the second escape.

Return
Keep your gear on until past one brief section of cable. The path then joins the return path from the Itinéraire du Rocher Marcelinas (see Stage A).

APPENDIX A

Routes listed in order of difficulty

Route		Stage	Grade	Exposure	Seriousness	Page
29	VF d'Andagne	A	1	1	B	171
32	VF du Diable	A	1	1	A	181
38	VF de St-Colomban-des Villards	A	1	1	A	213
55	VF de la Schappe		1	1	A	291
25	VF de Pralognan	B	1	1	A	151
17	VF La Grotte du Maquis		1	3	B	118
4	VF du Rocher de la Chaux	C	1(3)	2	A	65
60	VF du Torrent de la Combe		1(2)	1	B	310
35	VF de Poingt Ravier		1	1	A	200
43	VF de l'Alpe du Grand Serre	A	1	1	A	241
15	VF École de Rossane		1(2)	1	A	109
24	VF du Plan du Bouc	B	1	2	B	146
34	VF du Télégraphe	A	1	2	B	196
11	VF d'Ugine		1	2	C	89
52	VF du Rocher du Bez		1	1	A	280
57	VF de l'Horloge		1	1	A	298
14	VF Roc du Cornillon	B	1	2	A	108
48	VF de St-Christophe-en-Oisans	B	1	1	B	266
43	VF du Grand Bec 1ère Partie	B	1	2	B	243

Route		Stage	Grade	Exposure	Seriousness	Page
37	VF de Comborsière		1(2)	2	A	208
33	VF de L'École Buissonnière		1	1	A	193
20	VF du Levassaix		1	1	A	132
64	VF de Fort Queyras		1	1	A	327
65	VF des Rochers La Clapière	A 1ère Partie	1	2	B	331
24	VF du Plan du Bouc	A Parcours en Arête	2	2	B	144
21	VF du Lac de la Rosiere		2(1)	2	A	134
26	VF des Bettières	A Eperon des Croës	2	2	B	153
14	VF Roc du Cornillon	A Parcours Primevère à Oreille d'Ours	2	3	A	106
2	VF Jacques Revaclier		2	3	A	52
61	VF des Gorges d'Ailefroide	A Via Facile	2	2	A	314
27	VF Roc de Tovière	A 1ère Partie	2	2	B	159
53	VF du Rocher Blanc	A Voie Facile	2	3	C	284
31	VF du Pichet		2(1)	2	A	177
30	VF du Col de la Madeleine		2	3	A	174
54	VF de la Croix de Toulouse		2	2	B	288
58	VF des Gorges de la Durance	A VF Initiation/Verte	2	1	A	302
45	VF Cascade de la Fare	A Les Passerelles	2(3)	2	B	253
51	VF l'Aiguillette du Lauzet		2	3	C	276
45	VF Cascade de la Fare	B La Cascade	2(3)	3	B	255
1	VF Fort l'Ecluse		2	2	A	50
44	VF de l'Alpe d'Huez	A Itinéraire des Gorges de Sarenne/ Découverture	2	3	B	248

Route		Stage		Grade	Exposure	Seriousness	Page
18	VF de Roche Veyrand	A	1ère Partie	2	3	B	122
47	VF les Perrons			2	2	A	260
3	VF des Saix de Miolène	A	Tronçon du Cabri	2	2	A	56
32	VF du Diable	B	VF les Diablotins	2	2	A	183
42	VF du Croix de Chamrousse	A	VF Les Trois Fontaines	2	3	B	236
49	VF des Mines du Grand Clôt			2	3	C	267
19	VF du Cochet			2	2	B	129
29	VF d'Andagne	B	Itinéraire Guy Favre	2	4	B	172
56	VF Les Vigneaux	A	La Voie du Colombier	2	4	A	294
62	VF de la Falaise	A	1ère Partie	2	3	B	318
65	VF des Rochers La Clapière	B	2ème Partie	2	2	B	333
7	VF de Curalla			2	3	B	74
12	VF Le Roc du Vent			2	3	C	93
34	VF du Télégraphe	B	Fort du Télégraphe	2	4	B	198
50	VF d'Arsine			2	3	A	270
4	VF du Rocher de la Chaux	A	La Tête de l'Éléphant	3	5	A	61
42	VF du Croix de Chamrousse	B	VF les Lacs Roberts	3	2	B	238
62	VF de la Falaise	B	2ème Partie	3	3	B	320
6	VF du Mont			3	3	A	70
66	VF des Orres	B	Itinéraire du Rocher Marcelinas	3	2	B	337
39	VF de l'Adret	A	La Passerelle	3	3	A	217
63	VF d'Arvieux	B	VF de Pra Premier	3(2)	3	B	325
9	VF Yves Pollet Villard			3(4)	3	B	81

Route		Stage		Grade	Exposure	Seriousness	Page
25	VF de Pralognan	A	VF de la Cascade de la Fraîche	3(2)	3	A	149
13	VF de la Guinguette	A	Itinéraire de la Grotte	3	2	A	102
26	VF des Bettières	B	Grand Pilier and La Vire des Barmes	3	3	B	154
32	VF du Diable	F	VF La Montée au Ciel	3	4	A	189
36	VF du Rocher Saint Pierre	B	2ème Partie	3	3	A	207
48	VF de St-Christophe-en-Oisans	A	1ère Partie	3	3	B	264
5	VF du Saix du Tour			3(4)	3	B	66
58	VF des Gorges de la Durance	D	VF Sportive/Noire (Second part)	3	5	A	306
22	VF de la Croix des Verdons			3	4	C	136
44	VF de l'Alpe d'Huez	B	Itinéraire de Pierre-Ronde/Sportif	3	3	B	250
27	VF Roc de Tovière	B	2ème Partie	3	4	B	160
40	VF de la Cascade de l'Oule	A	Parcours par la Vire des Lavandières	3	4	A	225
32	VF du Diable	E	VF la Traversée des Anges	3	4	A	188
58	VF des Gorges de la Durance	B	VF du Siphon/Rouge	3	4	A	303
38	VF de St-Colomban-des-Villards	B	VF de la Chal	3	3	A	214
28	VF Les Plates de la Daille			3	5	B	164
32	VF du Diable	D	VF le Chemin de la Vierge	3	4	A	186
59	VF de Tournoux			3	3	B	308
41	VF les Prises de la Bastille	A	Falaises VICAT	3	2	A	231
46	Cascade de la Pisse			3	5	B	256
26	VF des Bettières	C	Le Surplomb Jaune	4	3	B	156
8	VF de la Tour du Jallouvre			4	5	C	77
63	VF d'Arvieux	A	VF des Crêtes de Combe la Roche	4	3	B	323

Route		Stage	Grade	Exposure	Seriousness	Page
61	VF des Gorges d'Ailefroide	B	4	3	A	316
13	VF de la Guinguette	B	4	5	A	103
18	VF de Roche Veyrand	B	4	5	B	124
43	VF de l'Alpe du Grand Serre	C	4	4	B	245
16	VF Savoie Grand Revard	A	4	3	B	114
3	Tronçon du Chamois/Tronçon du Bouquetin	B	4	3	A	58
32	VF La Descente aux Enfers and La Montée au Purgatoire	C	4	4	A	184
39	Le Bastion	B	4	4	A	219
53	Voie Sportive	B	4	4	C	286
56	La Voie de la Balme	B	4	4	A	296
36	1ère Partie	A	4(1)	3(1)	A	204
58	VF Sportive/Noire (First part)	C	4	4	A	305
10	1ère Partie	A	4	3	A	86
41	Falaises de la Bastille	B	4(3)	2	A	233
4	L'Oeil de l'Éléphant	B	5	5	A	63
32	VF les Rois Mages	G	5	5	A	191
10	2ème Partie	B	5	4	A	87
66	Itinéraire de la Cascade	B	5	3	B	337
23	3ème Partie		5	3	A	140
27		C	5	5	C	161
40	Parcours par le Grand Dièdre	B	5	5	A	228
16	Parcours Grotte à Carret	B	5	5	B	116

APPENDIX B
Glossary of via ferrata terminology

Arête	Narrow ridge of rock.
Belvedere	Platform prominent from the rock-face.
Buttress	Broad steep ridge that juts out from a rock-face or mountain.
Cirque	Half-open steep-sided hollow at the head of a valley or on a mountainside.
Chimney	Vertical cleft in the rock, wide enough to fit into.
Couloir	Steep gully or gorge.
Crux	The most difficult passage of a route.
Dihedral	An inside corner of rock, with more than a 90° between the faces.
Flake	Thin slab of rock partially detached from the main face.
Low-angle	Steep section of rock that is angled noticeably below 90°.
Off-vertical	Steep section of rock angled at a little below 90°.
Overhang	Section of rock angled beyond 90°.
Pinnacle	High, pointed piece of rock.
Scrambling	A type of climbing somewhere between walking and graded rock climbing, necessitating the use of hands.
Scree	Small, loose, broken rocks, normally forming a slope beneath a cliff.
Smearing	Using the friction on the sole of your footwear against a flat surface, in the absence of any useful footholds.
Stemple	Metal rung normally used on via ferratas to aid progress.
Traverse	To progress in a more-or-less horizontal direction.

APPENDIX C
Useful French words and phrases

French	English
Everyday	
Bonjour	Hello
S'il vous plait	Please
Merci	Thank you
Au secours!/Aide moi!	Help!
Attention!/Caillou!	Look out!/Below! (for rockfall)
Puis-je passer?	Can I pass?
Voulez-vous passer?	Do you want to pass?
Combien de personnes y a-t-il dans votre groupe?	How many people are there in your party?
Via ferrata equipment	
Absorbeur de choc	(Via ferrata) Shock absorber
Baudrier	Harness
Casque	Helmet
Corde	Rope
Gants/Mitaines	(Via ferrata) Gloves
Longe	Lanyard
Weather	
Brouillard	Fog
Foudre/Éclair	Lightning
Glace	Ice
Neige	Snow
Nuage	Cloud
Orage/tempête	Storm
Pluie	Rain
Prévision météo	Weather forecast

French	English
(Beau/Mauvais) Temps	(Good/Bad) Weather
(Fort) Vent	(Strong) Wind
On the via ferrata	
Aérienne/Vide	Exposed
Arrivée	(Via ferrata) Finish
Ascension	Ascent
Balisages	Waymarks
Barreaux	Metallic rungs
Câble	Cable
Chemin/Voie/Sentier	Path/Way/Trail
Chutes des pierres	Stonefall
Dangereux/Danger	Dangerous/Danger
Défense d'entrer/Interdit	No entry
Dénivelée	Height difference
Départ	(Via ferrata) Start
Échappatoire	Escape point/path
Échelle (inversée)	Ladder (outward facing)
Passerelle	Footbridge
Piste	Track
Pont (de Singe) (Népalais)	Bridge (two-wire) (three-wire)
Poutre	Balance beam
Prise	Handhold
Sauvetage	Rescue
Surplomb	Overhang
Tunnel/Galerie	Tunnel
Tyrolienne	Tyrolean traverse
Voie/Parcours/Route	Route

French	English
Topographical features	
Aiguille	Pinnacle
Alpe	Mountain meadow
Arête/Crête	Ridge/Crest
Barrage	Dam
Brèche	Gap
Bois	Wood
Cascade	Waterfall
Col/port/pas	Col/Pass
Colline	Hill
Corniche/Vire	Ledge
Dalle	Slab
Dièdre	Dihedral
Éboulis	Scree
Falaise	Cliff
Forêt	Forest
Grotte	Cave
Lac	Lake
Massif	Mountain group
Montagne	Mountain
Mur/Paroi/Muraille	Wall
Pente	Slope
Pic	Peak
Pré	Meadow
Rivière	River
Roche/Roc/Rocher	Rock
Ruisseau	Stream
Selle	Saddle
Sommet/Cime	Summit
Torrent	Mountain stream
Trou	Hole
Val/Vallée	Valley
General	
Autoroute	Motorway
Cabane/Refuge	Hut

French	English
Chemin local	Minor road
Court	Short
Croix	Cross
Dernier	Last
Droite	Right
Église	Church
Été	Summer
Fermé	Closed
Gauche	Left
Grand	Large
Haut/Hauteur	High/Height
Horaire	Timetable
Location/Louer	Hire
Loin	Far
Maison	House
Nord	Northern/North
Occidental/Ouest	Western/West
Office de Tourisme/ Syndicat d'initiative	Tourist Office
Oriental/Est	Eastern/East
Parc National	National Park
Parc Naturel Régional	Regional Natural Park
Petit	Small
Pierre	Stone
Plan	Map
Raide	Steep
Relief	Contours
Route Nationale	Main road
Stationnement	Parking
Sud	Southern/South
Téléphérique/ Télécabine	Cable car/Gondola
Télésiège/Remontées mécaniques	Chairlift/Ski lift
Tout droit	Straight ahead

APPENDIX D
Useful contacts

Maps
www.geoportail.fr

Stanfords
12–14 Long Acre
London WC2E 9LP
Tel: 020 7836 1321
sales@stanfords.co.uk
www.stanfords.co.uk

The Map Shop
15 High Street
Upton upon Severn
Worcestershire WR8 0HJ
Tel: 0800 085 40 80
themapshop@btinternet.com
www.themapshop.co.uk

Tourist information/Accommodation
France Tourism Development Agency
Lincoln House
300 High Holborn
London WC1V 7JH
Tel: 090 68 244 123
info.uk@atout-france.fr
www.uk.franceguide.com

Geneva and the Northern Alps
www.geneva-tourism.ch
www.haute-savoie-tourisme.org
www.savoie-mont-blanc.com
www.ain-tourisme.com
www.visitesenchablais.fr
www.aravis.com

Chambéry
www.chambery-tourisme.com
www.savoie-mont-blanc.com
www.lesbauges.com

www.parcdesbauges.com
www.ain-tourisme.com

Tarentaise
www.savoie-tarentaise.com
www.ot-moutiers.com
www.bourgsaintmaurice.com
www.parcnational-vanoise.fr

Maurienne
www.hautemaurienne.com
www.maurienne-tourisme.com
www.parcnational-vanoise.fr

Grenoble
www.grenoble-tourism.com
www.tourisme-oisans.com
www.bourgdoisans.com
www.sudgrenoblois-tourisme.com
www.ecrins-parcnational.fr
www.belledonnetourism.com

Briançon
www.ot-briancon.fr
www.paysdesecrins.com
www.ecrins-parcnational.fr
www.queyras-montagne.com

See route descriptions for local tourist
office contact details.

Travel
Trains
www.eurostar.com
www.voyages-sncf.com

Long-distance buses
www.eurolines.co.uk

Crossing the three-wire bridge between the two towers on Via Ferrata le Roc du Vent (Route 12)

Ferries
www.directferries.co.uk

Mountain road closures
www.choisissezvotrecol.com
www.letour.fr
www.infotrafic.com

Up-to-date information on via ferratas (in French)
www.viaferrata-fr.net

Via ferrata equipment
www.needlesports.com
www.decathlon.co.uk
www.ellis-brigham.com
www.gooutdoors.co.uk

Equipment safety check
www.theuiaa.org/certified_equipment

Weather
www.meteofrance.com

LISTING OF CICERONE GUIDES

For full information on all our
guides, and to order books and
eBooks, visit our website:
www.cicerone.co.uk.

Walking – Trekking – Mountaineering – Climbing – Cycling

Over 40 years, Cicerone have built up an outstanding collection of 300 guides, inspiring all sorts of amazing adventures.

Every guide comes from extensive exploration and research by our expert authors, all with a passion for their subjects. They are frequently praised, endorsed and used by clubs, instructors and outdoor organisations.

All our titles can now be bought as **e-books** and many as iPad and Kindle files and we will continue to make all our guides available for these and many other devices.

Our website shows any **new information** we've received since a book was published. Please do let us know if you find anything has changed, so that we can pass on the latest details. On our **website** you'll also find some great ideas and lots of information, including sample chapters, contents lists, reviews, articles and a photo gallery.

It's easy to keep in touch with what's going on at Cicerone, by getting our monthly **free e-newsletter**, which is full of offers, competitions, up-to-date information and topical articles. You can subscribe on our home page and also follow us on **Facebook** and **Twitter**, as well as our **blog**.

Cicerone – the very best guides for exploring the world.

CICERONE

2 Police Square Milnthorpe Cumbria LA7 7PY
Tel: 015395 62069 info@cicerone.co.uk
www.cicerone.co.uk